THE GENTLEMEN
THEOLOGIANS

E. BROOKS HOLIFIELD

THE GENTLEMEN
THEOLOGIANS

AMERICAN THEOLOGY IN
SOUTHERN CULTURE
1795–1860

DUKE UNIVERSITY PRESS

DURHAM, N.C.

1978

© 1978, Duke University Press

L.C.C. card no. 78–59580

I.S.B.N. 0–8223–0414–7

Printed in the United States of
America by Heritage Printers

To Vicky
and to Erin and Ryan

CONTENTS

Preface   ix

Introduction   3

ONE. The Town Setting   5

    1. *Urban Images*   7

    2. *A Wider Field of Usefulness*   13

TWO. The Gentlemen Preachers   24

    1. *An Elite Hundred*   25

    2. *Ministerial Economics*   28

    3. *"The Other Professions"*   31

    4. *The Ideal of Gentility*   36

THREE. The Vanishing Liberals   50

    1. *"A Dispute About Authenticity"*   52

    2. *Jefferson: Sensation*   57

    3. *Gilman: Understanding*   62

    4. *Miles: Reason*   66

FOUR. The Evidence for Faith   72

    1. *Traditions*   73

    2. *Preparing for the Word*   77

    3. *Validating the Word: The Evidences*   85

    4. *Interpreting the Word: Rational Hermeneutics*   96

    5. *The Catholic Critics: The New Thomists*   101

FIVE. Scottish Philosophy and Southern Theology   110

    1. *Knowing*   112

    2. *Believing*   118

SIX. The Moralists   127

    1. *Sense and Sensibility*   129

    2. *The Science of Ethics*   134

    3. *A Moral Sense and a Warm Heart*   138

    4. *Relations*   146

    5. *A Theological Ethic*   149

SEVEN. Seals of the Covenant   155

    1. *The Covenantal Condition*   157

    2. *The Conditional Covenant*   165

    3. *A Sign of Faith*   171

    4. *The Presence of Christ*   175

EIGHT. A Rational World: Theodicy   186

    1. *Calvinists and Arminians*   187

    2. *The Reasonableness of Calvinism*   193

    3. *Speculative Theodicy*   199

    Notes   209

       Manuscript Collections Cited   209

   Index of Persons   254

   Index of Subjects   259

PREFACE

American "rational orthodoxy" was one expression of a broader pattern of conservative European religious thought, which was manifest both in the religious traditions of the English and Scottish enlightenment and in the eighteenth- and nineteenth-century European debates over revelation and Biblical criticism. As a mode of religious thought it dominated the churches and seminaries of antebellum America. Hence instead of attending to the theologians who to a greater or lesser degree broke with rational orthodoxy and therefore attracted later generations, I have concentrated primarily on the "orthodox" thinkers whose names have been forgotten despite their enormous influence among their contemporaries. I have looked at Southern theologians because they have been largely ignored in published monographs and because I wanted to examine as closely as possible the relationship between theology and a concrete social setting. My major theme is the "rationality" of American theology and the relationship between theology and urbanity in the Old South.

I am especially indebted to the National Endowment for the Humanities, which provided a fellowship for independent study and research that enabled me to spend a year reading and writing. The Emory University Research Fund financed a summer of research in manuscript collections throughout the South. And Dean James Laney of Candler School of Theology not only provided financial assistance but also helped me arrange my schedule so that I could find time to write.

I am indebted, as well, to a small army of librarians at Emory's Woodruff Research Library, the Pitts Theology Library at Emory, Agnes Scott College, Louisiana State University, the University of Georgia, the University of Mississippi, the University of Alabama, Vanderbilt University, the University of North Carolina, Yale University, Harvard University, Princeton University, Duke University, the Historical Foundation of the Presbyterian and Reformed Churches in Montreat, North Carolina, the United Methodist Historical Archives at Lake Junaluska, Columbia Theological Seminary, the Federal Records Center in Atlanta, the Georgia State Archives, and Eberhard-Karls University in Tübingen.

Yale University Press and the *Journal of Presbyterian History* graciously extended permission to me to adapt for use in chapters six and seven material that they had previously published in other forms.

And I am grateful for conversations with Sydney Ahlstrom, Thomas Frank, Samuel S. Hill, Jr., Paul Fiddes, Garrett Green, Fred Norris, Jim Waits, and especially H. Shelton Smith. The three persons to whom I dedicate the book are fully aware of how much I owe to them.

THE GENTLEMEN
THEOLOGIANS

INTRODUCTION

The most noticeable feature of American religious thought in the early nineteenth century was its rationality. The eighteenth-century British enlightenment shaped the orthodox religious mind in America, implanting a distinctive though pervasive rational temper that left its imprint on theologians and revivalists alike. The context of their thought had its main anchorage in the seventeenth century, but the orthodox theologians also adopted forms and methods from the Christian rationalism of the eighteenth century and appropriated patterns of theology rooted in the early eras of the Church. They attempted to confront the enlightenment on its own terms; the more unyielding their solicitude for the Biblical revelation, the more did they strive for rational proof and explanation. To be orthodox was to assume the unity of truth and therefore to affirm a "natural theology" based on human reason as the normal prolegomenon, proof, and corollary of Scriptural revelation. The era of revivalism was also an age of reason in American religion, and in some respects the rationalism proved more durable than the fervor.

Such a claim has an air of both presumption and peculiarity when applied to the Old South. It seems self-evident that Southern churches have perennially assumed a special responsibility for inculcating feeling rather than thought, spontaneous affectivity rather than labored ratiocination. We hear from the historians that the religion of the Southern people on the eve of the Civil War was "truly a faith," not a "reasoned orthodoxy"; that religious development in the Old South was a transition from Jeffersonian liberalism to revivalistic emotionalism;[1] that the religious Southerner had no ambition "to perfect a system, or to tidy up a world doomed to remain forever deceptive, changeful, and evil";[2] that Southern faith was "almost totally" from the heart, not the head;[3] that strictly the Southerner had no mind, only temperament;[4] that he did not think, he felt.[5] Such descriptions are not entirely false, but they are only partially true, which means that the prevailing image of Southern

religion is empty of contrasts; we are left with a portrait of ubiquitous religious feeling and unremitting biblicism. To speak of the
mindlessness of antebellum Southern religion is to repeat a cliché;
even some historians continue to loiter on the outskirts of the camp
meeting and to conclude that religious mentality dissolved into
feeling. To inquire into an orthodox Southern religious "mind,"
and especially a "rationalistic" mind intent on intellectually tidy-
ing up the world, is to question a commonplace.

The cities and small towns of the Old South, however, were
populated by clergymen who viewed themselves as apostles of the
unity of truth, as architects of rational cosmologies and reasonable
psychologies. These men were convinced—as one Methodist theologian wrote—that God had "never enjoined upon man the duty of
faith, without first presenting before him a reasonable foundation
for the same."[6] The clerical gentlemen tried to establish orthodoxy
on that foundation. Indeed, they believed that rationality should
pervade human existence. So they asserted that reason was the
formal criterion even of revelation; they taught the intellect to
superintend the internal affections of the Christian convert; they
sought to integrate the whole of society—from the internal life of
the individual to the impersonal structures of the state—into a
harmonious cosmos governed by omniscient wisdom. In one sense
they were naïve idealists who believed that the propagation of
correct ideas could subdue the recalcitrant vitalities of the natural
self and of the social organism as well—granted the assistance of
divine grace. The unity of truth, they believed, entailed the ultimate orderliness of reality; such was the verdict of Scripture and
reason. For the prominent urban clergy, therefore, theology seemed
both a reasonable and a rational enterprise, designed to commend
Christian faith to an expanding class of educated and aspiring
Southerners.

CHAPTER ONE

THE TOWN SETTING

In 1826 James Taylor, twenty-two years old and newly ordained, made a tentative step toward joining the clerical elite of the Old South: he moved to town. Despite an unusually brief apprenticeship as a missionary in rural Virginia, he received and accepted an invitation from the Second Baptist Church in Richmond, a struggling congregation in search of respectability and refinement as well as spiritual renewal. Richmond in 1826 was a modest community of twelve thousand people, and it still bore the marks of a disastrous economic depression, but for Taylor it was a new and exciting world with an enviable reputation among colleagues in the countryside. An old friend sketched his new image: "I imagine to myself that you have become quite a great preacher. Situated in the metropolis of the state, in the foundation of polite knowledge, having intelligent companions, recourse to many books, everything to make you diligent in studying, you have improved, I expect, considerably."[1]

The description embodied an implicit warning against pride and vainglory, but Taylor would have agreed that a tenure in Richmond should "improve" him. The son of an English cabinetmaker, he had sought self-improvement ever since the days of his intimate youthful friendship with the president of a small Virginia college. After being licensed to preach in 1824, he departed immediately for rural missionary tasks but resigned after a year to be "more at leisure to pursue his studies" and to write essays in theology for the *Columbian Star*, a Baptist paper published in Washington. His articles attracted the attention of the Richmond Baptists, and his stay with them confirmed his zeal for improvement. Taylor purchased the library of an older minister, began a program of diligent study, and in 1830 helped organize a group of ministers "friendly to the improvement of the ministry" into an education society to establish a Baptist seminary in Virginia: "Something must and will be done," he wrote, "for elevating the standard of improvement among the ministry of our denomination." By 1832 he could watch proudly as the Virginia Baptist Seminary, known later as Richmond College, arose on the outskirts of the city.

Taylor then turned his attention to the gentlemanly pursuit of writing history and biography, but his craving for "literary and scientific improvement" led him in 1839 to resign his pastorate temporarily and become chaplain at the University of Virginia, where he met regularly with the professorial club and attended daily lectures on Latin, Greek, natural philosophy, and chemistry for a year before returning to Richmond. He had thus become, in the words of his son, a "city pastor" within a rural society, a position of signal importance in the development of religious thought in the antebellum South.[2]

Taylor was one of a small but influential group of clerical gentlemen who were responding, in groping and half-conscious ways, to important changes in the Southern social order, as well as to the intellectual problems that accompanied the cultural transitions of post-Revolutionary America. His career exemplified the complex interrelation between religious thought and its social setting in the nineteenth-century South. He was sensitive to the aspirations of townspeople within a plantation culture; that sensitivity informed his attitudes toward theology and theological learning within a revivalist culture. Taylor typified an influential group of Southern theologians who inherited, modified, and propagated "rational orthodoxy."

The articulation of rational orthodoxy in the Old South coincided with the slow proliferation and growth of towns and cities; the quest for theological reasonableness was one component in a search for the meaning of urbanity. But the denominational theologies were also the product of traditions that antedated the nineteenth century and intersected various social settings. Theology has never been an isolated endeavor existing in antiseptic abstraction from the world, and no theologians were more firmly embedded within a social world than the urban clergy of the nineteenth-century South, but they were also self-conscious guardians of tradition. One must therefore attend to both the social location of the theologians and the ways in which they appropriated and used intellectual traditions. Southern theology in the nineteenth century was the product of a dual impulse: it reflected both intellectual commitments and social compulsions.

1. Urban Images

Though towns developed early during the settlement of the Southern frontier, the expansion of town life in the Old South was undramatic; the region remained rural throughout the nineteenth century. The first wave of immigrants into the piedmont and trans-appalachian South, the mobile seminomadic frontiersmen, were indifferent to urban amenities. The second wave, farmers and planters, built self-sufficient agricultural institutions that seemed to make the towns economically superfluous.[3] In 1810 only 4 percent of Southerners were urban dwellers; by 1850 the number had risen to 8 percent, located in forty cities scattered throughout the region. But that statistical report, which defines a city as merely a collection of 2500 or more persons, ignores the cultural and social diversity of the cities, it fails to suggest the panoply of attitudes and expectations among urban dwellers, and it overlooks the smaller towns. By 1850 the South also contained over 130 small towns, each having between 500 and 2500 identifiable inhabitants to attract the ministration of doctors, lawyers, teachers, and clergymen.[4] And although townspeople constituted only a small proportion of the Southern population, a few Southerners discovered in the forms and rhythms of the towns a new vision of themselves and their place in the world. The history of theology in the South was inextricably bound to that vision.

In 1860 J. D. B. DeBow, who spent his career as an editor defending and publicizing Southern city life, felt sanguine about the attractions of urbanity. "Within the last forty years," he said, "country life has quietly and almost imperceptibly undergone a great change," as the rural South became dependent on the town as a source of ideas and information, a business center, and a respite from boredom. "Whether in the pursuit of business, pleasure, or information, men leave the country and visit some neighboring city."[5] James Taylor, the young Richmond minister, believed that the economic power of merchants enabled the Southern towns to exercise such "large influence on the surrounding country," but Philip Lindsley, a clerical college president in Nashville, also helped to explain the attraction of town life when he praised the "refined society" and "eminent professional characters" in large communities.[6] In any case, a small but growing number of Southerners could have confessed with DeBow in 1860 that "our bodies are in the country, our souls in town."[7] And the townsfolk themselves became conscious of the differences: "I like the country people very much," wrote a Virginian in 1858. "I think there is much truth and simplicity about them. But then they have not the allurements that we Town People have to contend with."[8]

Amelia Montgomery of Belmont, Mississippi, experienced the tension of having her body in the country and her soul in town. Acclimated to New Orleans but then isolated in rural Mississippi, she complained bitterly:

> I am heartily sick of this kind of life, it is too laborious for me. . . . No school for our boys and no preaching to go to. . . . Oh for a pleasant home in the city, where we could enjoy each others society, and have our boys at some regular school or business. They will be ruined if we bring them up this way . . . I will try to cheer up.[9]

Other townsfolk thrust into similar isolation were even less adaptable. "I only spent one week in New Orleans," wrote one indignant urbanite exiled in the outer reaches of Louisiana, "and have been in this hole ever since. . . . I shall return to the city this fall."[10] Amelia Montgomery's aspirations may seem at first glance to have little relation to the abstractions of formal theology, but when a sufficient number of Southerners began to think of themselves as "Town People," the clergy felt obligated to bind together social aspiration and theological truth.

Town life in the Old South produced an incipient boosterism, an insecure civic pride composed of diverse elements: reaction against the condescending antiurban ideologues of the plantation culture, protest against the prevailing images of urban pestilence and mortality, and the desire to project, for economic and other reasons, an aura of enterprise, opportunity, culture, and refinement. Builders and promoters of new towns strove to overcome indifference and hostility through a promotion campaign, conducted after 1845 in the pages of J. D. B. DeBow's *Commercial Review of the South and West*, which after its founding in New Orleans became the organ of a veritable crusade for urbanization. DeBow opened its pages to town boosters throughout the South, and the publicists who submitted articles rarely limited themselves to commercial statistics or reports about the physical advantages of town life. They spoke also of the "spirit of improvement," "intellectual achievements," and "public taste" in the Southern cities. Spokesmen for the towns associated them with intellect and culture, wealth, energy, and talent.[11] A hopeful Texan exhibited the booster spirit in a letter to a young teacher:

> There is a new town called "Salado" just being laid out seven or eight miles below Belton.... The principal object in building the town is to get together a cultivated refined community and for educational purposes. There is now in process of erection a large roomy building for an academy and a teacher of high order is required even now for the beginning. It is intended that no place in the state shall boast of superior advantages to this.... All denominations enter into the arrangement.... We wish to know if you would accept a professor's chair in the college if it were offered you.[12]

Other towns boasted of their own superior advantages, and local newspapers proclaimed the urban gospel. The Lynchburg *Daily Virginian* took pride in its hometown as a "seat of learning" and art as well as of trade and manufacture; the editor of the Athens, Georgia, *Atheneum* announced in his prospectus that in his community "a disposition to patronize literature and science" was "extensively manifested."[13] From such self-appraisals one learns that the Southern towns were, in the estimation of their own journalists, "enlightened" communities, "not only rapidly acquiring all the facilities and necessities of social life, but also not a few of the attendants on refinement and elegance," and that refined townsfolk had achieved a triumph of civilization, intelligence, and order.[14] Outsiders often criticized the narrow commercialism of the Southern towns, but at least one contingent of urban dwellers yearned for a broader image.

One of James Fenimore Cooper's fictional characters once observed that an American town ordinarily passed through several stages of development, during which a casual mingling of classes gradually gave way to a subtle struggle for local superiority as contending families, emboldened by wealth, by beginning the struggle for "place" multiplied the gradations of social station.[15] As the clergy often noted, the Southern towns exhibited similar social patterns, loosely woven to be sure, that drew the educated and respectable citizenry first into informal and then into increasingly formal and structured relationships: clubs, churches, lyceums, professional organizations, thespian societies, library companies, debating clubs, literary societies, and, on occasion, exclusive neighborhoods.

Baltimore in 1800 was a city of 26,000 persons whose housing patterns reflected the social differences: the wealthy lived in the center of town, within sight of St. Paul's Episcopal Church, while the poor huddled around the edges of the city.[16] Charleston in 1850 was a city of 42,985 persons whose literary institutions symbolized the achievements and pretensions of its social elite; visitors admired the massive red brick and white marble Library Society building, the College of Charleston, and the Medical College. After visiting the city's elegant homes, where she conducted conversations about English poetry, the Swedish novelist Fredrika Bremer concluded that she had found a new "aristocratic world."[17] New Orleans, with 116,000 inhabitants in 1850, was the region's most cosmopolitan city; Louisville, with 43,194, was one of the most commercially energetic; and Richmond, with 27,570, still impressed tourists with its imposing capitol and grand churches "filled closely with the beauty, the fashion, the wealth of the city."[18]

What the Southern towns achieved or failed to achieve, however, is, for our purposes, less important than how they appeared to the Southern clergy and laity. Tuscaloosa was a modest community indeed, but to the Methodist Landon Garland its citizens seemed strikingly "intelligent and refined": "Perhaps few places of its size can boast of better society."[19] To one minister, Florence, Alabama, seemed to be filled with "more respectable and intelligent men than I have ever known in the same proportion in any other place."[20] To another, Nashville was a city of "intelligent, polished and hospitable" ladies and gentlemen.[21] Even the small towns appeared to be blessed with a plenitude of "intelligent and wealthy citizens."[22]

These literate and respectable townsfolk were a part of what Daniel Hundley, an Alabama planter and banker, contemptuously called the "middle classes," a motley grouping of well-to-do farmers, merchants, artisans, manufacturers, and professionals who stood in the Southern pecking order somewhat beneath the aristocratic gentlemen and the newly rich "cotton snobs" but yet above the yeomen farmers, the "white trash," and the slaves. The small-town and urban "middle-class lawyers, doctors, school-teachers, parsons and the like" were part of a broader group who were, in Hundley's view, imbued with a visible sense of "pride and self-importance" and disposed to "fancy that they are cultivated in the highest degree." Yearly, he said, they were becoming more wealthy and influential.[23] In other words: among the mercantile and professional classes in the Southern towns were growing numbers of people who aspired to gentility.

The town clergy accepted such aspirations—and the social and economic distinctions on which they were based—as natural, even providential. Their sermons and other expositions exhibited a consistent, albeit rough and unhewn, description of society as a gradation of aristocrats, middling classes, masses, and slaves. The ministers called for benevolence to the poor, criticized aristocratic display, and chastised unseemly and rapacious economic behavior, but they approved the social ranking. It became established dogma, confirmed by the fight over slavery, that there would always be "different classes and conditions of human society," indeed that social inequality was a divine contrivance.[24] On that dogma Protestants and Catholics could agree: Bishop John England of Charleston declared that it would be a lamentable mistake to bring about "the destruction of distinctions in society."[25] The concept of "the masses" or "the multitude," a collection of faceless souls ever hovering on the verge of barbarism or ripe for evangelistic outreach, permeated clerical writings on the social order.[26] The clergy could not ignore the social distinctions of town life: "With all the republicanism in our country," wrote Bishop William Meade of Virginia, "there is as much of social and religious prejudice, caste, and division among us as in any nation of Christendom, though it differs considerably in some of its modes."[27]

Thomas Smyth (1808–1873), the pastor of the Second Presbyterian Church in Charleston from 1830 to 1870, argued, in typical fashion, that the social and economic hierarchy expressed the immutable divine will. A native of Ireland, Smyth had graduated from Belfast College in 1827 with a brilliant record, studied for a year in London, and then emigrated to New Jersey, where he enrolled in Princeton Theological Seminary. When he began his pastorate in Charleston he quickly won widespread celebrity, but despite his personal popularity Smyth distrusted "the people" and felt uneasy with democratic rhetoric. Alexis de Tocqueville's *Democracy in America* confirmed his dislike of the unreflecting, revolutionary multitude, and he opposed any universal extension of manhood suffrage because he doubted whether "the entire mass of the people" were prepared to vote properly.[28] He also resisted any scheme that reduced the commercial prerogatives of the emerging Southern mercantile class. Only "speculative and philosophizing economists," he said, would suggest that the redistribution of wealth might bring happiness to a race entangled in sin. After Adam's fall, "poverty became the normal condition of man and the actual state of the great mass." Christian principles precluded any egalitarian order, for God himself ordained the "inequalities of condition and diversities of rank," which permanently and inevitably divided not only ruler from subject and master from servant but also rich from poor.[29] Smyth's personal vision of the social order accorded with a standard perception of Southern society among the elite clergy.

The social ladder therefore leaned heavily against the church house door, and a consciousness of social position affected the tone of Church life as well as its external trappings. When Frances Trollope toured the South in 1827 she observed that Church gatherings were the occasions when "all display is made, and all fashionable distinction sought." A stranger from Europe would be inclined, she said, to suppose "that the places of worship were the theatres and cafes of the place."[30] Urban congregations advertised their pre-eminence by erecting imposing physical structures, ranging from the large Monumental Church built by Richmond Episcopalians and the celebrated Round Church of the Charleston Presbyterians to dozens of "elegant" and "splendid" brick, Gothic, and Grecian buildings that began to grace the "excellent neighborhoods" of the newer transappalachian towns during the 1840s.[31]

Toward the end of the antebellum period a Catholic critic of Southern Protestantism ridiculed the trend:

> And if a traveler from some distant clime should chance suddenly to enter one of our *fashionable* meeting houses; if he should look at its splendidly cushioned seats . . . he would almost conclude that he had entered, by mistake, into some finely furnished lecture room. And if he were informed that this edifice had been erected and furnished by a joint stock company on shares, and that these shrewd speculations looked confidently to the income from the rent of the seats as a return for their investment, his original impression should certainly not be weakened. But the conclusion would be irresistible, if he were told still farther, that in order to secure a good attendance of the rich and fashionable, the owners of the stock had taken the prudent precaution to engage, at a high salary, some popular and eminent preacher! Those who have watched closely the signs of the times, will admit that this is not a mere fancy sketch, and that it is not even exaggerated.[32]

The description was a caricature, but it captured a recognizable image.

2. A Wider Field of Usefulness

To one segment of the clergy the town churches seemed to contain "the talent, the wealth, and the enterprise of our country."[33] The ministers may have bemoaned any traces in themselves of excessive ambition for eminent urban pulpits, but they also agreed that the city churches, especially the "more respectable and intelligent" congregations, constituted a "wider field of usefulness," of both symbolic and strategic importance.[34] The young Episcopal clergy who revived their Church from its post-Revolutionary stupor were among the first to exploit the possibilities of the city. Their carefully orchestrated efforts to lure Richard Channing Moore away from New York and into the Virginia Episcopal office focused on the potential of a bishopric in Richmond. William Holland Wilmer, the rector in Alexandria, wrote Moore in 1813 that

Richmond would offer unexampled opportunity for a bishop: "in its relation to the other parts of Virginia, [the city] is an infinitely important situation."[35] Wilmer's young ally, William Meade, subsequently reassured Moore that Richmond was the center of gravity for Southern Episcopalianism because if offered access to influential people.

> And if Episcopalianism dies there, at the heart, of course it dies elsewhere. This is the central place: here each winter the Assembly of the state sits. The supreme court, and the convention of the clergy meet here also. You would have a large and respectable congregation.[36]

Eventually some of the bishops had second thoughts. After rising to the episcopacy in 1841 Meade complained that the young priests in his diocese were content only in "the largest fields," and in an 1855 address Bishop Stephen Elliott of Georgia charged that the Episcopal clergy were utterly unqualified to "enter upon the arena of a rural parish." But even Elliott's allies demurred at his proposal to substitute fervor for style and learning in an effort to reach the rural masses.[37] Despite a brief period of debate during the 1850s, with attendant soul-searching, the abler Episcopal clergy stayed in town.

Urban congregations were not uniformly fashionable, and even Episcopalians, who recognized that they were "regarded as the Church of a class," had to contend with problems of status and style.[38] A Natchez minister named M. R. Babcock expressed a common feeling when he tried to persuade his colleague John Freeman Young to decline an invitation from St. Luke's in New Orleans in favor of one from the church in Natchez. The members of St. Luke's, he warned, could not provide "the sort of intellectual stimulus which you feel the need of."

> Is not a fourth or fifth rate city parish about the poorest thing imaginable? Where the feeling of social caste is so strong as it is in New Orleans, is there any reasonable prospect for making St. Luke's—at least for many years to come—what you hope?

Babcock suggested that Natchez, in contrast, would offer "the pleasantest possible associations" and "the consequent advantages (by no means small) of such society."[39] For similar reasons the Reverend Samuel Montgomery decided to stay in Canton, Mississippi, rather than to accept an invitation from neighboring Plains: "There can never be much of a church down there, as the place is not susceptible of much enlargement or importance." The "field for usefulness" in the larger town was more "flattering," he added.[40] Such considerations were not lost on ministers within the denominations of more modest social standing. Reflecting on his father's early years as pastor of Richmond's Second Baptist Church, George Taylor observed that although the title of "city pastor" had a grand sound, a city church "overshadowed by other and more powerful ones" could be a discouraging field of labor.[41]

In such a setting the town clergy of necessity became sensitive to the values and expectations within the urban social hierarchy. Some of them fretted openly about the danger that the image of clerical indigence (or even the impression that the clergy had emerged from poverty) might undermine ease of access to the influential classes. During the 1840s Southern Presbyterians debated the merits of various programs that had since 1806 provided funds to educate "poor and pious youth" for the ministry. The prestigious stalwarts of the denomination—Robert J. Breckinridge, James Henley Thornwell, Robert L. Dabney—complained of a "class ministry, and what is still worse, an eleemosynary class ministry." As late as the General Assembly of 1856 Peyton Harrison of Virginia was still condemning "the current notion that only indigent young men are to be expected to offer themselves to the Lord. . . . The sooner we get rid of a class ministry the better."[42] But Presbyterians did not object to a class ministry so long as the class was sufficiently respectable, and their humbler competitors envied their ability to attract and mingle with lawyers, doctors, politicians, judges, and others who symbolized "strength in high places."[43]

The great popular denominations, Methodists and Baptists, found it especially difficult at first to establish their clergy securely in urban pulpits. Largely the offspring of rural yeomen, they had long cherished and nurtured the traditions of the "plainfolk." Many of them had entered the ministry in the aftermath of the frontier revivals that swept the region after 1801, when they were confident that their fervor could substitute for, and even improve upon, such traditional ministerial qualifications as education, doctrinal understanding, and mastery of ancient languages. Most of the Methodist and Baptist clergy seem to have conformed to the stereotype of the frontier exhorter: disdainful of technical theology, frequently illiterate, indifferent to cultural refinement, and preoccupied with the stimulation of emotional excitement in camp-meeting revivals or the preservation of disciplined moral behavior in tightly regulated religious conventicles. But some of the town churches felt reservations about frontier exhorters—a fact that began to disturb a small coterie of aspiring clergy who were themselves embarrassed by the prevailing image of "popular preachers."[44]

Of all the Southern churches, the Methodists made the most ambitious institutional effort to adjust to the changing character of towns, initially with mixed results. When their traditional pattern of large circuits containing several congregations proved inadequate, they tried to modify the circuit system within the larger towns by rotating preachers among the various congregations inside the city boundaries. The physical proximity of the churches, however, permitted "overwhelming crowds" to rotate along with the gifted preachers, leaving only a handful to hear those of "less pleasing talent." Such selectivity proved intolerable both to the Church authorities and to the lesser clerical brethren, who were subject to spells of discouragement and envy.[45] Gradually, therefore, each town congregation became a "station," served by a single minister or two, rather than part of a larger circuit—a process under way by 1810.[46]

The Methodists had a difficult time, however, finding men qualified to serve the new stations. As early as 1815 William McKendree, the denomination's first native-born American bishop, began keeping private lists of clerical names, often distinguishing between men who were "qualified to fill any *station*" and others of "ordinary talents" whose educational and cultural deficiencies precluded their being accepted by town churches. The people were prone to look "too high," complained one minister, and to expect a "station preacher" to do "everything."[47] The Methodists made progress in the next quarter century, but during the forties William Winans of Mississippi, who oversaw the Church's progress in New Orleans, was still complaining that "the prospect of filling the stations tolerably is very gloomy." We have many important town churches, he confided to a friend, including congregations in New Orleans, Natchez, and Vicksburg, but "comparatively few suitable men to fill them."[48] "Our greatest want, in human means, is a supply of suitable preachers for the *Stations*, of which we have a number that are both difficult and important."[49] At the end of 1842 Winans reported that the number of preachers capable of occupying an urban pulpit was increasing. But he continued to write letters to urban clergy outside the South, urging them to "transfer immediately" to Southern cities.[50]

Aspiring Baptists were less sanguine: "We shrink with an instinctive dread from the crowded city," announced the *Southern Baptist and General Intelligencer* in 1835. "Look at our great city churches, few and feeble for want of a greater number of competent pastors."[51] The minister at Nashville's First Baptist Church, Robert Boyté Crawford Howell, who for years occupied the president's chair in the Southern Baptist Convention, complained that few Baptist clergymen were even acceptable in cities and towns. That was tragic, he said, because "these centres of influence are like the fortresses and strongholds of a country," and the party that possesses them possesses power.[52] In Alabama Basil Manly, Jr., who held prominent positions in urban Baptist churches throughout the South, also lamented that the denomination had "few men fitted" to serve in the "centres of greatest activity," and his father, a clergyman who was the president of the state university, fully agreed: "It is easy to get *a* man a city ch[urch]—but to obtain *the* man is another thing." As late as 1850 the elder Manly was searching for ministers who possessed "the qualities requisite for a successful pastorate in a city or town."[53] By that time the Southern Baptist Convention was describing the cities as the "fertile fields" of the religious South, bemoaning the melancholy fortunes of urban Baptist clergy, and planning to establish home missionaries in "the most prominent and important towns, possessing the most commanding influence."[54]

The great point of interest to which we would call the attention of the Convention [announced the Board of Domestic Missions in 1853] are the cities scattered throughout the South and South-west. These are the great centres of influence throughout our land for good or for evil. . . . It is a fact, which deserves the serious attention of this Convention, that while in the country we are comparatively successful, in the cities of the South and South-west we are comparatively feeble. . . . We are prepared to recommend these cities and towns as the prominent points of interest in our Home Missionary department.[55]

The Convention began to subsidize missionaries in such exotic locations as Vicksburg, Memphis, and Montgomery and by 1853 could claim some success in twenty-one Southern cities, which thereafter continued to receive a liberal share of the Convention's money and attention.[56]

The urban Methodist and Baptist pastors sometimes complained about the "assumption of superiority" among Presbyterians and Episcopalians.[57] They recognized, as did the Roman Catholics, that they were associated in the public mind with "the toiling classes of the community," or in some instances with "the middling interests" of society.[58] But ministers within the popular denominations could also have expansive ambitions. Although the Methodist clergy disagreed with one another about the propriety of accepting honorary doctor of divinity degrees, their General Conference of 1832 approved the practice after several speakers argued that it provided entree to a social class that Methodists might not otherwise reach: the doctorate, they assured themselves, offered "access to and influence over many."[59] Their efforts occasionally created tensions within local congregations. The educated clergymen who began arriving in Memphis after 1830 found themselves caught between "the intelligent," whom they desired to cultivate, and simpler members, accustomed to "noise and blunder," who felt uncomfortable with a conspicuous display of "reason" in the pulpit.[60] In Vicksburg the Methodists divided in 1849 into two parties, with the minority accusing the remainder of "Aristocratic" pretensions.[61] But the ambitions overcame the ambivalence, and Methodist and Baptist preachers within the towns increasingly noted with pride their success in attracting the "respectable" middle classes and in drawing "intelligent and wealthy citizens" to Christ.[62]

As the Methodist bishops had quicky learned, however, assigning a preacher to the "intelligent and wealthy" members of a town church was a delicate affair. In 1806 Augusta, Georgia, was a small community of 2400 inhabitants on the Savannah River. It boasted of wealthy merchants, wide streets, and handsome houses, in addition to an elegant academy graced with an ornamental cupola. The Methodists of Augusta were initially of low standing in the town's emerging polite society, which was said to be "well-informed" with "a considerable taste for literature." The local literary elite had plans for a Thespian Society and Library Company, which in 1808 became the first of several ephemeral associations.[63]

When Lovick Pierce became the Methodist minister in 1806, he consciously sought entry into "the best society" and thereby set an example for future ministers. A graduate of the medical college of Philadelphia, Pierce was said to be timid, distrustful of himself, and often impatient with others, but he compensated for his "limited cultivation" through the "grace of his manner" and soon altered the popular image of the Methodist circuit riders. By the time he returned to the church for a second appointment in 1823 the Methodists of Augusta were a bit more self-conscious about their social image and increasingly fastidious about their preachers. They "demanded such a pulpit supply as the conference could not always supply." In fact, they told the bishop that their next minister should be the courtly William Capers (1790–1855), an affluent planter's son who after leaving South Carolina College had studied law and then entered the ministry, moving quickly from rural circuits to pulpits in Charleston, Columbia, Oxford, and Savannah.

The bishop refused to honor the request, but he discovered that the congregation's perceptions were acute. In 1829 he sent to Augusta the earnest but undistinguished Elijah Sinclair—and the membership decreased by sixty. The following year he sent the equally unremarkable Henry Bass, and the church lost seventy-five more members. So in 1831 the bishop assigned the congregation to James O. Andrew, who was on his way to becoming a bishop himself, and to young George Pierce, Lovick's son, who had recently graduated with honors from the University of Georgia and who offended the old-fashioned clergy by refusing to abandon his fashionable attire when he entered the ministry. Within a year the Augusta congregation gained a hundred new members; the following year Pierce assumed sole responsibility and attracted a hundred more, thus financing a new brick edifice. But then the bishop made the mistake of returning Sinclair to Augusta. He struggled for a year, failed to attract a single member, and left. Sinclair's experience was not lost upon his successors. Isaac Boring accepted his subsequent appointment to Augusta with misgiving and self-doubt: "It was the first considerable city Isaac Boring had served."[64] By the 1840s a Methodist pastor could describe a rural appointment as "degrading," but anxieties were common among fledgling urban pastors, who were sometimes explicitly reminded that they were now preaching to "town-folks."[65] Even Leonidas Polk, later to become a famed Episcopal bishop, felt intimidated by his first city congregation in Richmond.[66]

The Augusta Methodists exemplified a pattern that transcended denominational boundaries, as urban congregations increasingly sought to impose their wishes on church officials. The Methodist patriarch Francis Asbury was distressed when Charleston Methodists claimed the unprecedented right to choose their own preacher and, being refused, formed a schismatic congregation designed to attract "the elite" in the city.[67] But Methodist bishops and presiding elders later became accustomed to receiving letters from urban churches with suggested nominees for pastoral appointment.[68] During the same period, moreover, Roman Catholic bishops had to face demands from lay trustees and wardens in urban parishes that threatened to plunge the Church into ceaseless litigation. Catholic congregations in Charleston, Norfolk, and New Orleans wanted not only to vest the ownership of Church property in local trustee boards but also to elect their own pastors and bishops. The Charleston Schism, beginning in 1818, lasted more than a year, and only with the arrival in 1820 of the new bishop, John England, did Church life there return to normal. Roman Catholics in New Orleans quarreled sporadically with the hierarchy for four decades, and only a papal condemnation of the lay trustees by Gregory XVI in 1844 could establish order there.[69]

The first Episcopal congregation in New Orleans proved so quarrelsome and independent that the General Convention initially refused even to recognize the newly formed diocese of Louisiana. Episcopal bishops in the South complained among themselves that local churches had "carried this lay element too far," indeed to such a point that they felt unable to assign a minister to a parish without permission from the lay vestry.[70] In practice, moreover, influential urban Presbyterians had free rein in the selection of their clergy, as also of course did the Baptists, who affirmed congregational autonomy as a matter of principle. In one way or another, officially or unofficially, urban congregations sought and usually won the right to judge the qualifications of prospective ministers.

That urban churchmembers could have high expectations is evident from the diary of Mitchell King, a Charleston Presbyterian who for over two decades commented profusely on the shortcomings and successes of the local clergy. A lawyer and member of Charleston's literary society, King was himself a match for his minister in knowledge of theology. He read Augustus Neander's *Life of Christ* to orient himself in German controversies over Biblical criticism, studied Pascal and seventeenth-century Jansenism, and conducted dinner conversations on the life of Luther. He read moral philosophy, along with works on the history of the crusades and such efforts in contemporary churchmanship as Stephen Colwell's *New Themes for the Protestant Clergy*, an early plea that ministers attend to social problems. King also studied sacramental theology, followed the controversies over Unitarianism, wondered aloud about the canonical status of the Book of Revelation, developed a passing interest in the Jewish Cabalistic tradition, and read French philosophy.

His evaluations of the Charleston clergy, therefore, could be penetrating and acerbic. One visitor to Charleston lauded the Presbyterian minister Dr. John Forrest as an accomplished preacher with polished manners and "varied acquirements in literature and science." From King's diary, however, we learn that Forrest's sermons ranged in quality from "good" and "fair" to "tolerable" and "unsatisfactory." Other ministers were subject to similar scrutiny. One preacher's discourse was "too ambitious," filled with "Celestialisms" and "Effloresce"; the argument of another was "able but unscriptural." One wrote an "excellent" polemical sermon, but another persistently failed to grasp the "logical consequences" implicit in his premises.[71] King was unquestionably exceptional, and few of the town pastors had to satisfy standards so exacting. But churchpeople who lacked King's erudition could nevertheless echo a demand for clerical gentility, which they justified purely on the basis of their status as townsfolk. The Methodists of Staunton, Virginia, complained in 1835 when their bishop assigned them an unacceptable preacher: "There was no place more important anywhere. . . . It had an able bar; judges of great distinction resided there; the stage lines centered there. In such a place a preacher of prominence and ability was needed to cope with the Presbyterians, who were very strong."[72]

A few ministers chafed under the demands. Basil Manly, Sr. (1799–1868) concluded that the religious and social expectations imposed on urban ministers were excessive. A member of a prominent North Carolina family, Manly was already licensed as a Baptist minister when a clerical colleague persuaded him to enter South Carolina College, from which he graduated as valedictorian in 1821. After five years of preaching in small towns, he accepted an invitation from the First Baptist Church in Charleston, where he remained for twelve years. In 1837 he accepted the presidency of the University of Alabama, a position that he filled for eighteen years, consistently rebuffing the periodic advances of Baptist congregations in New Orleans, Charleston, and Richmond. Manly had come to believe that it was "a prodigious slavery to be Pastor of a city church in these days." After turning down an invitation from Richmond in 1849, he explained why he had "seen enough . . . of the pastorate of our city churches." An urban pulpit, he said, offered a vacuous prominence, an empty notoriety, the tyranny of custom, subjection to continual judgments and comparisons, and, always, the pressure of competition with other clerical notables. The workload was unreasonable: townsfolk demanded proficiency in the pulpit, the lecture room, the Sabbath school, the prayer meeting, the mission board, the academic societies, the editor's table, the revival meeting, and the sick room. And the salary of $1500 was inadequate when a man was "*required* to maintain the *style* of a gentleman, and the generosity of a Christian." In 1855, though, the Wentworth Street Church in Charleston implored him to reconsider, and though his decision both "amazed" and "appalled" him, Manly accepted their invitation: "I know what the pastorate in a large city comes to. . . . What is the Lord carrying me to Charleston for?"[73] Ever sensitive to urban expectations, Manly spent the rest of his career crusading for theological education that would prepare Southern ministers to reach the region's "cultivated hearers."[74]

To outsiders the South's towns and cities often seemed modest, even meager, in appearance and arid in cultural achievement, but Basil Manly and many of his fellow Southerners had a different view. What was the impact of towns and cities on the Old South? A question so broadly phrased resists any coherent answer. But there are more modest ways of posing the issue. Which groups were influenced by the patterns of town life? How did they respond and with what consequences? Such questions illuminate the history of theology in the Old South because the region's clerical theologians—at least, the men who published their thoughts in books and journals—were, in the main, pastors of town churches and teachers in schools and colleges within towns and cities. Observing that fact and inquiring into its meaning need not imply that the theology was merely a symbolic manifestation of latent, mysterious social processes, or that it masked covert class interests, or that it appealed only to Southern city dwellers. But as town pastors within a rural society, the Southern theologians were naturally sensitive to their surroundings; their concrete relationships with other townsfolk engendered canons of selectivity that guided their appropriation of tradition.

CHAPTER TWO

THE GENTLEMEN PREACHERS

During the antebellum period the Southern clergy nurtured two conflicting images of themselves. The first was an image of the preacher as a man embodying the religious sentiments of the common folk, distinguished by fervor and commitment, sharing with his flock in a relationship of emotional warmth that was tempered by authoritarian command. The second was an image of the minister as a gentleman, exalted and elevated through character, erudition, and professional status. The images both mirrored and molded the emerging patterns of Southern religious life. By 1860 the amateur sociologist Daniel Hundley distinguished between the preachers of the yeoman class—ignorant, illiterate, and dogmatic—and the middle-class parsons who affected cultivation and learning.[1] From the latter group came the proponents of clerical gentility, a small and elite body, unequally divided among the major denominations, divided also among themselves over both fundamental and trivial questions, and occasionally uneasy about their own aspirations. Yet in numerous instances they made the decisions that governed the Southern churches, they staffed the Protestant colleges, taught moral philosophy, and wrote theology. They articulated the "orthodox" religious thought of the Old South.

It is hard to know how many ministers to include in the ranks of the elite. In 1817 John Holt Rice estimated that only ten or twelve of the more than four or five hundred Baptist preachers of Virginia were "men of some literary attainments," and that the Methodists were "about equal in point of learning." But he found within the Presbyterian Synod of Virginia some forty or fifty ministers "furnished with the best education that the literary institutions of the state will afford, and anxious to diffuse religious knowledge."[2] Methodists and Baptists made some gains in the next four decades, but even in 1844 only four of the fifty-one Southern delegates to the Methodist General Conference were college graduates (though college education was not invariably a sign of intellectual aspirations during a period when self-educated men rose to positions of commanding academic influence and collegiate studies often did little more than certify mediocrity).[3] According to the census of 1850, some 7514 clergymen were then active in the South. Three years later the Southern Aid Society reported that "one fifth of the preachers are regularly educated for their business," an estimate suggesting that as many as 1500 Southern clergy might by that time be numbered among the men of "literary attainments."[4] "Regularity" of education, however, is a hopelessly flexible notion; quantitative judgments about such qualitative matters can be little more than speculation.

1. *An Elite Hundred*

Rather than hazarding a guess as to the number of "literary" parsons, we might find it more helpful to look at one hundred Southern ministers whose activities and achievements constitute a rough standard for defining the term "elite": all held positions of regional and not simply local leadership; all were active in organizations, institutions, and movements to facilitate the educational and cultural "improvement" of the clergy; and all labored for a portion of their careers in towns and cities. Such a sampling does not reveal much about the typical preacher in the rural South. It does afford a perspective on the gentlemen preachers in the towns and hence on the social background of their style of religious orthodoxy.[5]

The thirty-seven Presbyterians in the group, with their fourteen Episcopal colleagues, helped establish the Protestant beachheads in the Southern towns. The eighteen Methodists and twenty-three Baptists sometimes discovered that social snobbery in the "populous places" could be as disconcerting as the rigors of the frontier, though the Methodists quickly found life in the towns quite to their liking.[6] The two Lutheran pastors were men of some learning who had access, each in his own way, to the educated, while the six Roman Catholics had dissimilar experiences in the cities: in Louisville, for example, they encountered rejection, even violence, from a nativist citizenry, while in Charleston they moved easily and confidently in the upper levels of polite and literary society.[7]

The denominational divisions within the sample do not correspond to the patterns of growth in the urban clerical population. By 1860 30 percent of the town clergy in the South were Methodists. They far outnumbered their nearest competitors, the Episcopalians, and fully justified the boast of denominational annalists that the "stationed minister" had saved "the new cities" for Methodism, although their numerical prominence was due in part to the fact that nearly three-fourths of Southern churchgoers in 1860 were Methodists and Baptists.[8] Only 16 percent of the town clergy were Episcopalians; 16 percent were Baptists; 14 percent Roman Catholics; and a mere 12 percent were Presbyterians.[9] Hence the sampling of one hundred elite clergy does not even necessarily reveal the character of the "typical" town preacher; it focuses, rather, on town ministers who became highly visible; it seeks to identify the intellectual leaders of the antebellum churches.

Most of the elite town ministers were native Southerners. Only twenty-eight were transplanted Yankees; only eight—including four of the Catholics—were born in Europe. As a group they were thoroughly imbued with Southern traditions: fully half of them were natives of Virginia and the Carolinas. They were active, though, throughout the entire region: fifty-five worked in the upper South and border states, thirty-seven in the lower South, and eight moved back and forth between the two areas. Their activities were not restricted to the eastern coast: sixty-three of them preached mainly to congregations in the piedmont and transappalachian country.

In family background they were a diverse lot. About half of them had spent their early childhood in towns and cities, so they were obviously not simply the offspring of the rural yeomanry. Slightly more than 40 percent were the sons of farmers and planters, but they rarely represented the wealthy planter aristocracy. Slightly less than 20 percent were the offspring of merchants, businessmen, or urban artisans; roughly another 20 percent were sons of professionals—lawyers, physicians, teachers—and civil servants; and almost 20 percent were following in the clerical footsteps of their fathers. The categories are imprecise, but they suggest that while the families of the clerical leadership occupied a variety of social positions, most of them would fit into Daniel Hundley's "middle classes."[10]

The range of educational experience was striking. At one end of the spectrum were a few Southerners trained in both American and European settings. The Baptist John Armstrong (1798–1844), a graduate of Columbian College in Washington, D. C., spent two years of study and reading in France and Germany before returning to a congregation in Columbus, Mississippi; the Methodist Edward Drumgoole Sims (1805–1845), a member of the Tennessee Conference, graduated from the University of North Carolina and then spent two years of research in classical and Semitic languages at the University of Halle; the Presbyterian Benjamin Mosby Smith (1811–1893), a graduate of Hampden-Sidney College and Union Theological Seminary in Virginia, studied theology and Semitic languages for two years in Prussia as a prelude to pastorates in Danville and Staunton, Virginia. At the other end of the spectrum were such self-educated clergy as the Methodist Henry Bidleman Bascom (1796–1850), who rose to regional fame on the basis of an oratorical ability that he undergirded through the discipline of reading "one or two hundred pages a day for forty years."[11]

Seventy-three of the one hundred ministers had some college training; nine more received a classical education in private academies; only eighteen were self-educated or instructed solely by private tutors. Thirty-two attended theological seminaries—thirteen at Princeton—while fourteen more received some formal postcollegiate theological training through the tutelage of older ministers.[12] Their educational experiences were also geographically varied: thirty-three attended Southern colleges, with private schools holding a slight edge over the state colleges and universities; thirty studied in the North; four tried both regions; and six went to college in Europe.[13] As a group, the clerical leaders in the town churches had far more exposure to formal education than most antebellum Americans, North or South.[14]

Our group of one hundred occupied positions of regional leadership throughout the early nineteenth century. They were officials or delegates in the various regional (or national) synods, presbyteries, conferences, conventions, and associations. They included twenty bishops, three national Baptist convention presidents, and two moderators of the Presbyterian General Assembly. Thirty-one edited journals or newspapers; thirty were college presidents; and sixty served on college or seminary faculties during some period in their careers. Although the uneducated clergy sometimes felt uneasy about the ambitions and ideals of their more educated brethren, they consistently elevated the town pastors to positions of leadership, or acquiesced in their elevation. The gentlemen preachers exercised an influence that far exceeded their numbers.

In drawing a group portrait of the clerical "elite," in any case, one glimpses the features of the ministers who wrote theology during the antebellum period. The theologians were—with few exceptions—the town preachers and professors. Their formal theology was not the only expression of Southern religious thought; the songs of the plain-folk, the spirituals of the African slaves, and the sermons of frontier preachers were also forms of religious thought that expressed the fear, hope, and dignity of human life. But the writings of the most articulate can on occasion reveal dimensions of a religious culture that are not so evident in other forms of religious expression, or can, better, expose the radical variety even within such a supposedly homogeneous religious culture as the nineteenth-century South. One function of religion in the Southern towns was to reassure men and women that they were reasonable people living in a reasonable world; the elite clergy were charged with the duty of both symbolizing and conceptualizing that vision. So one cannot understand their thought without locating them within their society.

2. Ministerial Economics

By the eve of the Civil War the town clergy had acquired impressive economic and social standing. They were not, as a group, marginal participants in the region's economy. While the average wealth of free adult males in the United States in 1860 was $2500, the average wealth of the Southern town pastors was $10,-600.[15] Clerical affluence was especially visible within some of the smaller towns. Among the five ministers in Athens, Georgia, one Presbyterian, Alonzo Church, had realty and personalty holdings of $27,500; the other, Nathan Hoyt, was worth $13,000; the Episcopalian Matthew Henderson had $12,000 in real estate and personal holdings; the Baptist minister, L. R. L. Jennings, was worth $6500; and the Methodist James Hinton had wealth amounting to $4000. Of the nine Protestant ministers in Natchez, Mississippi, one Old School Presbyterian, Perry Chase, had holdings worth $65,000; the Methodist W. G. Millsaps was close behind with $45,000; the second Methodist, W. H. Watkins, held $8500; the Presbyterian Thomas Cleland, $3000; and G. B. Perry, the Episcopal priest, $1500. Four of the Protestant clergy in Natchez were without accumulated wealth. To the east, in Spartanburg, South Carolina, a Methodist, A. N. Walker, stood atop the pyramid with holdings of $22,500; the Presbyterian pastor, Edmund Cates, had $17,280; then came three more Methodists, one with $16,500, two others with $15,000 in wealth. The Baptist minister was worth $1600; only two of the clergy had no holdings. But though clerical wealth was highly visible within the smaller towns, the clergy in the larger cities also stood high above the national average: in 1860 the average wealth of the ministers in Savannah was $7200; in Charleston it was $7383; in Richmond, $7689; and in Nashville, $10,350. As a class, the town clergy occupied a comfortable economic position.

Within the clerical ranks, however, there were enormous disparities. Fully half the urban Southern ministers in 1860 had wealth of less than $3200; 40 percent of them fell beneath the national average. While the upper 20 percent held wealth ranging from $15,000 to $290,000, the bottom 20 percent had no accumulated wealth. Denominational affiliation could make a difference: within some communities Methodist and Baptist preachers stood at the top of the ministerial economic ladder, but across the South the Episcopalians maintained their superior standing. In 1860 the average wealth of urban Episcopal clergy was $18,888; next came the Presbyterians, with an average of $11,605; they were followed by the Baptists, who averaged $9883, and the Methodists, with $9454 each.[16]

The disparities extended also to annual salaries: at the beginning of the nineteenth century, Methodist circuit riders received $80 a year; as late as 1840 many Methodist clergy were existing on a yearly income of $400 "quarterage" plus "traveling and table"

expenses, but by that time some Methodists received $1200 to
$1500.[17] Episcopalians and Presbyterians often received more—
but not always. A visitor to Savannah in 1808 found one Presbyterian minister who took in $10,000 a year from salary and pew
rentals; in 1839 the Presbyterian congregation in Tuscaloosa paid
$1500; in 1842 the church in New Orleans offered $2000; the theological professors at Columbia Seminary in 1847 also received
$2000; but during the 1850s there were twenty-one Presbyterians
within a single South Carolina presbytery whose wages were not
over $250 a year.[18] Baptists in Mobile in 1839 offered a salary of
$2500; in Richmond the offer was $1500; but many Baptist ministers within Southern towns had to work at two vocations.[19]
Throughout the antebellum period, assemblies of ministers im-
plored the churches to pay a reasonable salary, noting that clergymen of all denominations were compelled to support themselves
through outside occupations.[20] Economic stratification within the
clerical ranks was a persistent characteristic of antebellum Church
life.

The upper levels of the clerical hierarchy could, in any case,
easily afford to purchase slaves, living symbols of economic and
social status. Town ministers invested quite heavily. Three of the
five pastors in Athens, Georgia, were slaveowners in 1859; 45 percent of the clergy in Savannah held slaves in 1855; by 1860 at least
61 percent of the pastors in Macon, Georgia, were slaveowners,
as were at least 50 percent of the ministers in Spartanburg and
Beaufort, South Carolina, and 54 percent in Columbia. Most of
the ministerial masters seem to have held from five to eleven
slaves: eight pastors in Macon, for example, owned a total of forty-
nine; nine ministers in Columbia held ninety-nine. But some had
larger holdings: Basil Manly, Sr., who helped initiate the regional
split within the Baptist Church, owned thirty-eight persons while
he lived at Tuscaloosa; by 1860 Bishop James O. Andrew, who
had been the symbol of the slavery issue in the Methodist Church,
owned twenty-two; and the Episcopalian Stephen Elliott of Beaufort, South Carolina, represented the small body of clergymen
within the uppermost circles of the slavocracy: he owned one
hundred ninety human beings.[21]

Land was the visible token of economic power and social prestige, even for townsfolk, and by 1860 42 percent of the town clergy

had real estate holdings, valued at $500 to $79,000 and often complete with their own involuntary laborers. In fact, 38 percent of the town clergy who owned real estate had holdings valued at or above $10,000; 72 percent owned land worth $3000 or more.[22] Harriet Martineau attributed such clerical advancement to matrimonial successes: the ministerial profession was of such high honor, she observed, that preachers could often marry into landed wealth. "Not a few planters in the south began life as poor clergymen, and obtained by marriage the means of becoming planters."[23] But slaveholders were not necessarily landowners, and slaves served symbolic as well as functional purposes. They were symbols of prestige—even if they were also more than that—and they thus helped to determine the social relationships and associations of the clerical gentlemen.

3. *"The Other Professions"*

Town life brought the clergy into increasingly complex relations with other members of the professional classes, who were beginning in the early nineteenth century to constitute a new kind of elite in American society. The diminishing authority of the old colonial gentry in the aftermath of the Revolution prepared the way for the elevation of professionals in public esteem and influence—and also helped to change the patterns of professional activity.[24] Throughout the South lawyers ceased to traipse after judges from circuit to circuit and instead settled in towns, established specializations in such indispensable duties as bill collecting, and here and there began to outnumber the planters in the seats of political influence. At the beginning of the century the Virginian William Wirt concluded that "the bar, in America, is the road to honor," and as early as 1821 a young South Carolina Methodist minister, Stephen Olin, observed with interest that "honors and offices are wholly engrossed by lawyers." By 1850 some 7711 Southern lawyers were racing along that road to honor and office.[25] But legal expertise and political power were not the only forms of professional activity. In 1850 the region had 14,370 doctors who were so conspicuously successful that Olin described the South as "the paradise of physicians." And the decisions by state and local governments to establish tax-supported schools, though skimpy in vision and scope when judged by Northern standards, provided expanding opportunities for teachers; the census takers found 8559 of them laboring in the South.[26] Professionals were not significant because of their numbers; they constituted a small proportion of the Southern population. In North Carolina only 4 percent of the state's residents were lawyers, editors, teachers, or physicians. In Alabama, Virginia, Georgia, and Mississippi these professions constituted less than 1 percent of the populace.[27] But the very paucity of professionals ensured their visibility, especially in the towns.

Towns attracted them in disproportionate numbers, and their presence not only helped to set the style of town life but also stimulated a professional consciousness that rubbed off on some of the more sensitive ministers. By 1847 over 7 percent of the white adult males in Montgomery were practicing lawyers, and physicians outnumbered the attorneys almost two to one.[28] In the same year, fifty-one Tennessee lawyers—almost 10 percent of the total number in the state—lived in Nashville, which also boasted of thirty-six physicians and fifty-seven teachers.[29] In 1860 there were at least eighty-one doctors and fifty-seven lawyers in Memphis, but the professional presence in the smaller towns was probably more noticeable. There were at least eleven doctors and thirteen lawyers in Athens, Georgia; eight doctors and fifteen lawyers in Jackson, Tennessee; and eight doctors and twelve lawyers in Charlottesville, Virginia.[30]

The urban professionals possessed the economic power to extend their influence. The average wealth of the town preachers far exceeded the average of free white adult males in 1860, but the preachers as a group fell far short of their professional counterparts. The average wealth in 1860 of lawyers in the Southern towns and cities was $33,487, more than three times the clerical average, and physicians stood even higher, with holdings of $58,179 for each doctor. The affluent clergy could not avoid being aware of the differences and of their uncomfortable middle position as a professional class. They towered above the blacksmiths, draymen, and laboring men of the towns, who in 1860 were working for wages ranging from $1.00 to $2.50 a day. But they stood below the other professionals with whom they wished to compare themselves—and whom they wanted to attract.[31]

The patterns of association and discussion that urban life made possible for doctors and lawyers altered their perceptions of professional responsibility. Town lawyers took the lead in the formation of bar associations to maintain uniform standards of legal practice; the drive to improve the level of medical treatment also began with the formation of local medical societies, which during the 1840s then cooperated in the formation of state societies.[32] In short, the towns were centers of professional self-consciousness. The wealthy doctors and lawyers within the towns and cities initiated organized efforts to advance the usefulness and elevate the character of their learned vocations. And the clergy looked on with interest and at least a trace of anxiety.

As early as the twenties some of the town clergy began to be aware of the potential for adverse comparisons between the ministry and other professions. John Holt Rice (1777–1831) sounded an alarm in his *Virginia Evangelical and Literary Magazine*. A lawyer's son, he had been a tutor at Hampden-Sidney College before entering the Presbyterian ministry and plunging into a rural parish in Virginia, where he combined preaching and planting and accumulated both celebrity and a comfortable income. In 1823 he completed an eleven-year pastorate in the First Presbyterian Church of Richmond, during which he accepted the position of moderator in the General Assembly but declined an invitation to the presidency of Princeton. His accomplishments failed to diminish his unease about the future of clerical influence: "In sadness of heart I do believe that the other professionals are running before the clergy of the country. I foresee the evils which must result from this state of things; and, in my humble sphere, am laboring to prevent them. . . . Activity and vigorous exertion are necessary: so are science and learning."[33]

Within the next two decades Rice's complaint reappeared persistently. Although Mrs. Trollope found that the clergy in America were accorded "distinction and pre-eminence," and Fredrika Bremer decided that they constituted "one portion of the aristocracy," the Southern ministers often lamented the gulf between themselves and other professionals.[34] The Presbyterian George

Howe, a graduate of Andover who in 1831 became professor of Biblical literature at Columbia Seminary, warned his fellow pastors: "All the professions are advancing. We must at least advance with them, and if possible keep before them, or be despised."[35] The Methodist R. H. Rivers, a professor at LaGrange College in Alabama and eventually the president of Centenary, bemoaned the condescension of "the men who attained eminence in political and professional circles."[36] In 1840 the *Baptist Chronicle and Monthly Monitor*, published in Columbus, Georgia, contrasted the clergy to the "men of ability in . . . . the professions of law and medicine."[37] One group or urban pastors wanted to reclaim the traditional image of a professional ministry, which had seemed to vanish for a time on the frontier. Their proximity in geography and aspiration to other learned professionals both enhanced and threatened their own self-perceptions.

The term "professional" was more suggestive than precise in clerical comments, but clearly at its center was one ideal: the personal embodiment of knowledge. A clerical professional was a man of "sound scholarship." He was "learned and accomplished," capable of scaling "heights of knowledge" and possessed of "intellectual power."[38] The ministerial ideal was commensurate with the norms prevailing among progressives in law and medicine. Professionalism was not so much the refinement of technical skills as the mastery of a body of knowledge, whether scientific, legal, or theological, and of the foundational principles implicit in the application of the knowledge. Progressive lawyers spoke of transcending technical legal minutiae and grasping the reason and spirit of the law; the new medical schools in New Orleans, Charleston, Lexington, and Augusta taught largely through a lecture system designed to demonstrate the scientific principles of medicine. If ministers were divided over the desirability of such professional ideals, moreover, so also were their counterparts: some lawyers championed "instinct" while others called for erudition and learning and some doctors urged more "theory" while others called themselves empiricists who eschewed any pretense to scientific generalization. In each case, however, the advocates of professional improvement called for scholarship, learning, theory, and erudition. And though many of the clergy bewailed such worldly aspirations, others thought the title of "professional" no epithet but rather an honorific description.[39] They therefore took concrete steps to protect their own status and to impose regularity on the procedures of entry into the ministerial calling: increased attention among Baptists to the procedures of licensing clergy, clearer distinctions in Methodist circles between lay and clerical prerogatives and between the regular itinerant ministers and part-time local pastors, Presbyterian debates about the nature of professional education, and proposals for more effective ministerial education within all the major churches.

In addition to their interprofessional associations, there were ample occasions for urban clergy to compare themselves with other educated townsfolk. It was important that they were thrust into close continuing relations with other pastors: they exchanged pulpits, joined the same organizations, met for lunch and discussion, and listened to one another's sermons. Fond reminiscence of such association stands out in clerical memoirs, but the ministers recognized that an exchange of pulpits or an interdenominational service was also an exposure to evaluation, a testing, as well as a courtesy.[40] It was equally important that the ministers were expected to participate in a variety of secular organizations that stimulated intellectual and cultural activity. A few scattered local societies that promised to disseminate "useful knowledge" of belles-lettres, moral philosophy, natural history, and similar topics had existed in the South ever since the eighteenth century, and migrants into the Southwest established them promptly in the new frontier towns. Natchez formed a Society for the Acquirement and Dissemination of Useful Knowledge as early as 1803. But not until the popular lyceum movement emerged in America in 1826 in imitation of the British mechanics' institutes did Southern townsfolk embrace this pathway to instant culture. The construction of an imposing lecture hall for the Norfolk, Virginia, Lyceum in 1826 signaled a flurry of interest that lasted throughout the thirties, when at least twenty-five Southern towns formed lyceums, drawing their patrons largely from middle-class believers in the dogma of improvement. Between 1830 and 1860 Mississippians alone formed fifty-six such societies for mutual cultural edification. And the lyceums complemented other associations ranging from Charleston's pretentious Literary and Philosophical Society to the small debating club formed by the "gentlemen" of Athens, Georgia, in a spacious but unfurnished room located over the post office.[41]

Town pastors assumed leading roles in the societies, and for some of them a paper delivered to a local group was the first step in the production of a theological treatise or a pathway to local eminence.[42] A few, however, had to struggle to avoid embarrassment. In Greensboro, Georgia, the Presbyterian pastor, Archibald Scott, took the initiative in 1817 in forming the Moral and Political Society, which held weekly debates on religious, metaphysical, and political questions. The Methodist clergyman, Lovick Pierce, attended faithfully, but he later confided that in order to carry on the discussions with his better-informed peers he felt obliged to maintain a regimen of study in logic, moral philosophy, and "physics."[43] Whether by threatening embarrassment or promising eminence, the structures of town life could promote among the clergy the awareness that a certain "rationality" was expected of them.

4. *The Ideal of Gentility*

The habits of association in towns helped engender two ideals—gentility and rationality—which in their interconnection determined the ways theologians wrote and taught. The town pastors formulated their versions of orthodoxy with a constituency in mind. Their vision of the laity and of their position vis-a-vis the laity shaped their judgments about what was theologically appropriate and necessary. It was therefore of a certain intellectual significance that the clergy were sensitive to the impressions they made "on public sentiment, that is, the common judgment of society as to the proprieties of life and conduct."[44] It became a commonplace that a minister's usefulness depended on his reputation, especially in the eyes of the "improved and elevated" classes of society, the "best families."[45] The clergy were conscious of being under scrutiny—we are "observed with a microscopic eye," wrote one Episcopal bishop—and they warned one another against behavior that might make the ministry "appear ridiculous." The Baptist Jesse Mercer urged that every minister attend to the refinements that could "render him acceptable to his fellow men." Above all, said Philip Lindsley, a Nashville Presbyterian, one should never expose "the cloth" to "the contempt and derision of the intelligent and discerning."[46]

Sensitivity to appearances, in other words, was a virtue. The Methodist bishop, William McKendree, was commended for his attention to public opinion: "He was not one of that kind of men who do not care what others think of them."[47] Of course there were dangers: by having too great a respect for mere human approbation, one could fall prey to vanity and ambition, about which the town pastors worried publicly and privately. Even worse, one could become trapped in servile fear of one's congregation.[48] A visitor to the South in 1842 observed that the clergy, standing midway between rude fervor and eminence in learning, were (as a result of their uncomfortable "middle position") prone to "incertitude and timidity."[49] But despite the dangers the ideal perdured—reputation was essential to ministry.

While their sermons often dealt with guilt—the transgression of prohibitions—many of the clergy were more anxious about the threat of shame: fear of being exposed and found wanting. They worried that they could not live up to their ideal images. "Opposed to honor," wrote James Henley Thornwell of South Carolina, "is shame, which is either the contempt of others manifested in some external expressions, or the fear, on our part, of doing that which justly shall expose us to disgrace."[50] Thornwell associated shame with vice, but the fear of contempt and disgrace, of exposure and adverse judgment, could pursue even the most virtuous of ministers.

Such a sensibility was part of the intellectual tradition behind literate Southern culture. The British moral philosophers had taken for granted that the "consciousness of merited . . . Esteem" was one of the primary desires of humankind, that honor was inseparably connected with "the good Opinion and Love of others," while shame arose from "the unfavorable Opinions of others concerning us," and that social disapproval was rightly mortifying "beyond all measure."[51] Bishop Joseph Butler argued in a treatise widely read and admired by Southern preachers that human nature made disgrace as painful as physical torture and esteem as desirable as any material comfort.[52] In their collegiate courses on the elements of moral science, usually required for graduation, young Southerners learned that the subversion of another's reputation was a crime equivalent to robbery.[53] When combined with the cult of honor in the secular culture, the British moral tradition ensured that reputation was a treasure to be guarded, defended, worried about. Urban life was a nursery in which customary anxieties could bloom and flourish.

The psychological tension was heightened by conventional strictures against hypocrisy: appearances kept up for the purpose of deceiving were contemptible. A person had to be what he appeared to be. "The most serious form of hypocrisy," wrote Thornwell, "is that in which a man pretends to a character to which he is really a stranger." The essence of a lie was a misrepresentation of one's self. Thornwell appealed to Aristotle, who had written that the truthful man was one whose words and deeds represented him exactly as he was. So the clergy were in a dilemma. Obliged to be sensitive to society's judgments of propriety, they were also obliged never to appear to be what they were not. William Capers warned lest regard for social approval degenerate into a quest for "popularity" and a consequent obeisance before the prejudice of the masses, but he acknowledged the rightful authority of "public sentiment."[54] The conclusion was foregone: the minister was to become a public self. He was to conform, without hypocrisy, to the expectations of the improved and elevated classes. Indeed, he was to identify himself, without reserve, with his public role.

However complex its source, the consciousness of subjection to public scrutiny could be unnerving. The Reverend Joseph Cottrell, who in 1855 was the Methodist minister at Pensacola, Florida, recorded his distress in his diary. The son of a South Carolina minister and physician whose premature death left his widow penniless, Cottrell taught French and mathematics at an Alabama academy before entering The Citadel military academy when he was nineteen. After graduation he entered the ministry and soon became extremely self-conscious about the gaps in his education. So Cottrell began plodding through English and Latin grammars, "building compactly, surely, trudging through that which others think I am *au fait* in," fearing even to send a letter "lest some word has been misspelt." He sometimes bemoaned his efforts to keep up an appearance: "One half the labor spent in studying, which is thrown away endeavoring to hide ignorance, would make scholars of many." But each day Cottrell tried to arise at daybreak in order to study before breakfast. After a brief walk he spent the morning in study, reserving his pastoral duties until after dinner. Two more hours of study in the afternoon and an evening of reading and writing completed the day. In this way he began to master the rudiments of Latin, Church history, and theology, but he yearned for more. Cottrell had high ambitions; he wanted to "be far wiser and better than persons imagine—to surpass the ideal of the vulgar mind, and attain to heights to which they are wholly ignorant." And he was a man of worldly accomplishment. By 1860 he had accumulated wealth of $11,500 and purchased ten slaves as visible tokens of his achievement. But it was hard for him to escape a sense of intellectual failure. "Oh, that I had improved my time regularly, and studied with system! My advancement would have been much greater."[55] He believed that it was incumbent upon him to meet and even to excel the expectations of literate, refined laity and of his clerical companions.

A growing concern that the ministry might be unable to live up to expectations led during the 1840s to a concerted call for "clerical improvement"—especially among Methodists and Baptists. R. B. C. Howell in Nashville complained that Baptist ministers had not kept pace with the rapid progress of society. "It is not uncommon, especially in the South-west, to find the laity in advance, intellectually, of the clergy." The results "need not be described," particularly in "the populous places."[56] Howell's voice joined a chorus. Without ministerial improvement, wrote one Georgia Baptist, "the number and respectability of our hearers must and will continue to decrease."[57] The time is rapidly coming, said a Virginian, "when our congregations will not sit under an uninformed and uneducated ministry."[58] Another Virginian called it a scandal to ordain men without culture.[59] "We must do something towards the improvement of our preachers," echoed the editor of the *Southern Methodist Pulpit*, "or else our people will stray to other pastures. The ministry must be in advance of the people, leaders intellectually and socially as well as spiritually."[60] A minister, wrote another Methodist, must "put himself in connection with the age in which he lives, and keep abreast with the men of his time," or else relinquish his hold "upon the mind and public opinion of the time and country."[61] High evaluations of "improvement" were not universal; the aspiring brethren encountered ridicule, opposition, and indifference. But among the aspirants a nascent consensus about improvement took form around the ideal of the gentleman: "A minister is presumed to be a gentleman. He must be not only what might by possibility pass loosely by that designation, but he must always be found in the forerank of gentlemen."[62]

The ideal of gentility pervaded the private and public writing of the elite clergy: letters, diaries, sermons, tracts, and textbooks in moral philosophy. Nowhere did it find clearer expression than in the array of biographies and historical narratives, written by churchmen, that accompanied the emerging historical consciousness in Southern culture (the first of the Southern state historical societies originated in 1831 in Virginia and four more came into existence during the thirties).[63] But the biographies and histories also represented a species of "success literature," detailing achievements worthy of emulation and praise. The biographies, in particular, fused the aristocratic "life and letters" tradition with an older style of spiritual biography, and thus combined a literary genre that catered to and memorialized men of rank and station with another genre that preached of piety and humility and exalted the virtues of the simple Christian.

On the one hand, the biographies elevated the clerical profession to a level of equality with statesmen, military leaders, and notable professionals, who were the typical subjects of biographical adoration. "While it is profitable and proper," wrote one clerical biographer, "that the lives of men should be preserved for the benefit of the state, and for the advancement of learning, and for the improvement of the arts, it is especially proper that they should be embodied in a permanent form for the benefit of the church."[64] On the other hand the biographies were devotional tracts, providing examples of virtue and piety for inspiration and guidance. Through their double character, they provided role models for men who wanted to adapt to cultural change while preserving older forms of piety. They appealed to a constituency who still read and admired Richard Baxter's *Reformed Pastor* and Isaac Watts's *Rule of Ministerial Conduct*, classic productions of an earlier era, but who also valued Samuel Miller's *Letters on Clerical Manners and Habits* (1828), a popular guide, written by a Prince-

ton professor, to care of the hair, dinner manners, and social nice-
ties, or *The Preacher's Manual* (1800), an attempt by the English
Methodist Adam Clarke to explain away John Wesley's rule that
ministers should not "affect the gentleman." Clarke wanted to
show that Wesley had in fact been an early advocate of clerical
gentility.[65] Though the biographies sometimes took the form of
artless chronicles, their purpose was not to relay facts but to promulgate ideals. The rhetoric of the clerical biographies therefore
exposes the lineaments of the gentlemanly ideal.[66]

James Taylor's *Lives of Virginia Baptist Ministers* (1837) promoted the union of piety and refined intelligence as one mark of a
clerical gentleman. Despite their frequent lack of formal education, he pointed out, the abler Baptist clergy of the eighteenth
and early nineteenth centuries had dedicated themselves to the
"cultivation of intellectual powers." While Taylor duly noted and
commended the lives and activities of earnest but undistinguished
exhorters, his personal heroes were clearly ministers who possessed
"urbanity" of manners, who sought "every available means for
intellectual cultivation," who pored over their books by candle-
light and tried to establish schools and seminaries, and who sought
"the advantage of an improved mind" even though they knew that
learning was not an indispensable qualification for ministry. In
short, they were men whose actions manifested Taylor's dictum
that "want of learning is a great disadvantage and misfortune."[67]

Since that dictum was unacceptable to some of Taylor's fervent but uneducated fellow clergymen, his friend Jeremiah B.
Jeter, the pastor of Richmond's First Baptist Church, wrote an
introduction to the book that turned aside possible criticisms. Jeter
seemed at first to be deprecating the "mental cultivation" of the
younger ministers by comparing it unfavorably to the zeal of the
fathers. "Our modern preachers know more of books and adopt
sounder principles of Biblical interpretation than did our early
preachers; but probably they know less of the contents of the
Bible." Yet precisely when it seemed that Jeter was undercutting
Taylor's call for a union of piety and intellect, he enlisted the authority of the forefathers on behalf of the new ideals.

We have no reason to be ashamed of our ancestors; they were
true, earnest, godly, useful men. We love to give them honor.

Whether, if they could revisit the scenes of their devoted labors, they would be proud of their sons, is doubtful. They would have much to learn, and many prejudices to subdue, before they could appreciate the present order of things. Our plans for spreading the gospel, our colportage operations, our seminaries for the education of young ministers, and our Sunday-schools, would be new to them, and would not meet their approval without careful examination. The result of that inquiry is not doubtful.[68]

In sum, Jeter claimed that the proponents of ministerial improvement were the rightful heirs of the Baptist patriarchs.

While Taylor's *Lives* uplifted the ideal of clerical learning, Thomas O. Summers's edition of the *Biographical Sketches of Eminent Itinerant Ministers* (1858) exemplified another feature of clerical gentility: dignity and polish. An English immigrant to New York in 1830, Summers had overcome his religious doubts by reading Adam Clarke's *Commentary on the Epistle to the Romans*, a revered essay in Methodist Biblical interpretation, whereupon he began traveling a circuit in rural Virginia. Before long he ascended to the Methodist pulpit in Charleston, where his voluminous writing and omnivorous reading, it was said, made him "a marvel to those cultured and dignified Carolinians." Summers believed that ministers should be men of "intellectual capacity" who knew languages, logic, rhetoric, philosophy, and physical science, and in 1853 he received the opportunity to circulate his views throughout the denomination when he accepted an appointment to become the editor of the Methodist publishing concern in Nashville. He applied himself to editing, revising, and writing treatises and commentaries before finally moving into the first chair of theology at Vanderbilt.[69]

As editor of the *Biographical Sketches*, Summers tried to obtain a short biography of one minister from each of the Southern Methodist conferences; the geographical diversity highlighted the unity of purpose among his biographers. From his sketches we learn that the Reverend Robert L. Kennon of Alabama was admirable "as a gentleman. . . . He kept up his relations with society . . . knew political men, literary men, men of business, and was universally popular." We discover that William Capers of South Carolina combined "the elegance of a finished gentleman" with "the simplicity, purity, and benevolence" of a pious Christian; that Ignatius Few of Georgia was a man of "polished manner, courtly bearing, and unsurpassed courtesy and refinement"; that William McKendree of Tennessee never regarded "roughness, coarseness, and bluntness, as insignia of internal piety, but allowed no one to behave more handsomely than himself"; and that William Kennedy of South Carolina served "the large towns and cities" with impeccable dignity and "urbanity." The biographies exhibited the values of their authors; the clergyman worthy of biography was a gentleman.[70]

Biographies and histories were not the only literary genres in which ministers could express their loyalty to the ideals of gentility; respectable urban preachers considered their sermons as potential contributions to "the standard literature of the Church."[71] Die-hard clerical populists decried the tendency to minimize practical results as the measure of homiletic excellence, but the gentlemen persisted in advancing other criteria. No sermon, wrote a Mississippi Methodist, should offend "an audience of good taste and intelligence."[72] In concert with allies in England the elite preachers launched an attack on "allegorical" sermons that spiritualized the text in fanciful ways; they insisted, rather, on "sound canons of scriptural interpretation."[73] And they believed that sermons should teach doctrine as well as move the emotions. By 1859 the Southern Methodist *Quarterly Review* was belittling popular orators who "put the merest modicum of theology into their sermons—they never tax their hearers with the drudgery of thinking." The multiplication of such "popular preachers," the journal charged, would be of dubious value to the Church.[74]

The mark of gentlemanly preaching was attention to "method." The elite clergy sought to weave the elements of the sermon "into an elegantly-wrought piece of network that awakened admiration by the skill of the arrangement, engaged attention by the felicity of the thought, and produced conviction by the irresistible logic of the conclusions."[75] They distrusted flourish, rhetorical display, splendid metaphors, and literary elegance; the hallmarks of their method were order and system, precise discriminations, tasteful language, irresistible logic, and elocutionary dignity. In a period when American popular speech was fluid, spontaneous, often unruly, innovative, and even vulgar in its vitality, the language of the urban pulpits embodied the characteristics that Tocqueville found in the more refined examples of American language. It was "abstract rather than concrete, general rather than specific, periphrastic rather than direct."[76] Tocqueville attributed the speech patterns to the insecurity naturally engendered in a fluid, mobile, democratic society. The gentlemen clergy seemed tailor-made to confirm his explanation. The wording of their sermons did indeed serve the function of distinguishing the elite from rural exhorters and therefore elevating their ministry in the eyes of their watchful parishioners. To Harriet Martineau, visiting the South in the 1830s, it seemed that "gentlemanly preaching" bogged down in "harmless abstractions."[77] With something of the same insight, Basil Manly warned his son to leaven his preparation for a career in the pulpit by withdrawing for a time from a "congregation in a city," with its rigid demands that the minister follow "methodical rules in constructing sermons," in order to experience the freedom of being a "preacher to people not accustomed to preaching."[78] Many of the younger preachers, though, were disdainful of such "old-fashioned" preaching; they preferred "models of pulpit oratory."[79]

Publication of a sermon therefore became an index of clerical success and prestige, especially after the 1820s when such publications as the *Virginia Evangelical and Literary Magazine* began to print an occasional sermon. By the mid-nineteenth century the South was awash with printed sermons; books of sermons competed for attention with a growing periodical literature devoted to worthy examples of pulpit artistry. The books were well-received: the public purchased over twenty thousand copies of Henry Bidleman Bascom's collected sermons. So by the 1830s the Southern churches were sponsoring an array of journals: *The Protestant Episcopal Pulpit* (1835), *The Southern Preacher* (1837), *The Southern Baptist Preacher* (1839), *The Southern Baptist Pulpit* (1839), *The Baptist Preacher* (1842), *The Southern Methodist Pulpit* (1848), *The Southern Pulpit* (1848), *The Southern Baptist Review* (1849), *The Southern Presbyterian Pulpit* (1853), *The Methodist Pulpit South* (1853), and others.[80] Written mainly by town pastors and codifying what was recognized as "a great change in the manner of preaching," the sermons were designed to "contribute something" toward a new Southern "literature," which some ministers wanted to model after the classic and urbane essays of Joseph Addison in the eighteenth-century English *Spectator*.[81]

Similar ideals prompted a few ambitious pastors to found theological journals. During the early nineteenth century most magazines were class publications for gentlemen, restricted to men of rank, station, and respectable ancestry. They maintained the tone of an upper-class defending itself against leveling tendencies. In such an atmosphere, theological journals that combined "religion and sound learning" would naturally bear an aura of distinction and therefore enhance clerical prestige.[82] The self-consciousness of the ministerial editors continually expressed itself in the comparisons they made between their journals and Northern or European counterparts. *The Virginia Religious Magazine* (1804) was an attempt to emulate, if not surpass, the successful *Connecticut Evangelical Magazine*. When John Holt Rice founded his *Virginia Evangelical and Literary Magazine* (1818), he patterned it after "the best" Scottish literary journals.[83] The theological magazines were symbols of both regional and professional status. The Southern Methodist *Quarterly Review* (1846) became a token of that denomination's "respectability," especially when it could be said that the journal had "attained rank and reputation with the best Quarterlies of the country, and . . . elicited flattering commendation from men and periodicals of the first class." *The Southern Presbyterian Review* (1847) came into being as the counterpart of and competitor to the dignified and elevated *Princeton Review*.[84] During the tense regional conflicts of the 1840s, as churches were dividing into Southern and Northern branches, the new journals signified the intellectual independence of the Southern theologians, but the magazines were symbols of social as well as regional pride. They were means for communicating not only information but also an image.

In building bridges between their denominations and Southern colleges, the pastors made an even more ambitious effort to combine religion and learning. In 1820 there were only about a dozen colleges—with some thousand students—within the Southern states. By 1850 there were over a hundred colleges training more than nine thousand students. Indeed by 1860 more than 25,000 Southerners were attending college somewhere in the United States or Europe—a number proportionally far greater than the Northern states could boast. Though often inferior to the best academies, the Southern colleges symbolized the hopes of the middle and upper classes. To a large extent, moreover, they were an extension of urban ambitions and tokens of local enterprise. Until well into the 1850s, local communities were far more active than religious denominations or state governments in the formation of colleges. Promoters usually located a college in a specific community in return for pledges of local support; the churches initially provided little more than sanction and encouragement.[85]

In 1820 the South had only one church-sponsored college; within the next forty years the churches agreed to sponsor more than twenty-five and developed close relationships with still others. The new schools had a myriad of cultural functions, from sectarian self-aggrandizement and the preservation of orthodoxy to character formation and mental growth. To isolate an evangelistic impulse as the sole motive for the clerical support of colleges would be to overlook the pervasive assumption that Christianity and cultural advancement were two sides of the same coin. The colleges were safe avenues of advance for the middle classes, including the fledgling preachers called upon to satisfy "the taste" for an "educated minister" in urban congregations.[86]

Despite objections from traditionalists, the colleges, in alliance with the new theological seminaries, began to transform the clergy. To understand the transformation one must recall that the schools promised to provide their students with an encyclopedic grasp of the world and yet to fit the diversity into a unified pattern that was consistent with the Christian tradition. There was an implicit logic to the course offerings in the Christian colleges, namely, an assumption that all of reality, from inorganic nature to the society of godly men, could be comprehended as within a series of concentric circles of which the Biblical revelation was the center. Consequently to touch any one circle was to find oneself en route to that center.

Nowhere did this reasoning receive clearer expression than in Jesse Mercer's 1834 address to the Georgia State Baptist Convention: "Knowledge Indispensable to a Minister of God." A pastor in Washington, Georgia, Mercer had received his only formal education at his father's classical school in North Carolina, but his knowledge of ancient languages and his passion for ministerial learning distinguished him from most of his brethren. The address to the Georgia Baptists followed closely upon the decision to build Mercer University, which opened its doors in 1833 as a "classical and theological school" intended primarily to train clergymen. The project created some unease, so Mercer tried to assuage anxieties by elaborating the religious import of even the "secular" curriculum. Each of the academic disciplines, he said, exhibited the truth of God: to study geography, chemistry, history, or philosophy was to study "the works of God, in creation, and providence, and grace." Geology revealed the divine wonders, astronomy the divine glory.[87] Every academic discipline was, at heart, theological—a claim which suggested that theology itself was an academic, a reasonable, enterprise.

Mercer assumed that both education and reason could be kept under control as subordinate servants of faith, and he offered an apt metaphor.

> We consider education to the minister, what clothes are to a man. They have no power in them to make the man, and yet they are very necessary both to his comfort, and to render him acceptable to his fellow men. So education is very necessary to the happiness and acceptance of a minister in the course of his ministry.[88]

A considerable group of clerical populists, however, believed that the clothes might, indeed, make the man. They sensed that the institutions and innovations proposed by their gentlemanly friends embodied an implicit agenda for a certain social class, and they were uneasy when Stephen Olin, the Methodist president of Randolph-Macon College in Virginia, argued for theological education as a means of preparing clergy to reach "the rich and influential." They felt it more important to sway the masses, with whom they felt at home.[89]

Throughout the antebellum period, therefore, the churches were wracked by theological and ecclesiastical controversies that were made even more intense by cultural resentments. Citing both theological and Biblical warrants, more than nine hundred "Primitive Baptist" preachers rebelled between 1820 and 1850 against "the learned gentry of the day, who swarm out of the theological institutions like locusts, and are ready to devour the land."[90] Cumberland Presbyterians withdrew from the Synod of Kentucky when it insisted that education and doctrinal understanding were as important as inward religious experience in the preparation of a minister, and even within the older Presbyterian churches there were reports of "envy and jealousy" between the clergy who had learned their craft under the individual tutorship of older ministers—the field-school method—and those who had "better opportunities."[91] Methodists fought over education and ministerial attire as well as church organization: the younger progressives complained about having to continue dressing in "the style of a clown."[92] When the "Protestant Methodists" departed from the denomination in 1830, complaining about the tyranny of the hierarchy, they also implied that the Church was falling under the sway of "rich men"—"learned gentlemen and gentlemen's sons."[93]

By 1855 the Methodist William J. Sassnett of Emory College issued a monograph on *Progress* that conducted a rear-guard battle against the deterioration of the old ideals. Sassnett could support some innovations, but he complained that the younger clergy had begun to seek "a reputation among men for talent and taste," and the resulting tensions had produced party alignments.

> The younger class displayed that absence of suitable reverence for age, though associated with long, laborious, and useful service, everywhere so common in these times. That there is such a want of reverence . . . that there is a young class, who, claiming to constitute a party of progress, discredit the claims of the older, simply because they are old, must be obvious to all who notice the movements of individuals in the affairs of the Church. Such manifestations are to be witnessed in the common intercourse of the society, in the various council-boards of the Church, in her deliberative assemblies—indeed, under all circumstances, and on all occasions, where by possibility there can be competition between the claims of the younger and the older.

The new generation, he charged, had perverted their calling "from the great end of pleasing God to that of pleasing men merely—in the tendency to make the office of the ministry a theatre for human display."[94]

The populists directed their attack explicitly against the ideal of gentility. They bemoaned "chaste and classic" sermons fashioned "to please the refined ears and cultivated tastes of the age." They scorned "neat and fashionable" clerical dress that was calculated to grace the "genteel pulpit" and "secure the attendance of genteel people."[95] A subscriber to the *LaGrange Herald* in Georgia complained that the ministers favored the rich, succumbed to fashionable style, and even wore black silk gloves in the pulpit. "They dress as fine and as fashionable as any body. Their houses, furniture, carriage and horses must be as fine or a little finer than any body else's."[96] The populists also deplored "mongrel theological and literary institutions" and ridiculed the benevolent societies through which many of the elite clergy wished to advance the cause of missions, Sunday Schools, temperance, and religious literacy.[97] They despaired at the rage for "science, arts and letters" among the gentlemen. And they complained of the power in the hands of the urban clergy.[98] Alexander Campbell, one of the founders of the "Christian Movement," attracted many of his early converts by denouncing "the extravagance, show, and pomp of city congregations" and their "aristocratic" clergy. Baptists and Methodists, he charged, had now become decent and fashionable, with clergy who claimed "homage and respect." To Campbell it seemed that they were affecting "the fine gentleman," and to him the word was a damning epithet.[99]

In one sense the critics were correct, for in commending Christianity to the professional and educated classes who thought of themselves as reasonable people, the clerical gentlemen were willing to abandon some of the revered patterns of rural piety. And their program did have theological consequences: in choosing to be and to attract persons who valued "reason," the leading clergy turned for guidance to the theologians who had in the past demonstrated the reasonableness of orthodox Christianity. Their social setting compelled them to emphasize the rationality of faith; their religious traditions confirmed their certainty that Christianity was reasonable. Both experience and tradition promoted adherence to a "rational orthodoxy."

CHAPTER THREE

THE VANISHING LIBERALS

The orthodox town pastors thought of themselves as reasonable men; their liberal critics accused them of irrationality. The liberals considered themselves men of faith; the orthodox charged them with infidelity. The lines of conflict seemed clearly drawn: reason was opposed to revelation, orthodoxy to heterodoxy, and faith to rationality. The question of "reason"—our own and the world's—was the hidden agenda in half the theological disputations in the Old South and an explicit issue in the conflict between orthodox and liberal theologians. Both groups viewed their differences as irreconcilable, and the traditionalists were exultant when it became clear during the 1830s that the South's nascent liberal movements were on the verge of collapse. Yet in retrospect the boundaries seem not so precise and sharp as they appeared in the nineteenth century. One is struck by the similarities between the liberals and the orthodox clergy, by the common presuppositions that marked their controversies. A core of shared assumptions underlay their differences, and a glance at the Southern liberals therefore illuminates the assumptions of orthodoxy.

The Old South in post-Revolutionary America was no Bible Belt. Fewer than 10 percent of the population were church members in 1776, though larger numbers probably attended services, and the low figures reflected the rigor of the churches as well as the prevalence of religious indifference. Yet many of the clergy were appalled and frightened by the skepticism and infidelity that they found in their midst. Both Protestants and Catholics reported that Kentucky was a cauldron of unbelief; one newspaper there speculated that "the infidel part has a considerable majority," and in 1793 the Kentucky legislature dispensed with the services of a Christian chaplain.[1] The pious Joseph Caldwell, president of the University of North Carolina, believed that politicians in the region east of Chapel Hill felt compelled to disavow the Bible in order to collect votes, and churchmen felt unmitigated "gloom" at the indifference and hostility they encountered in Virginia.[2] By the 1790s the Presbyterian General Assembly was officially warning against deism and the Methodist General Conference was proposing a day of fasting and prayer to repulse deist advances.[3]

Infidelity seemed especially visible in the towns and cities. There were "Deistical Clubs" in Lexington, deist newspapers in Baltimore, and debates over deism in Richmond. Even toward the end of the antebellum period one minister in Charleston saw theological errors moving from "the cities and large towns" to the villages and hamlets; a Virginia urban pastor described "the populous towns and cities" as the last bastions of liberalism.[4] It was equally disturbing to the orthodox ministers that unorthodox views seemed enticing to the upper levels of society. In the eyes of some clergy, "almost all the people of education" were predisposed to heterodoxy: the "rich and educated," the "intellectual and influential" were, it often seemed, either silent unbelievers or vocal critics of Christian doctrine.[5] In the early nineteenth century, recalled Bishop Meade of Virginia,

> Infidelity was . . . rife in the State, and the College of William and Mary was regarded as the hotbed of French politics and religion. I can truly say, that then, and for several years after, in every educated young man of Virginia whom I met, I expected to find a sceptic, if not an avowed unbeliever.[6]

During the Jeffersonian period, complained another minister, infidelity was "reputable, it was literary, it was scientific."[7] And it always seemed to appeal to the very people whom the town ministers wanted to attract: "There were few men in the professions of law or physic," wrote one clergyman, "who would avow their belief in the truth of Christianity."[8] When Jasper Adams of Charleston wrote his *Elements of Moral Philosophy* in 1837, he was still complaining that an aura of "infidel feelings and sentiments" seemed endemic among physicians.[9]

The accuracy of the woeful clerical jeremiads is not open to conclusive evaluation; one suspects overstatement. But the complaints delineate the clerical consciousness. And to many preachers the power of liberalism, for good or ill, must have seemed manifest when the deists united temporarily with evangelical dissenters after the Revolution to disestablish Anglicanism in the Southern states. It was an "unholy alliance," claimed a later Episcopal historian, and within a decade after their victory the erstwhile dissenters were already voicing a similar judgment; it seemed that their old allies bore a demonic visage.[10]

1. "A Dispute About Authenticity"

No single literary event disturbed the orthodox more than the publication of Thomas Paine's *Age of Reason* in two parts in 1794 and 1795. An attack on Biblical revelation, the book also exhibited a pattern of argument that made it more than simply a negative critique. Paine's criticisms of Christianity had their own internal logic. Time and again in his argument he returned to one theme: religion must exhibit "consistency." In particular, he called for a theology that was consistent with the attributes of God, especially God's immutability and morality. Because God was immutable, Paine said, his governance occurred through fixed and unalterable principles, manifest in the eternal truths of the human sciences. A reasonable theology, consistent with God's changelessness, would therefore take the form of a scientific explication of the structure of the universe. It followed that no written book could be a divine revelation, for no language was immutable or universal. A Bible was unable in principle to establish a reasonable religion because by its very nature as a linguistic product it was incommensurate with the divine attribute of immutability.

Because God was perfectly moral, moreover, the Christian and Jewish Scriptures, replete with human rapacity and ungodly commands by the deity to execute captives, murder infants, and debauch virgins, patently exhibited their own spuriousness and threatened the moral order of society. So to ensure that religion be consistent with both the morality and unchangeableness of God, Paine had to undermine belief in the authority and authenticity of the Bible. He did so by uncovering its inconsistencies, disproving the traditional ascriptions of authorship, and exposing the irrationality of the Biblical narratives.[11]

Paine repeated the arguments familiar to Englishmen who had read Matthew Tindal against revelation, Conyers Middleton against miracle and myth, Thomas Morgan against the Old Testament, Thomas Woolston against miracles, and Thomas Chubb against Christian morality.[12] And his claims for rationality were circumspect; he acknowledged that reason could not discover all the divine attributes. But his book popularized deism as a rational religion founded on God's "universal display of himself in the works of the creation" and verified by human reason through "the principles of science." "For the Creator of man is the Creator of science; and it is through that medium that men can see God, as it were, face to face."[13]

When he published the second part of *The Age of Reason*, Paine complained that his opponents had confounded a "dispute about authenticity with a dispute about doctrines"—a judgment echoed by later historians.[14] And there indeed was an hysterical quality in the clerical obsession with Paine. "His *Age of Reason* would never have been known in this country if the clergy had suffered it to rest," argued the poet Philip Freneau in 1799, "but they dragged it into publicity—let the text be what it would, animadversions on Paine made a part of the sermon. The clergy wrote— the people read."[15] What may have been the first book printed in Mississippi was a polemic against Paine in 1799, and the campaign continued well into the late nineteenth century.[16] When Frederick Law Olmsted toured the South in 1853, he observed crude attacks on Paine by uneducated clergymen.[17] But even in the early polemic there were traces of continuity between the deists and their orthodox opponents. The more articulate Southern clergy argued that Paine's deism, with its subversion of revelation, was unacceptable because it was less reasonable than the alternative. On the surface the anti-deist arguments appeared to present a brief for theological irrationalism, but the appearance was misleading.

Andrew Broaddus (1770–1848), a Virginia Baptist, was one of the first Southerners who tried to turn the tables on the deists by demonstrating their irrationality. A tense, finely wrought, self-taught man who disciplined himself through language study, Broaddus served for a time as the assistant pastor of the First Baptist Church in Richmond, to the dismay of his father, who had intended his son to enter the Episcopal ministry. Tiring of Richmond, he moved into rural Virginia, declining invitations to prominent pulpits in Boston, Philadelphia, and Baltimore, and in relative solitude he constructed his refutation of Paine in a small treatise entitled *The Age of Reason and Revelation.*

Broaddus admired Paine's political views and intellectual ability, but he found his philosophical assumptions naïve. "Christians know something of *philosophy* too, as well as Deists," he wrote, and then he proceeded to a criticism of what he considered the primary presupposition of deism: the doctrine of rational self-sufficiency. If men were purely rational creatures, as the deists seemed to imply, then natural religion grounded in the investigation of the created order would be defensible. But in fact rational investigation shows, he continued, that human beings are creatures of passion and prejudice, sufficiently reasonable to recognize their dilemma but not to transcend it. A rational analysis of the self, in other words, demonstrated the limits of reason and established the need for revelation. But this did not mean that the revelation was irrational, even though it exceeded the grasp of reason, and it did not mean that reason had for the Christian a merely negative, critical function. Broaddus believed that reason could not only describe the human situation but also discern the power and majesty of God in the works of creation and even provide confirmatory evidence for the truth of the revelation.[18]

Against Paine's doctrine of the mutability of language, Broaddus argued that there was an underlying, immutable "substance" of meaning ingredient within diverse forms of expression. As evidence he pointed out that "the substance of what is conveyed in one language, may be faithfully conveyed in another language."[19] Speech was variable but meanings could perdure within various linguistic forms; an immutable idea could therefore reappear in different languages and cultures. Against Paine's contention that the Scriptural narratives were inconsistent with the moral perfection of God, Broaddus offered a countervailing assertion. Revelation, he said, illustrated "more" of the divine perfections than did the creation; it depicted the mercy, graciousness, and forgiveness of God in ways that "the volume of creation" could not. And against Paine's argument that revelation lacked a reasonable foundation, Broaddus, who agreed that "rational evidences are necessary," counterposed three arguments. He said that miracles and prophecies validated the Scriptures, that the intrinsic worth of

Scriptural teaching demonstrated its truthfulness, and that the historical progress of Christianity despite seemingly insuperable adversities evidenced the supernatural character of Christian doctrine.[20] His book would hardly have been persuasive to someone who was not already convinced, but whatever the merits of his arguments about selfhood, language, divine morality, and the traditional "evidences," Broaddus recognized that he was engaged in a dispute about authenticity, not simply a debate about doctrines, and he sought rational criteria for undergirding Christian apologetic. In fact, he adumbrated the logic of later rational orthodoxy.

Other Southern clergy offered similar replies to Paine, derived for the most part from the English anti-deistic writers: Richard Watson, William Paley, and Charles Leslie. In 1795 James Muir, a Presbyterian minister from Alexandria, Virginia, printed *An Examination of the Principles Contained in the Age of Reason*, and two years later Samuel McCorkle, a Presbyterian who helped organize the University of North Carolina, published his *Four Discourses on the General First Principles of Deism and Revelation Contrasted*, both authors repeating the argument that reason itself demonstrated the limits of rationality. In 1797 the president of the new Presbyterian seminary at Hampden-Sidney College, Moses Hoge (1752–1820), edited a series of anti-deistic treatises by Richard Watson, the Regius Professor of Divinity at Cambridge. A number of Virginians urged Hoge to add his own arguments to the series, and he did so in *The Sophist Unmasked*, a treatise, he wrote, that verified its claims through both "the light of nature" and the Scriptural revelation. Hoge believed that he was able to derive religious truth from the visible creation, human science, "and every other source," and that Paine therefore had no philosophical advantage. He did point out that natural philosophy could not establish the doctrine of immortality; at that point rational arguments were inconclusive. The created order did not reveal, therefore, "all that man wants to know" about the divine economy. But that revelation, once given, was perfectly congruent with reason.[21] Hoge was typical of the educated Southern clergy at the dawn of the nineteenth century; he was certain that reason was on his side.

The revivalists were undoubtedly more effective than the theological pamphleteers in rejuvenating popular religious interest in the South. Beginning in 1800, the frontier camp meetings became a major means of coping with the vast shifts in population that accompanied the westward migrations. Critics of the revivals claimed that they failed to deal with the prevailing "skepticism, deism, and atheism," but even the critics acknowledged a change in religious attitudes. In the three decades following the onset of the new revivalism, they noted, infidelity and heterodoxy became covert, silent, and unpopular.[22] The transition coincided with the expanding sectional defensiveness about slavery; it reflected the movement into the churches during the 1820s of the English upper classes, who were widely admired in the South; it also paralleled a shift in economic and political power as the tobacco fields and rice plantations that had supported the tidewater aristocracy became less productive than the newer westward lands. Whatever the reasons, by 1836 the president of William and Mary College, Thomas R. Dew, acknowledged in the *Southern Literary Messenger* that skepticism was no longer "respectable."[23]

Despite revivals, censorship, and economic shifts, several varieties of theological liberalism maintained a tenuous hold, primarily in the towns and cities. About 1819 the apostles of New England Unitarianism began to attract followers in the region's coastal cities. In that year William Ellery Channing preached in Baltimore his celebrated sermon on "Unitarian Christianity," in which he argued that a rational interpretation of Scripture entailed belief in the unity and moral goodness of God and hope in the moral restoration of humanity through the influence and example of Jesus Christ. The new Baltimore Unitarian pastor, Jared Sparks, promptly launched a preaching tour of the Southern towns, established a liberal magazine with agents throughout the South, and exulted as liberal societies temporarily flourished in Charleston, Augusta, Louisville, Savannah, Richmond, New Orleans, Mobile, Nashville, Wheeling, and other towns.[24] "We do not hear now-a-days of such things as the *Age of Reason*, parts first and second," complained the *Virginia Evangelical and Literary Magazine* in 1822, "but of Unitarian books and pamphlets, and even preachers, we hear a good deal."[25]

By the middle of the century the number of Unitarian congregations had shrunk to six, but for a time the urban visibility of Unitarianism imposed on the orthodox town clergy an exaggerated sense of its potential. Unlike their rural colleagues, who may never have actually seen a living liberal, they regularly associated and debated with the South's few liberal clergy and in fact competed with them for the allegiance of the mercantile and professional classes in the towns. Unitarian congregations were often small but, from the orthodox perspective, disconcertingly respectable.[26]

The orthodox clergy believed that they had a reasonable alternative to Unitarianism. In fact, their presuppositions about rationality were much closer to Unitarian positions than they could have comfortably acknowledged. Their kinship begins to appear when one contrasts Unitarianism with other forms of liberal religion—deistic or romantic. One can distinguish a liberalism of sensation, understanding, and reason and thereby begin to illustrate the point that both the Unitarians and the orthodox, in their common devotion to "understanding," were also committed to shared assumptions that shaped their views of theology.

2. Jefferson: Sensation

Thomas Jefferson has been associated with the New England Unitarian impulse, partly because he urged Harvard Unitarians to venture southward and predicted that the movement would sweep the country: "Missionaries from Cambridge would soon be greeted with more welcome, than from the tritheistic school of Andover."[27] But despite his admiration for Channing, Jefferson epitomized an idiosyncratic English and French deistic temper, broadened by ethical insight, chastened by speculative humility, and dedicated to the proposition that sensation established religious truth. Jefferson thought that the only way to restore the moral simplicity and thus the practical relevance of Christianity was to promulgate the notion that knowledge came from seeing, hearing, touching, smelling, and tasting. Only through sensation could the religious man, by a circuitous route, recover the ancient purity of Christian teaching and thereby restore the authority of the moral sense in the religious life. Religious reform for Jefferson entailed a tenuous journey: from sensation to a purified tradition and thence to a renewed moral sensibility.

Jefferson's odyssey began with the belief that "on the basis of sensation, of matter and motion, we may erect the fabric of all the certainties we can have or need." Abandon "the basis of sensation," he wrote John Adams, and "all is in the wind."[28] Hence he plunged into the early nineteenth-century French debate over Ideology, a philosophical movement named and nurtured by Destutt de Tracy, who between 1796 and 1803 managed to circulate his ideas throughout the educational and intellectual establishment in France—a philosophical hegemony cut short only by Napoleon's disenchantment with recalcitrant philosophers.[29] Jefferson read, edited, translated, and publicized Tracy's books; he considered him "the ablest living writer on intellectual subjects."[30] An attempt to construe philosophy as a biological science rather than a metaphysical quest, Tracy's Ideology represented a French appropriation of English Baconian and Lockean empiricism; yet it was intended not simply as an epistemology but also as a "science of methods," which reduced all ideas to elemental feelings, activities, or sensations that could be directly experienced and verified.[31] Jefferson believed that Tracy provided a method to retrace the mind's modes of action and deduction and thus offered a new way of approaching the study of government, economics, logic, and morality.[32]

Tracy was indifferent to religious doctrine, but Jefferson combined his ideological loyalties with a religious vision. For him, to embrace the senses was to possess ample evidence for "design, consummate skill, and indefinite power" in every atom of the universe.[33] More important, to embrace the senses was to spurn the allure of spiritualism, the bane of religious life. Jefferson's exaltation of sensation was almost indistinguishable from his materialism. In 1803 he commended Tracy's French colleague, P. J. G. Cabanis, for having "taken us as far as we can go" in showing that thought is "a faculty of our material organization." He continued to pursue the issue with his friend Thomas Cooper, who wanted to translate Cabanis's writings into English but refrained out of uncharacteristic deference to public sensibilities.[34] Cooper's outspoken views kept him off the faculty of the University of Virginia, much to the dismay of Jefferson, who blamed meddling Presbyterians, and also cut short his tenure as president of South Carolina College. Cooper's difficulties strengthened Jefferson's distaste for the "spiritualists," and he rejoiced in 1825 when a French researcher, Pierre Flourens, seemed to have demonstrated through experiments on animals that "the cerebrum is the thinking organ" and therefore that matter was capable of thought.[35]

The issue was not for Jefferson merely a matter of intellectual curiosity. He believed that materialism and sensationalism, taken together, guaranteed the certainty and the utility of ideas. "The business of life is with matter," he wrote a friend in 1825. "That gives us tangible results."[36] Jefferson admitted to Adams that he failed to read all of Tracy's works because he was "not fond of reading what is merely abstract, and unapplied immediately to some useful science."[37] He wanted trustworthy and useful knowledge as contrasted with esoteric and indistinct speculation. Like the Puritans who yearned to be assured of their salvation, Jefferson also wrestled with a problem of assurance; but the Puritans sought a freedom from sin that would provide inner peace; Jefferson wanted a freedom from doubt that would release him for confident moral activity in the world.

Neither his sensational epistemology nor his materialistic ontology can be isolated, therefore, from Jefferson's distaste for "indistinctness."[38] Plato was his arch villain because Platonic spiritualism led to incomprehensible nonsense and thence to an immobilizing skepticism. By resting knowledge on sensations, of which we are "very certain," he wrote, Tracy had erected an irresistible barrier against the skeptics.[39] Matter and the senses stood opposed to mysticism, speculation, obfuscation, dreams, fantasies, and skeptical immobility, whether in governmental theory, morality, or religion. An esoteric and indistinct religion was "artificial." Jefferson wanted to restore religious faith by exposing the platonizing conspiracies of the "priesthood"; in eliminating incomprehensibility from the Christian faith he would restore its moral authority. He therefore felt enormous gratitude for Joseph Priestley's *History of the Corruptions of Christianity* (1782). An English Unitarian minister and scientist who spent his last years in America, Priestley had attributed to philosophically minded Hellenistic theologians the responsibility for "platonizing" and corrupting primitive Christianity. Jefferson read the book repeatedly, for it confirmed his conviction that the "incomprehensible jargon" and "artificial scaffolding" of Greek philosophy stood in the way of discipleship.

> The religion-builders have so distorted and deformed the doctrines of Jesus, so muffled them in mysticisms, fancies, and falsehoods, have caricatured them into forms so monstrous and inconceivable as to shock reasonable thinkers, to revolt against the whole, and drive them rashly to pronounce its founder an imposter. Had there never been a commentator, there never would have been an infidel.[40]

By demolishing the Platonic vagaries that lay behind such absurdities as the doctrine of the Trinity, or the virgin birth, or the resurrection, Jefferson hoped to erase misconceptions about Jesus. Sensation was for him an historical tool; the certainties of the senses cut through all the overgrowth of Platonic obscurity that masked the genius of Jesus.

Jefferson's polemic against obscurity revealed the extent to which "simplicity" was for him a primary desideratum of Christian thought. It was the simplicity of primitive Christian teachings that recommended them for nineteenth-century society. Jefferson anticipated no difficulty in discerning the genuine teachings of Jesus; he knew that they would reflect the razor-sharp simplicity of religious genius: "It is as easy to separate those parts, as to pick out the diamonds from dunghills."[41] The doctrines of Jesus were "pure and simple" in content, style and spirit; they were unsophisticated and plain. Demolition of the artificial scaffolding would reveal the "simple structure of Jesus," which was itself mainly a purifying and simplifying of a Judaism in need of reformation.[42] Jefferson's admiration for primitive Christian simplicity reflected his confidence in the economy of a natural order in which every reality, including swamps and mosquitoes, found its rightful place. Nature itself manifested to Jefferson the unity and simplicity of the Creator.[43] But his Christianity was not an afterthought of his cosmology. Jefferson's vision was also historical; he was intent on recovering primitive simplicity by discovering the teaching of an historical figure. It is true that he transformed Jesus into an eighteenth-century deist with exalted notions of the unity of God, a high moral sensibility, confidence in a future state, and concern about the heart. Though he sometimes disagreed with Jesus and even concluded that his doctrines were "defective as a whole," Jefferson was a bona fide primitivist.[44] In searching for primitive Christian doctrine he ironically aligned himself with a variety of orthodox Protestants who were claiming to have recovered the earliest layers of Christian thought and practice.

The orthodox sought the primitive in order to conform to it; Jefferson sought it in order to liberate the spontaneous moral sensibility. To sweep away the "gossamer factitious religion" was to recover the ability to "moralize for ourselves, follow the oracle of conscience." The larger purpose behind Jefferson's iconoclastic historiography was ethical, for the moral sense stood near the center of his religious vision. As early as 1809 he reported that his religious reading "had long been confined to the moral branch of religion," and while he was in the White House he began work on his abridged New Testament, an octavo of forty-six pages entitled the "Life and Morals of Jesus of Nazareth," which depicted Jesus as a refined ethical teacher who had presented "the most sublime edifice of morality which had ever been exhibited to man."[45]

His admiration for the "universal philanthropy" in Jesus's ethics enabled Jefferson to call himself a Christian. Yet he was indifferent to most of the concrete moral teachings of Jesus; he found in pure Christian ethics a plea for universal benevolence, but it is hard to find much discussion of specific New Testament admonitions and prescriptions. He told Priestley that Jesus had reformed Jewish ethics according to the standard of reason, justice, and philanthropy, yet clearly Jefferson was preoccupied with only two of Jesus's moral insights: his demand for benevolence to the whole family of mankind rather than merely friends and kindred, and his accent on inwardness and purity of motivation. Jefferson valued the ethical teachings of the New Testament because they seemed to confirm his own belief in a moral sense within human nature, analogous to the senses of hearing, seeing, and feeling. When unencumbered by Platonic tradition and artificial rules, the moral sensibility could be trusted to ensure tranquillity and justice in society.[46]

Jefferson struggled against artificiality within the Christian tradition because the Platonic encrustations blocked the moral sensibility. Jeffersonian empiricism purified the tradition of its Platonic dross and cleared the way for the moral genius of Jesus to shine through and confirm the dispositions of our own inherent moral sensibility. In religious matters the senses were the servants of the moral sense; epistemology was the handmaiden to ethics, which was the driving force of religion. "To the corruptions of Christianity I am indeed opposed," Jefferson said, "but not to the genuine precepts of Jesus himself. I am a Christian, in the only sense in which he wished anyone to be; sincerely attached to his doctrines, in preference to all others; ascribing to himself every *human* excellence; and believing he never claimed any other."[47]

Jefferson conceived of himself, then, as a rational Christian who believed that reason was the "only oracle" provided by heaven, and by reason he clearly meant *reasoning* grounded in sensory experience of the world.[48] Yet the objects of such reasoning were not simply the events and regularities of nature but also an historical tradition. It was precisely the senses that enabled the historical reason to formulate an accurate view of the past by clearing away the metaphysical haze. The depiction of the past then confirmed and emboldened the moral self to trust its own sensibilities.

3. Gilman: Understanding

Jefferson kept his religious views to himself most of the time, sharing them with only a few friends and correspondents, but he believed that he had devised a Christian philosophy that would displease "neither the rational Christian nor Deists." None of the rational Christian Unitarians who infiltrated the South after 1819, however, could have entertained Jeffersonian ideas about revelation, the miraculous, and matter. Jefferson lived in a world populated by material selves and a material God.[49] The Unitarians strove for spiritual perfectibility in a world constituted by restless human spirits drawn by the one divine Spirit. Jefferson's piety was far removed from the spirituality of the Boston liberals, who were as distressed as the orthodox when the deists disparaged the Scriptures. The Unitarians agreed with the anti-deistic theologians that reason was not to be exalted above the Biblical revelation. In fact they were at one with the orthodox when it came to describing the formal relationship between reason and revelation: both groups agreed that revelation was reasonable, though it might transcend reason. But the Unitarians believed that the orthodox anti-deists had failed to see the implications of their formal principle. The denominational theologians believed a doctrine to be reasonable if it was an integral part of a system of revealed truths for which there was persuasive rational evidence, even if the particular doctrine was itself incomprehensible. The Unitarian liberals insisted that a doctrine could be considered reasonable only if it stood alone before the bar of rational scrutiny. They did not insist that the autonomous and unassisted powers of reason could have independently deduced the truths of the Christian revelation. They simply believed that every individual doctrine was to be tested by the canons of reason.

By "reason" they had in mind something different from the Jeffersonians. G. W. Burnap, pastor of the Unitarian church in Baltimore, summarized the typical view in a sentence: reason is "a sentinel at the entrance of the human mind, to determine what is true and what is false, what is to be admitted and what is to be kept out." Reason was, as Burnap put it, "the understanding," an internal "faculty of the mind" with its own inherent laws.[50] His description revealed his indebtedness to Scottish "Common Sense" philosophy—an eighteenth-century reaction against the empiricism of both Hume and Locke. At the center of the Scottish epistemology, as developed by Thomas Reid at Edinburgh and expounded by Dugald Stewart, was the conviction that the mind contained innate constitutive principles that enabled thinking men and women to describe the world accurately. Such principles were logically prior to sense experience; indeed they regulated and organized all experience. They were axiomatic assumptions inherent in all thought, and they influenced the religious consciousness as well as every other cognitive endeavour.[51]

The most articulate Southern representative of New England liberalism was Samuel Gilman (1791–1858), who journeyed from Harvard in 1819 to become the minister of the Second Independent Church in Charleston. He was a self-conscious disciple of the first generation Unitarian patriarchs: Channing, Henry Ware, President Kirkland of Harvard. He was also a man of cosmopolitan sympathies who admired the social reforms of Dorothea Dix during a period when most Unitarians were social conservatives and appreciated the Biblical scholarship of Moses Stuart at Andover despite his polemic against liberalism. For a period Gilman also spent an hour every morning with Jasper Adams, the Episcopal president of Charleston College, reading German Biblical criticism. He ordered thirty volumes of Albert Eichhorn's critical studies, which argued that the Old Testament was a compilation of numerous layers of tradition. He also admired Johann Griesbach's New Testament criticism, from which he could learn to recognize and compare the ancient manuscripts behind the Biblical text and to understand the newer literary analysis of the Gospels. But Gilman still found his major intellectual sustenance in Scottish Realism. He admired Locke, he said in 1829, but he felt closer to Reid's philosophy of the mind and to "the thorough scholarship of Dugald Stewart."[52] His commitment to Scottish thought remained strong throughout his career in Charleston.

Gilman believed that Scriptural revelation addressed "the judgment and reason" and thereby impressed itself upon the "religious capacities and tendencies" that formed part of the human mental constitution. Revelation did not impart the religious capabilities but simply invigorated ineradicable native instincts that were a part of human nature "long before one word of the Bible was written, or revelation had uttered and miraculously enforced a single truth or command." Among the "principles" that the Scottish philosophers found underlying all concrete knowledge, Gilman included a "religious appetency," an instinctive impulse toward and receptivity to divine revelation.[53]

Gilman's argument for a religious principle within human nature did not lead him to question the superiority of Scriptural revelation. His Dudleian Lecture at Harvard in 1848 was a sustained defense of "a special, supernatural revelation," an effort to show that the most refined doctrines of Christianity transcended the normal religious capacity. Gilman disapproved of the radical German Biblical critics, who had, he believed, reduced the gospel accounts to "impalpable myths." He believed that Scripture consisted of historical records that offered a plain and conclusive revelation, even if the ethical and philosophical imperfections in the Bible required occasional correction. Scripture contained the "highest truths of absolute religion": without the Bible there would be no Unitarian Christianity.[54] Gilman assured his fellow Southerners that Unitarianism had no relation to Deism, that "an immeasurable distance" separated him from the disreputable Paine. The Unitarian embraced revelation "with his whole heart" and believed "devoutly in the truth of his Bible."[55]

Yet Gilman's conviction that revelation addressed the judgment and reason led him to believe that the Bible had to be read in a "broad, comprehensive, reasonable light." He identified Biblical interpretation as the primary issue dividing liberal and orthodox theologians. Echoing Channing's 1819 sermon, Gilman claimed that the distinctive mark of liberal religion was its preference for the clear and reasonable—as opposed to the "mysterious"—interpretation of Scripture. A revelation that defied understanding was no genuine revelation.[56] And that meant that few orthodox doctrines could stand scrutiny. Gilman denied that men and women were totally depraved or that God imputed Adam's guilt to his descendants; he denied that Christ had died as a substitute for the race; and he criticized the imposition of creeds. He believed that one could abstract from the various estranged denominations of Christians a common essence, a central core of eternal truths that underlay the temporary, contingent, contradictory forms of expression that divided them. The aim of Unitarianism was to unite all persons who could "possess and exhibit the true spirit of the Savior," who cared more for behavior than for speculative beliefs, and who sought the spirit of the Bible rather than its letter.[57]

Gilman called for devotion to a progressive future in place of idolatrous commitment to a "faded past." He directed his call to a congregation of urban merchants and professionals who could well understand a religion of progress. His congregation had originated in 1817 following a schism in the older Independent Church in Charleston. Sixty-nine Calvinist subscribers moved into the Circular Church, one of the finest buildings in the city. But the Unitarian group consisted of "a fair proportion of the worth, the piety, and the respectability of the former united body." Eventually they constructed a splendid Gothic building, with a tower and buttresses, stained glass and finials, and elaborate fan tracery in the ceiling of the nave. It was such an elegant structure that the Unitarian clergy felt obliged to deny that it was extravagant, that mere vanity and aesthetic taste prompted its erection, or that its "expensive adornment" was a waste. It was fitting, said John Pierpont, Jr., of Savannah, that Church architecture "should keep pace with the wealth, the taste, and the culture of our age."[58]

Both the building and its pastor symbolized Unitarian strategy in the South. Like the physical structure, Gilman was a showpiece. A Harvard graduate, he and his wife Caroline were both literary figures who published popular fiction and poetry, and his slave-holding illustrated his status and success within the Southern way of life. He was one of the bright stars in a small galaxy that included Theodore Clapp in New Orleans, James Freeman Clarke in Mobile, John Pierpont of Savannah, G. W. Burnap in Balti-more, John Heywood in Louisville, Jared Sparks in Baltimore, Horace Holley in Lexington, and Stephen Bullfinch in Augusta. These men did not expect to attract the masses. They hoped to reach people who were educated, cultivated, and influential—or who wanted to be. But the orthodox town pastors were intent on persuading the same constituency.[59]

4. *Miles: Reason*

In 1815 George Ticknor of Boston began the migration of young New Englanders to German universities: there and elsewhere they discovered the new "romantic" feeling, which had a narrow but profound impact on American theology. In Boston, Emerson and Theodore Parker tried with limited success to lead the clergy beyond the restrictive authority of Scripture and Scottish episte-mology and to push forward with the help of a higher intuitive Reason into a realm of eternal truth. But romantic ideas could also inform more conservative churchmen. The new interest in the art, pageantry, and culture of the Middle Ages permeated the high-church movements within the Episcopal Church, and at Mercers-burg Seminary in Pennsylvania a talented group of Reformed theologians who were imbued with a metaphysical vision drawn from the German Hegelians and a corporate consciousness derived from the school of Schleiermacher began during the 1840s to de-scribe Christianity as a vital corporate "life" mediated through the sacramental Church rather than as a set of doctrinal propositions.

Gradually romantic ideas penetrated the South, creating new literary tastes, infusing Southern "nationalism" with new strength, and occasionally altering religious sensibility. "Romanticism" embraced such a broad spectrum of thinkers that some historians have found the label useless, but, at a bare minimum, it can serve to mark a distinction between theologians who remained satisfied with an empiricism drawn from Locke or the Scottish philosophers and other theologians for whom empiricism was a confining barrier. For the romantic liberal, "experience" and "reason" both suggested an intuitive grasp of supersensuous reality that involved the self as an organic unity of thought and feeling. For them, Reason was not limited to discursive ratiocination, but it embraced a range of feelings, a quality of awareness, and an aesthetic sensibility that earlier deists would have consigned to the region of mere "emotion."

Among the few Southern clergy who could be numbered among the romantics was James Warley Miles (1818–1876) of Charleston, who during his lifetime roamed across the entire spectrum of romantic religion, in both its conservative and its radical forms. As a student in General Theological Seminary in New York he helped instigate the establishment of an Anglican monastic establishment, Nashotah House in Wisconsin, that would recapture an ascetic medieval spirituality; thus he stood for a time with the English Oxford Movement that tried to restore Catholic tradition within the Anglican Church. In 1841, though, he moved back to his home state of South Carolina, where he lost his confidence in Oxford Anglo-Catholicism and embarked on an Episcopal mission to Constantinople and Mesopotamia, where he remained four years. In 1847 Miles returned to the parishes of South Carolina, eventually coming as interim pastor to St. Michael's Church in Charleston.

There he built a library of works in more than thirty languages and found new intellectual mentors, especially Samuel Taylor Coleridge in England, Victor Cousin in France, and John Morrell, an English philosopher of religion who had drawn together the themes of Continental and British thought in his influential *History of Modern Philosophy*. Miles purchased and admired the works of Schleiermacher and of such German "mediating" theologians

as Augustus Neander and Carl Nitzsch, who were trying to reconcile traditional Christianity and nineteenth-century Idealistic philosophy. He associated himself as well with the English Broad
Churchmen—Thomas Arnold, R. D. Hampden, and Richard
Whately—who wanted to reinterpret Anglican thought in the light
of new scientific and historical learning. Finally in 1849 he published his *Philosophic Theology*, a work that received the rare
compliment of being immediately translated into German by one
of Neander's students who was impressed by his mentor's commendation of it as an "important publication." But the negative
response among the orthodox clergy in America helped drive Miles
from his parish, whereupon in 1850 he assumed a new philosophical chair in the College of Charleston.[60]

Miles believed that one test of a theologian's insight was his
capacity to distinguish "Reason" from both understanding and
sensation. The "understanding," he said, had a limiting function:
it merely filtered and formed the material of knowledge, which
was derived from other sources. He had learned from Immanuel
Kant that the understanding was a repository of innate categories
and forms that imposed a structure on experience, which otherwise
would be a buzzing chaos. But the material of knowledge came
from the senses and, more important for the theologian, from the
"Reason," a direct, spontaneous apprehension of reality. The intuitive insight of Reason was not in the strict sense "knowledge" until it was filtered through the understanding, which com-
pressed the intuition into a limited range of logical forms. But
Reason nevertheless transcended the reach of the merely "logical"
understanding.[61]

Miles's epistemology was an eclectic mixture drawn from Kant
and Coleridge, but he diverged from Kant in believing that Reason
could apprehend ultimate reality. Reason was the realm of "necessary convictions": its conceptions were not empirically verifiable
but they were logically necessary. In conceiving of a "Perfect Being," for instance, the Reason provided intimations that a real
Infinite Being was manifest in the world, for the idea of perfection
entailed existence, manifestation, and personality. It was not absurd, morever, to conclude that the Infinite was incarnate in an
historical person, and Miles in fact believed that God revealed

himself in Jesus, reconciling and connecting the finite and the Infinite. In so formulating the issue, he was following the European mediating theologians—especially Hans Lassen Martenson of Copenhagen and Carl Nitzsch of Bonn and Berlin—who also had described the Incarnation as a logical necessity and the substance of Christianity as the reconciliation of finitude and infinity.[62] He was the only Southern theologian whose vision was fundamentally formed by the post-Kantian and Hegelian discussions in Germany.

Seen in a wider European perspective, Miles was a conservative who agreed with the "right wing" speculative theologians that God was incarnate not only in the development of generic humanity but also, uniquely, in the person of Jesus. But in America he seemed radical, mainly because he thought of revelation as a "power" for kindling "life" rather than as a propositional datum enclosed in sacred books. To be sure, Miles believed that the Gospel accounts in the New Testament were historically accurate, as Andrews Norton of Harvard had argued in *The Genuineness of the Gospels*. Yet Miles thought that Christian faith, even its notion of God, had emerged from Reason, and the Biblical records were therefore to be judged by general religious and moral criteria, including the "religious sensibility." Miles believed that the Christian consciousness was logically prior to Scripture, so it was inconsequential that the Bible might contain myths, false notions, or narrow prejudices. He read the famous *Life of Jesus* (1835) written in Tübingen by David Friedrich Strauss, who had argued that the gospels were the products of an unconscious religious impulse that was expressed in forms peculiar to the mythological world-view of the first century. While disagreeing with Strauss's antisupernaturalism and with his assumption that mythological legends could have arisen so quickly, Miles believed Strauss to be correct in his conviction that the New Testament expressed an antecedent Christian consciousness.

> Profound and philosophical insight! It is not in the record of the letter, but in the spiritual sanctuary of the heart, that Christianity is enshrined and lives. And if it were possible to destroy the record, the Christian consciousness would then,

perhaps, form glorious legends of the mighty Christ, whose power and truth will ever continue to be accentuated in the experience of man. . . .[63]

Miles eventually interpreted the Old Testament by means of categories familiar to the disciples of Strauss. The fables of Genesis, he wrote, embodied philosophical truths of which the authors were unconscious: the story of Eden expressed the mysterious strife between the finite free will and the infinite Absolute Will; the creation story contained the insight that the human spirit was the finite manifestation of an infinite creative Intellect.[64]

Historical authenticity, then, was secondary, and the authority of the Bible came solely from its capacity to evoke and enlarge moral and religious sensibilities, its inherent "religious power," and its capacity to mediate reconciliation. The Christian consciousness preceded the written records and could exist without them. The Bible was revelatory insofar as it could awaken "man's intuitive consciousness to the direct apprehension of the religious truth and power of Christianity," and the Christian faith was worthy of acceptance insofar as it enlarged and empowered the consciousness of humanity.[65]

Miles had some thoughts in common with the New England transcendentalists, who also grounded religion in Reason and sensibility, but compared to Emerson he was a traditionalist. The transcendentalists considered it unimportant whether one believed in Biblical miracles, which in any case they doubted; Miles still defended belief in the miracles, though he denied the orthodox and Unitarian contention that they confirmed Christian doctrine.[66] The transcendentalists removed the person of Jesus from the center of Christianity; Miles tried to keep him there. They had no use for Trinitarian doctrine; he thought there was ground for belief in a plurality within the divine personality. Emerson believed in the divinity of the individual self; Miles had a bleaker sense of human moral irresponsibility. He would have not felt at home in Emerson's Concord—he much preferred Berlin or Cambridge.

He felt especially isolated in the South. Miles was appalled by "the emptiness and ignorance" of the orthodox ministers who opposed him, and he suffered from their antagonism. "You have no notion of the suspicion with which I am regarded," he wrote to a friend in 1851. By 1854 he felt himself to be a broken man: "I feel every day, almost, feebler in both mind and body. . . . I have no confidence whatever in my judgment and criticisms."[67] It is true that the South seemed particularly hostile to religious liberals, partly because many Southerners grew to associate religious liberalism with dangerous social innovations, especially with abolitionism, and partly because of the agrarian environs.[68] Yet Miles would have been uncomfortable also in Connecticut or Illinois, for he stood outside the patterns of theological thought that dominated antebellum American religion.

Instead of flocking to the theologians who attracted the interest of later generations—Bushnell, Emerson, Channing, Nevin—most educated clergy learned their theology from conservative writers whose names have largely been forgotten despite their enormous influence among their contemporaries. These theologians, deeply conscious of their denominational ties, felt certain that rationality supported orthodoxy. They were also convinced, for the most part, that theologians enamored with sensation or Reason would inevitably fall into error. "Locke's philosophy, called Sensationalism, and the more opposing scheme, called Transcendentalism, err on opposite extremes," wrote a prominent antebellum Methodist.[69] The orthodox sought, therefore, to show that revealed theology, as they understood it, had the sanction of the "understanding," which they interpreted much in the same fashion as the Unitarians.

CHAPTER FOUR

THE EVIDENCE FOR FAITH

Every orthodox theologian in the Old South would have asserted that the foundation of faith was the Bible, but few would have rested content with the mere assertion. They wanted to demonstrate the authority of Scripture by appeal to an external criterion, not fully recognizing that their methods subtly shifted faith's foundation. Their rational orthodoxy had a circular logic: revelation undergirded reason, but reason verified revelation. On this seeming paradox the orthodox rationalists built their theology. Few of the town pastors, moreover, would have claimed that the Bible was the sole foundation for the Christian religion. Certainly they believed Scripture to be sufficient and necessary, but they also believed that all experience adumbrated the truths of Scripture; the discoveries of reason approximated the mysteries of revelation. Every rational person could perceive the signs of divine activity in the natural and social orders of existence, could indeed discover the clues that validated the special Biblical revelation, which merely fulfilled and perfected the natural reason. Persuaded of the unity of truth, the Southern theologians believed that human experience overflowed with analogies that anticipated, confirmed, and illuminated the facts of revelation.

The ministers were confident that rational orthodoxy would commend itself to the educated and influential classes whom they found in the towns and cities. Therefore they proclaimed their scholastic gospel not only in polemical treatises and theological texts but also in innumerable sermons with such revealing titles as "The Reasonableness of Faith," "Trinitarians Rational," "The Reasonableness of Religion," and "The Credibility of the Gospel."[1] But their fondness for reasonableness was no innovation. Despite their preoccupation with eighteenth-century issues they were also following an example that originated in the New Testament's adaptation of Stoic and Hellenistic categories and arguments. Ever since the early second century there had been Christian theologians who accorded honorific status to rationality, and each of the five major traditions of religious thought in the Old South—Catholic, Lutheran, Reformed, Anglican, and Wesleyan —reflected that heritage. The social imperatives of urban society prompted the Southern town pastors to recover an older apologetic theology.

1. *Traditions*

As early as the second century the Christian Hellenistic apologists, trying to demonstrate the commensurability of faith and reason, inaugurated the tradition of "Christian evidences." Justin Martyr (*fl.* 150) and Origen of Alexandria (*ca.* 184–253) exemplified the style of argument when they tried to prove that Jesus was the Christ and that his teachings were true by pointing out that he performed miracles and fulfilled Jewish prophecies. Their arguments were circular, but they suggested that Christian truth-claims were subject to an extrinsic mode of verification, logically antecedent to the doctrines themselves.

The confidence in rational argument reached its apex in the thirteenth century when Thomas Aquinas tried to present Christian truth in such a way that pagan philosophy could be seen as preparatory to faith. Just as Thomas argued that grace did not destroy but rather perfected nature, so he also claimed that theology presupposed, used, and perfected natural knowledge. To sustain the claim he pointed out that there were two classes of religious truths. The first was demonstrable by rational reflection on the created world; the second—embracing such doctrines as the Trinity and Incarnation—transcended the reach of rational inquiry. Yet even these suprarational truths were not irrational. Aquinas believed that reason could show them not to be absurd and in some instances could even demonstrate their probability. And Thomas also agreed with the older apologists that Scriptural truths transcending natural knowledge received additional confirmation from the fulfillment of prophecies and the performance of miracles. Nineteenth-century Catholic theologians still quoted the Thomistic injunction: "Men would not believe, if they could not have a ground for belief through signs and wonders or similar things."[2]

The fourteenth-century Nominalists helped to persuade Martin Luther that reason could not penetrate into the truths of faith, but by the nineteenth century Luther's American disciples could claim, with some justification, that they were as confident as any Thomist about the rationality of Christianity. As early as 1536 Luther's close friend Philip Melanchthon was speaking of philosophy as a prelude to true Christianity and arguing that reason could demonstrate both the existence and the attributes of God. During the Age of Orthodoxy in the seventeenth century the Lutherans returned to Thomistic theses, established with Aristotelian metaphysics. In his celebrated *Loci Theologica* (1610–1621) John Gerhard of Jena not only adduced the older "evidences" of faith but also spoke of revelation as being "above" but not opposed to reason—a recovery of scholastic hierarchical imagery. It was no revolution when the South Carolina Lutheran Synod (1824) required its ministers to study natural and moral philosophy; the synod was merely following orthodox tradition.[3]

The Southern Reformed theologians—the heirs of John Calvin and Ulrich Zwingli—inherited an even higher estimation of rationality. Calvin had never completely shared Luther's distaste for rational demonstration. To be sure, he said that reason deprived of the grace of revelation would misinterpret the clues to a divine presence in the universe and fall into idolatry. And he insisted that apart from the special inward testimony of the Spirit the Christian could not know the Scriptures to contain a supernatural revelation. But Calvin also thought that an innate awareness of divinity permitted even the pagan to perceive dimly the divine power undergirding the world and that proofs from reason could assist the Christian to confirm the inward testimony by rendering the Scriptures credible. Calvin used a number of arguments to "prove" that the Scriptures contained a divine revelation; their antiquity, their style, their confirmation by miracles and fulfilled prophecies, and their universal acceptance in the Church validated their truthfulness.

Calvin's successors were even more optimistic about rational argument, and no seventeenth century theologian had greater influence in the Old South than the Genevan Reformed dogmatician Francis Turretin (1623–1687), whose *Institutio Theologiae Elencticae* (1679–1685) was a theological textbook in the three major

Presbyterian seminaries in the South—Columbia, Union, and Danville—and at Princeton as well. When the Baptists opened their Southern Seminary in 1859 they also had their students in theology read Turretin, along with Anselm of Canterbury and Thomas Aquinas.[4] To praise his writings, wrote one Presbyterian minister on the occasion of a new Latin edition of Turretin's works, "would be as idle as to eulogize the sun."[5]

In Turretin the Reformed clergy had an authoritative voice for a "rational" orthodoxy. He believed that Lutherans, Anabaptists, and even Roman Catholics gave inadequate scope to "the light of right reason." The first part of his *Institutes* consisted of an argument on behalf of natural theology and philosophy; because truth could never be contrary to truth, he said, even the "mysteries" of faith were ultimately rational. Turretin believed that reason could demonstrate the existence and attributes of God, serve as a "competent judge" of religious teachings, and prove the Christian Scriptures to be authentic and divine. The proofs of Scriptural revelation were both "extrinsic" and "intrinsic": the antiquity of the Bible attested to its credibility, for instance, as also did the sublimity and efficacy of its teachings.[6] The continuing popularity of Turretin, his Dutch counterpart Witsius, and the English Reformed theologians Richard Baxter, Stephen Charnock, and John Owen served to justify and validate the nineteenth-century quest for rationality among Presbyterians, Baptists, and some Episcopal clergy.[7]

Anglicans needed no prompting from Geneva to mount a platform on behalf of the reasonableness of faith. After the Glorious Revolution of 1688 the clergy of the English establishment seemingly came to believe that their special mission was to prove the credibility of revelation. More than any other group of theologians they created the intellectual world inhabited by the Southern clergy. In the late seventeenth century a few Anglican preachers complained about deists, and thereafter almost every Anglican theologian who had anything to say tried his hand at confuting deism. A nineteenth-century theologian ruefully surveyed the history of postrevolutionary religious thought in England:

There is scarcely one, perhaps, of our more eminent divines who has not in a greater or lesser degree distinguished himself [in writing on the evidences of revelation] and scarcely an aspirant for theological distinction who has not thought it one of the surest paths to . . . eminence to come forward as a champion in this arena.[8]

A few lonely voices protested: Henry Dodwell proclaimed in *Christianity Not Founded on Argument* that rational religion was a form of pride, and William Law wrote that the renunciation of argument and evidence was *The Way of Divine Knowledge*. But in their reservations Dodwell and Law were eccentric figures. The oft-quoted judgment of Mark Pattison still stands: "The title of Locke's treatise, *The Reasonableness of Christianity*, may be said to have been the solitary thesis of Christian theology in England for the great part of a century."[9]

The patriarch of Methodism, John Wesley (1703–1791), confronted the English enlightenment by counterposing an internal "spiritual sense" against a fallen "natural reason," but instead of proceeding to irrationalist conclusions, he, too, had taken for granted that anyone who departed from "genuine reason" departed from Christianity. Wesley harshly criticized Dodwell and Law and he borrowed from Locke to explicate the relation between the inner sense and rationality: just as physical sensations were the necessary ground of natural reasoning, so the internal sensation of faith was also a "way of seeing," a "taste," enabling the mind to "reason concerning spiritual things."[10]

As a consequence of his fascination with internality, Wesley considered abandoning the "external evidences" of revelation, and he objected to the purely rational theology of the deists, but in fact he continued to use the older "evidences" and he assumed that even deists could arrive at some religious truths. He acknowledged that it was reason, relying upon evidences, that knew the Christian revelation to be divine, but he also went further: "Christianity requires our assent to nothing but what is plain and intelligible in every proposition."[11] English Methodist theologians appended qualifications to their affirmation of natural theology, for they believed with Wesley that rationality presupposed always an appropriate "sensation" as its foundation, but Richard Watson, whose prominence in America gave him a reputation as "the Calvin of the Methodists," maintained in his *Theological Institutes* the

Wesleyan insistence on intelligibility.[12] As the standard theological authority for antebellum American Wesleyans, Watson's institutes also undergirded the nineteenth-century quest for theological rationality.

In eighteenth- and early nineteenth-century England, wrote Mark Pattison, "the rationalizing method possessed itself absolutely of the whole field of theology."[13] And the English experience indelibly colored the outlook of the Southern town clergy; it taught them what a rational theology should look like. Encouraged by their traditions, they boldly assigned to reason a threefold task: the preparation, validation, and interpretation of revelation. Holding firmly to orthodoxy as they understood it, they put the older formulations to new uses and thus changed the force and meaning of inherited doctrines. Without knowing it, they were not only preserving tradition but also transforming it.

2. Preparing for the Word

No Southern theologian defended the priority of a special Biblical revelation more profusely than Thomas Ralston (1806–1885?), a native of Kentucky who in 1827 began traveling one of the state's rural Methodist circuits. Despite poor health he advanced by 1835 to the town churches, first Versailles, then Frankfort and Maysville, and then in 1839 to the state's largest Methodist church in Louisville. Two years later he became the principal of a Methodist school for women in Lexington, where he began writing his *Elements of Theology*, which at its first appearance in 1847 was intended as a popular but systematic explication of Southern Methodist doctrine.[14] The denomination continued to issue reprints long after the Civil War, as the book became mandatory reading for ministerial candidates, and Ralston published an expanded and revised edition as late as 1871. Even then the Methodists were still describing the book as a landmark of doctrinal instruction: "a body of theology which is unsurpassed, if equalled, outside the pages of the Bible, and which has given to the illustrious author an immortality of fame."[15]

On the surface Ralston often sounded like an implacable critic of natural theology, for he denied that reason, independent of revelation, could even produce a conception of God, let alone fathom the essence of the divine nature. Yet he found a way to justify natural theology. During the prelapsarian period, he said, Adam and his sage and pious family had a direct and spontaneous knowledge of God. Rational notions of the deity among the Romans and Greeks resulted from "the dim light" that remained from this primal and general revelation, and the light still burned in the nineteenth century, enabling the theologian to look up "through nature's works to nature's God."[16]

Ralston's notion was a commonplace: ingredient in the primeval innocence of humanity was a supernatural revelation, a deeper wisdom, and the fall did not entirely obliterate its presence in the consciousness of the race.[17] This idea, which Philip Melanchthon had resuscitated in the sixteenth century, provided a justification for reassembling all the traditional rational arguments for the existence of God based on the harmony of the natural order, the mutual adaptation of its parts, its complexity, the necessity of a sufficient cause for its existence, and the universality of religious belief.[18] The insights thus garnered constituted a "natural" knowledge of God, independent of a special Biblical revelation.

Although the theologians believed that natural theology was insufficient without a supplementary Biblical revelation, they always posited a complementary relationship between natural and revealed theology. One of the clearest statements came from Henry Bidleman Bascom (1796–1850). Because he angered Methodist traditionalists by refusing to abandon his elegant attire, Bascom spent several years in the isolated circuits of rural Tennessee, but eventually he moved into the fashionable pulpits of Danville and Louisville before becoming a professor of moral science at Augusta College and, by 1842, the president of Transylvania University in Lexington. He was much in demand in educational circles, and he turned down invitations to the presidencies of both Missouri University and Louisiana College, but he did accept the editorship of the Southern Methodist *Quarterly Review* and in 1850 became a bishop in the Southern wing of the denomination.

He was a man of influence both in and out of the Church, and during the twenties Henry Clay sought and received his political support. In gratitude Clay established Bascom as Chaplain of the United States Congress for two years, but Bascom immediately embarrassed his patron with a two-hour sermon against the Unitarians, who were heavily represented among the senators and representatives. Clay said later that the two hours seemed like three.[19] Bascom was extremely sensitive to such disapproval: his friends described him as a man of "morbid sensitivities," anxious and apprehensive of failure, burdened with an unhappy marriage.[20] But in the Southern cities he was a sterling success. When he lived in Lexington the city still called itself "the Athens of the West," and many of its six thousand inhabitants were said to have acquired both wealth and "a taste for polished society and for all the useful appendages of civilized life."[21] Bascom was apparently a useful appendage, for when he preached in Lexington and other cities huge crowds flocked to hear him.[22] His appeal to urban audiences accounted largely for his rise to the episcopacy.

Bascom wanted to present to his admirers an argument for Christianity "based exclusively upon the facts and principles of Natural theology." He feared that the mass of Southern Church members were unprepared for the intellectual labor of such an enterprise; the public mind, he said, had been so "drugged with the familiar dogmas of the pulpit" that it had begun to exhibit "a kind of dyspeptic debility," but Bascom was by 1837 sufficiently confident of success to begin a series of lectures on natural theology in cities throughout the South. With each repetition he refined his arguments until finally he came to consider his "Lectures on the Relative Claims of Christianity and Infidelity" as the "master production of his life." His fellow Methodist theologians were pleased. Ralston believed that the lectures were unanswerable and that Bascom had secured a position among "the most profound philosophical thinkers, and the ablest logical reasoners of the age."[23] The *Quarterly Review* described it along with his other writings as "part of the permanent literature of the church."[24]

Bascom tried to unfold a three-part schema to show that natural theology, properly understood, furnished a foundation for revelation. First, he said that revelation was *congruent* with natural theology: there were analogies in the natural order to the revealed mysteries of Christianity. Both for example taught that the most substantial benefits of life came only through the voluntary sacrificial instrumentality of others. The cross was not only an historical saving event but also a paradigm of natural experience. Second, he said that revelation *completed* natural religion, which otherwise remained partial and imperfect. The truths of natural theology always appeared as heralds of still higher truths, of "something beyond, more enlarged, and better defined." The natural theologian could present analyses of human sinfulness and of disorder, but only revelation could furnish a fitting solution. The natural theologian could discern God's existence but not his nature. And Bascom's thoughts about the completion of natural knowledge led him to the third level of his schema: *correlation*.[25] A general philosophical theology, using human reason, posed and defined the central questions of human existence, and Christian revelation supplied the corresponding answers.

> It is a fact which must always compel the admiration of intelligence, that all the great difficulties, and most perplexing problems stated, and formally, or by implication, hypothecated by natural theology, are defects resolved by Christianity.[26]

At the crucial point, then, natural theology was helpless, but its very defects pointed to the remedy. The natural theologian revealed the "irresistible relevancy in the Christian revelation," whether he recognized it or not.[27]

Bascom expressed a broad consensus about natural theology when he said that it could demonstrate God's existence and a general sense of our relations to him but could provide no consistent notions of God's nature or his scheme of redemption. Any rational person, wrote A. B. Van Zandt, a Presbyterian minister in Petersburg, Virginia, could grasp the reality of "an invisible, almighty power, the disposer of events and the arbiter of destiny," but this formal and abstract conception of God the Creator and Judge was incomplete without a special revelation of the divine mercy in Christ.[28] The fragmentary character of natural theology, however, did not detract from its importance. The partial truth pointed to and participated in the whole truth; moral and religious experience could approximate in varying degrees to the revealed Word; right reason moved toward faith.[29]

Their confidence emboldened by the doctrine of primal revelation, the Southern theologians maintained a careful and hopeful watch over the physical sciences, with every assurance that "natural philosophy" would provide the nineteenth century's distinctive prospectus on divine truth. The clergy thought that modern science was both the product and the protector of the Christian tradition. Van Zandt explained to a university audience in 1851 that natural science presupposed purpose and rationality in the cosmos: "The maxim that 'Jehovah has created nothing in vain,' we hold to have been the basis of all those minute investigations of the scientists."[30] And if modern science was the offspring of the Christian West, there was every reason to believe that the child would honor and obey the parent.[31] Natural science would be one more weapon in the apologetic armory of Christendom.

To become an amateur scientist was to extend and enrich the ministerial calling. When John Holt Rice became the first Professor of Theology in the Presbyterian Seminary at Hampden-Sidney, Virginia, he was instructed to raise up a generation of scientifically minded clergymen: "And also as the cavils and objections of infidels have been more readily answered as *natural science* has been enlarged, that branch of knowledge should form a part of that fund of general information, which every minister of the Gospel should possess."[32] The nascent Church-sponsored colleges tried to develop courses in chemistry and natural philosophy, sometimes in geology and astronomy, and their science instructors—such men as the Methodists Landon Garland of Randolph-Macon and Alexander Means of Emory, the Presbyterian W. C. Kerr of Davidson, Father Andrew Cornette of the Jesuit Spring Hill College in Alabama, W. G. Simmons of the Baptists' Wake Forest—had every expectation of demonstrating the harmony of religion and science.[33] The clergy also joined the movement to enhance the scientific offerings at state colleges and universities, and their journals always reviewed the growing body of scientific literature, as well as the apologetic treatises written to prove "the harmony between the system of nature and that of revelation, through the entire course of the sciences."[34]

One Southern pastor became known as an accomplished scientist in his own right. The South Carolina Lutheran John Bachman (1790–1874) said that he felt constrained by a sense of clerical duty to investigate the sciences, and his research eventually brought him an honorary doctorate from the University of Berlin.[35] Bachman came to South Carolina in 1815 as pastor of St. John's Church in Charleston. By 1831 he was collaborating with J. J.

Audubon; he wrote the text of the celebrated *Viviparous Quadra-peds of North America* (1845–1849), a book that struck Jean Louis Agassiz of Harvard as having no equal in America.[36] In the South Bachman became better known as a scientific defender of the theory of the unity of the human race. Between 1847 and 1853 Agassiz delivered several lectures in Charleston defending a poly-genetic account of human origins. During the same period a small group of Southern naturalists advanced the same hypothesis, partly to demonstrate that whites and blacks were not members of the same species. Bachman believed that they were subverting the Biblical account of a single creation, so in 1853 he published *The Unity of the Human Race* to show that humankind constituted a single species with an infinite number of varieties. He resolved to discuss the issue without any appeal to Scripture, and he confined his argument largely to demonstrating the existence throughout nature of variation within species, but he also wrote as a conservative Christian intent on proving the congruence between "the book of nature" and the revealed "truths of heaven."[37] He was engaged in an enterprise that preoccupied dozens of ministers who published articles on science and religion in the Church journals; by 1851 it was possible to speak of a "theology of natural science" that was supposedly in perfect harmony with the Bible.[38]

The primary motive for all this activity was to demonstrate the compatibility between Genesis and geology, but the clergy also wanted to show that scientific investigation, properly conducted, provided a vast and grand extension of the traditional argument that design and order in nature demonstrated the existence of God.[39] They therefore admired inordinately "the remarkable Mr. Hugh Miller," a Scottish naturalist whose combination of piety and geological acumen found expression in a series of popular treatises: *Footprints of the Creator, Popular Geology,* and *The Testimony of the Rocks.* Miller not only tried to prove the compati-bility of geology and the Old Testament but also to show the order-liness of nature under a superintending providence. He found even a numerical order in the creation: vertebrates always had ten digits, mammals always had seven neck vertebrae, and the leaf appen-dages of plants exhibited similar mathematical patterns.[40] Na-ture was filled with pattern and regularity and therefore with intelligence.

The Southern clergy had not lost interest in "physico-theology." In the early eighteenth century a small army of English and German theologians had produced an array of books on Astro-, Pyro-, Hydro-, and Litho-theology, even on Insecto-, Phylo-, Petino-, and Bronto-theology, all intended to display the glory, wonder, and purposefulness of nature.[41] The high point was the publication in England in 1802 of William Paley's *Natural Theology*, which brought a new conceptual sophistication to the genre. Paley argued that nature, in its purposeful regularity, was similar to a watch, except that the contrivances of nature, the structural adaptations within organisms and the adaptations of living beings to their environment, were so numerous, subtle, and complex that anyone who believed in watchmakers should believe even more in an intelligent Creator of the natural order.[42] In subsequent years the argument from design assumed increasingly complicated and even fanciful forms. *The Southern Presbyterian Review* carried articles during the 1850s that based the proof of God's existence on the intricate modifications of the chemical elements.[43]

It was easy for the clergy to overlook the flaws in the argument because so many leading scientists found it compelling. Yale's geological star, Benjamin Silliman, was also a conservative Christian apologist. The naturalist Edward Hitchcock of Amherst studied for the ministry and wrote a theological account of *The Religion of Geology and its Connected Sciences* (1851), which received enthusiastic reviews in the Southern denominational journals.[44] Joseph LeConte combined scientific and theological interests at Oglethorpe College in Georgia, as did Matthew Fontaine Maury in Virginia. The naturalist James Woodrow even accepted a position on the faculty of Columbia Theological Seminary. It was during this period, after all, that the *American Journal of Science* devoted itself to demonstrating "the supreme intelligence and harmony and beneficence of design in the Creator," and *The Columbian Star*, the leading Baptist newspaper in the upper South, carried on its masthead the picture of a star flanked by two words: "religion" and "science."[45]

A few discordant notes marred the harmony. Ever since 1795, when James Hutton of Edinburgh explained rock stratification as the consequence of erosion throughout vast epochs of time, the geologists had split into warring factions. "Uniformitarians" believed that the strata resulted from the slow operation of natural processes, while "catastrophists" argued for a series of natural disasters, each leaving a different layer of debris. The geological controversy was the first great scientific trauma of the American churches, and the clergy generally leaped to the defense of the catastrophists, whose account seemed more compatible with the chronology of Genesis and the Biblical flood story. But the divisions among the geologists meant that natural science was not an invariably trustworthy ally. By the 1850s the *Presbyterial Critic* was speaking of the alliance as "a very delicate point in the present posture of opinion." We are too sensitive about the pretensions of science, wrote the journal's editor Thomas Peck.[46]

In 1857 the Tombecbee Presbytery in Mississippi complained of insidious scientific attacks on religion and recommended the establishment of chairs in the theological seminaries to ensure the continued harmony of religion and science. Among the clergy who favored the proposal, some felt defensive about the sciences, others had every expectation of maintaining cordial relations between the disciplines. James Lyon (1814–1882) of Columbus, Mississippi led the drive. A graduate of Princeton Theological Seminary who had interrupted a series of urban pastorates to spend two years traveling in Europe, Lyon hoped that the new chair would preclude the "indiscreet zeal" of ministers who were unequipped to defend the faith. He was confident about the apologetic potential of the sciences, for he believed that the works of nature constituted "the first great revelation that God has made of himself," and that therefore the revelation in nature was fully as authoritative and inspired as the Bible itself. Scripture, he said, was simply a "supplement" to nature, made necessary by human sinfulness.[47]

Others were uneasy, and Robert L. Dabney of Union Seminary in Virginia spoke for them when he complained that the proposed chair would have "a tendency towards naturalistic and anti-Christian opinions."[48] But in 1859 a member of Lyon's congregation, Judge John Perkins, donated $50,000, and the denomination promptly called James Woodrow to the "Perkins Professorship of Natural Science in Connection with Revealed Religion" in the seminary at Columbia. Woodrow's inaugural address spoke of the "harmony" of Scripture and science, but almost immediately he shifted his language to refer to the absence of "contradiction" between them, and within three decades Woodrow was the defendant in a heresy trial occasioned by his acceptance of evolutionary theory.[49]

The Perkins Professorship symbolized the end of an era, and the debates attending its formation signaled the breakdown of clerical optimism about the sciences. Indeed the sad conclusion of the affair portended the anti-scientific temper of later Southern Protestantism. Throughout the antebellum period the gentlemen clergy had found in the sciences the data for a natural theology that prepared the mind to receive the Biblical revelation. The study of the natural world enabled the theologian, so it was thought, to approximate by degrees to the level of revealed truth. The very effort assumed a continuity between natural and revealed religion; it assumed that truth was one.

3. Validating the Word: The Evidences

The "rationalism" of the Southern clergy meant more than simply an affirmation of natural theology; they also believed that reason established the criteria for recognizing and validating the Biblical revelation itself. They defended the traditional formula: revelation was above reason though never contrary to it. While they often depreciated the religious capacities of the mind, they usually added a disclaimer. One sees the pattern in the theology of Thomas Smyth, the pastor of the Second Presbyterian Church in Charleston. Smyth was a learned minister: in 1857 the Synod of South Carolina purchased eleven thousand volumes from his personal library for the seminary in Columbia. As a spokesman for theological conservatism as well as an internationally known clerical voice on social issues, Smyth felt a special responsibility to puncture liberalism in Charleston, and he maintained a close watch over the Unitarians. When his friend Samuel Gilman issued a public condemnation of Calvinism in 1852, Smyth moved quickly to publish his "Unitarianism Not the Gospel" which along with his "Articles on the Trinity" appeared in serial form for several years in *The Southern Presbyterian Review*.[50]

Smyth claimed that reason was limited not only by sinfulness but also by finitude and that the liberals had pridefully overstepped the limits. He wrote as an empiricist who thought that the mind was subject to the domination of the senses, which were the only inlets of perception. Reason was therefore trapped within a limited field of observation and could not comprehend transcendent realities. Smyth thought that the errors of the European Hegelian theologians illustrated the futility of an overweening rationalism. Precisely because the finite could never comprehend the infinite, the essential doctrines of Christianity rested of necessity on revelation. Reason could neither originate nor demonstrate the notion of an infinite personal Godhead existing in a triunity of subsisting Persons and incarnate within history. The Unitarian variety of rational theology was therefore a presumption; the liberals could recognize the existence of God and affirm Jesus as Messiah, perhaps, but as nothing more, for only "the special divine influence" of Biblical revelation could undergird belief in his divinity.

> On all subjects on which it alone can give evidence, the testimony of God is the highest reason, and outweighs all possible objection and cavil, since these are all based on the absurdity that the finite can comprehend that which is infinite and infinitely incomprehensible and beyond our capacity to understand.[51]

Smyth's conclusion seemed to diminish decidedly the scope of reason in theology. Yet he prefaced his criticisms of reason with three disclaimers: he acknowledged that reason could recognize a revelation; it could also certify that the Scripture was the voice of God; and it could interpret the revealed Word.[52]

The testimonies on behalf of reason that appeared as a mere qualification to Smyth's arguments against the Unitarians received more detailed elaboration in the work of other Southern theologians. The Bible, claimed *The Southern Presbyterian Review*, "submits its credentials to be judged of by reason. It only demands, that its claims be decided according to the ordinary laws of evidence."[53] The clergy denied that they issued any call for "unreasonable credulity."[54]

The Methodist Thomas Ralston was as convinced as any nineteenth-century rationalist that truth was a "harmonious system." Though revelation stood above reason, a perfect vision would reveal "the consistency of sound reason with the sublime revelations of Heaven," and discrepancies between them were merely apparent. In fact, reason in Ralston's theology was the precondition of faith, for only reason could judge "whether God has given us a revelation or not."[55] Ralston's arguments were often circular and question-begging, but his major point was clear: reason could identify the divine Word over against the plethora of merely human words. Reason supplied the criteria for identifying the revelation as a truly divine message.

If reason identified revelation, or certified its validity, or interpreted its content, was not then reason the measure of revelation? Were the Southern theologians, so often consigned to the ranks of pure biblicists, covert and unconscious devotees of "rationalism"? Such questions occurred to the ministers, who were not disposed to give a uniformly negative response, though they deplored the term "rationalism." In one sense they acknowledged that reason was the measure of revelation; even the most zealous religious conservatives to some extent shared that conviction.

A precise analysis of the issue appeared in the theological lectures of the conservative Presbyterian Robert Lewis Dabney at Union Seminary in Virginia. Dabney was a graduate of the seminary and he spent seven years as a rural missionary before joining the faculty in 1853 as a professor of Church History and Polity. He soon began lecturing on other theological topics and by 1859 became an Adjunct Professor of Systematic Theology. But from the beginning he made his professorship one of the most influential positions in Southern Presbyterianism, and he became known as a champion of unyielding conservatism, both as a churchman and as a social thinker.

As a philosopher Dabney was a Scottish Realist who believed that laws of reason inherent in the mind structured the processes of both sensible perception and abstract conception. Having thus dismissed a fragile empiricism that was vulnerable to skeptical criticism, Dabney felt safe in claiming that even the possibility of a Scriptural revelation presupposed "the authority of our native, fundamental laws of thought."

The claim which the Scripture addresses to us, to be the one authentic and authoritative revelation from God, is addressed to our reason. This is clear from the simple fact, that there are presented to the human race more than one professed revelation; and that they cannot be authoritative witnesses to their own authority prior to its admission. . . . The evidences of inspiration must, therefore, present themselves to man's reason. . . . He who says he believes, when he sees no proof, is but pretending, or talking without meaning.[56]

Dabney did not mean to suggest that reason should be permitted "to make the interpretations of Scripture square with the teachings of human philosophy," for that would have been "German rationalism." He denied that reason could judge the material content of Scripture. But in a formal sense reason was the measure of revelation. It alone could judge which of the competing revelations was genuine; it verified and established the revelation by determining whether the Bible was the authentic Word of God.[57]

Dabney was a man of his age; a distinction between the formal and material functions of reason, though never expressed explicitly in those terms, was one of the presuppositions of rational orthodoxy. Once having certified the revelation as genuine—thus making the formal judgment—the intellect was morally and religiously obligated to accept it, even if it contained incomprehensible mysteries.[58] But reason was first to identify the formal characteristics that might be expected to accompany a divine revelation, to verify their authenticity, and then to interpret the revelatory material.

Verification proceeded through the guidance of a "principle of externality." The Methodist clergy learned it from their English mentor, Richard Watson, whose *Theological Institutes* was prescribed reading for every man seeking ordination. Watson was "the text-book of Methodist theology,"[59] and he elaborated the criterion of externality without any equivocation: "The principal and most appropriate evidences of a revelation from God must be external to the revelation itself." The evidence must be "addressed to our reason, the only faculty which is capable of receiving it."[60] The externality-principle guided even theologians who would derive all their precepts immediately from Scripture, for they felt obliged to show that their biblicism stood on a reasonable foundation.

The first step in their argument was to establish that the concept of revelation was itself rational. At any rate, they believed, no deist or theist could deny the possibility of a revelation. "Upon the supposition that there is any God at all," wrote one minister in 1851, "there is no antecedent improbability that he would make a revelation of himself to his rational creatures."[61] And that assertion had its positive side: any theistic hypothesis entailed the probability of a revelation. A. B. Van Zandt tried to persuade the students and faculty of the University of Virginia that anyone assuming the existence of a deity who provided for the physical wants of mankind —as the deists assumed—could also reasonably conclude that the same deity would care for intellectual and religious needs as well. God would reveal himself. The conclusion was only probable, but "establishing a probability, that probability may serve as a link in the chain of induction, which leads us down to a positive and unavoidable conclusion." The deist who argued from the adaptations of external nature to a designing cause should have no objection to the claim that the adaptations of Scripture to the felt wants of our internal and spiritual nature provided evidence for its supernatural and divine origin.[62] But Van Zandt's argument subtly shifted the locus of authority from an infallible Scripture to the internality of the rational self. The Bible was authoritative, according to his logic, because it could fulfill conditions implicit in human existence. Elsewhere Van Zandt argued that the Bible was true because it was a revelation; here he said that it was a revelation because it was true. The latter claim embodied the covert logic of rational orthodoxy.

Having determined that self-revelation would have been a reasonable recourse for God, however, the clergy felt constrained to demonstrate, as the second step in their argument, that he had in fact revealed himself in the Christian Bible. To do so they appropriated the ancient second-century evidential arguments, as expanded and refined by the theologians of the Enlightenment. The Southern apologetic rested in large part on the so-called internal and external evidences, and for this reason no theologians received greater attention in the antebellum South than the English repristinators of the evidential tradition, especially William Paley and Joseph Butler.

The "internal" argument can be summarized in a maxim: Scripture is both consistent and compelling. The argument was amenable to profuse elaboration, however, as Bishop Butler proved beyond doubt in his *Analogy of Religion, Natural and Revealed, to the Constitution and Course of Nature* (1736). Though he constructed an intricate series of interlocking arguments, Butler advanced one central theme: the Biblical revelation was thoroughly consistent with the manifestation of God in nature. The God of nature resembled the God of Abraham and Isaac; the deist who accepted the one should therefore accept the other. At least, the deist who criticized Scripture for its darkness and ambiguities should face up as well to the dark mysteries of nature. For every putative error in Scripture, Butler argued, there was a seeming evil in nature, for every paradox an incomprehensible mystery, for every enigma a conundrum. Christian commitment, then, was no more irrational than natural religion—or any other mode of commitment. Butler also developed a positive argument from analogy. The pattern of moral regularity in human affairs, according to which virtue conduced to pleasure and vice produced misery in the long run, suggested a transcendent moral constitution regulating the eternal destiny of humankind. Our earthly ethical destinies thus corresponded to the revealed teaching that we would be rewarded or punished for our deeds.[63] But it was Butler's polemic against deism that continued to attract disciples. It made sense to remind the deist that revealed truth was one with his truth, that it was neither more obscuring nor less revealing. "Let the skeptic first go and settle his quarrel with the God of nature," wrote Ralston, "and then his cavils at revelation will be less inconsistent."[64]

Consistency was the watchword. There were other kinds of internal arguments, most of them appealing in one way or another to a principle of consistency. Biblical truth was internally consistent; it was consistent with human need and thus capable of transforming the heart; it was consistent with the highest ethical ideals of the race; it was consistent with science.[65] The arguments were derived from a motley group of eighteenth-century Anglicans: Soame Jenyns, Samuel Clarke, John Chapman, Richard Watson, and others. But Butler was the center of interest, and the Methodist *Quarterly Review* testified in 1854 to the continuing influence of his *Analogy*: "Its celebrity gives it currency everywhere. . . . It is a standard work, an acknowledged authority; it is read as a matter of obligation," even if not always well read.[66] Through Butler the principle of externality firmly entrenched itself in Southern theology, for his book was an argument that reason could and should judge of the meaning, morality, and evidence of revelation.

The eighteenth-century apologists had also found the internal argument useful against deism, but by 1748 the discussion in England had shifted. A Cambridge librarian and critic named Conyers Middleton published in that year *A Free Inquiry into the Miraculous Powers which are Supposed to have subsisted in the Christian Church.* His historical critique of early Christian pretensions to miraculous powers was aimed at Rome, but he struck, at first inadvertently, the tender underside of Anglican apologetics as well. His historicizing method left few if any criteria for distinguishing false from true miracles—and thus little basis for believing that miracles could serve to verify the supernatural quality of the Christian revelation.[67] In the same year David Hume published his essay "On Miracles" as a part of his new *Philosophical Essays concerning Human Understanding*, and its impact was lasting. "It still lives in the world," Ralston lamented.[68] Hume shifted the argument from nature to history; he also shifted attention away from the internal to the external evidences of Christianity. The Reverend George Campbell's hasty reply, his *Dissertation on Miracles*, initiated a polemic against Hume that reached a climax in the writings of the so-called "evidential school" of Cambridge theologians: the Norisian Professor, John Hay; the Regius Professor, Richard Watson; and above all, William Paley, who never occupied an endowed chair, remained at the university only nine years, from 1766 to 1775, and published his answers to Hume after he left Cambridge to become archdeacon of Carlisle. He wrote his *Horae Paulinae* in 1790, his *Evidences of Christianity* four years later, and they brought him a Cambridge doctorate of divinity and international celebrity. No small amount of Paley's popularity in the nineteenth century was due to the belief that he had provided an answer to Hume.[69]

According to the evidential school, a miracle was an interposition of divine power against the regular course of nature. As such it was a confirmatory sign external to the content of the revelation itself. "Without an external sign from God," wrote one Southern minister, "no man can certainly distinguish a Divine revelation from what is purely human. . . . Without the criterion of miracles we might confound the revelations of the Holy Spirit with the

dreams of the enthusiast and the inventions of the imposter."[70]
It was therefore happily providential that the miracles of the Bible
attested to the veracity of its revealed truth. But what, Hume had
asked, can attest to the veracity of the miracle accounts? Was there
evidence that would compel belief in miracle? Specifically, was
testimony, from the apostles, for example, a sufficient reason for
belief in the miraculous? Hume thought not. As a violation of the
laws of nature, a "miracle" was by definition an exception to uniform experience, which provided the only criteria for evaluating
testimony. Attestations to the miraculous were therefore intrinsically dubious:

> No testimony is sufficient to establish a miracle, unless the tes-
> timony be of such a kind, that its falsehood would be more mir-
> aculous, than the fact, which it endeavours to establish; and
> even in that case there is a mutual destruction of arguments,
> and the superior only gives us an assurance suitable to that
> degree of force, which remains, after deducting the inferior.[71]

In other words, experience was the criterion of testimony, and the
uniformity of experience amounted to a presumptive proof against
any testimonial on behalf of the miraculous.

The theologians did not take Hume's argument lightly. Ralston
offered grudging testimony to their concern:

> Such has been the fame of Hume's arguments against mira-
> cles, that scarce a treatise has appeared on the evidences of
> Christianity, since the first enunciation of that gilded sophism,
> in which it has not been brought upon the arena for discussion.
> . . . [No] treatise on the question can ignore it entirely with-
> out being viewed by many as incomplete.[72]

To prevent impressions of incompleteness, Southern theological
writings abounded in refutations of Hume, invariably taken from
earlier English critics. The clergy concentrated on his claim that
only experience could validate a testimony and that no reasonable
person could believe an account that contradicted uniform experience, as every account of the miraculous undoubtedly did. His
principle, they said, begged the very question it presumed to answer. Rather than having demonstrated the absolute uniformity of

experience, he merely assumed it. Hume's principle, moreover, precluded all belief in the radically new; any discovery contrary to the uniform past experience of the race was, by Humean canons, false by definition. And he had covertly and illogically translated his credible claim that experience validated testimony into an erroneous claim that the absence of an experience invalidated testimony, or that our failure to experience the miraculous in everyday affairs warranted our disbelief in miracles anywhere and anytime. But the absence of miracles in ordinary experience, they responded, was not a positive proof of the impossibility of miracles. Hume demanded positive experiential verification for belief; the orthodox demanded the same for disbelief.

They then added some positive arguments of their own. After all, they wrote, miracles might eventually be found to accord with the laws of nature (an argument, one should observe, that shifted the definition of miracle). And in the meantime, any rational person would accept the testimony of honorable men whose word was sealed in suffering and privations. That was Paley's favorite argument: the apostles were trustworthy men whose testimonies about miracles evoked scorn and persecution. They could be believed.[73] Both Hume and his opponents thus assumed that men of the first century viewed the world in much the same fashion as men and women of the eighteenth and placed the same value on "rationality." So the orthodox continued to believe that the miracles stood as external proofs validating the truth and supernatural origin of Christian teaching.

There was, moreover, a second traditional external proof: the argument from "prophecy." Christians had always interpreted the Old Testament prophecies as veiled references to Christ's advent. The pattern of prophecy and fulfillment demonstrated the messianic character of Jesus. By the eighteenth century the prophetic utterances had assumed an even heavier burden. The vindication of the prophecy-fulfillment pattern, it was argued, would also validate the Christian belief that the Biblical authors spoke and acted by divine inspiration, since unerring predictive power indicated supernatural guidance. But in 1724 the English deist Anthony Collins argued in his *Discourse on the Grounds and Reasons of the Christian Religion* that the prophecies referred not to Christ but to a variety of contemporary expectations that in fact had often failed to materialize. Collins set the English apologists to the task of authenticating the predictive accuracy of the prophetic literature.[74]

In his attack on the proof from prophecy, Collins expanded an earlier discussion about the meaning and interpretation of Biblical texts to include a broad range of historical questions: What were the conscious intentions of the Biblical writers? Did they mean for their prophecies to refer to Christ? And was the resemblance between the prophecy and its alleged fulfillment sufficient to justify the customary Christian interpretation? Both the questions and the variety of answers exhibited an emerging pattern, for the debates invariably focused on general rational criteria that were compatible with the demand for external verification. The conservative apologists contrasted pagan and Biblical prophecies, extolled the purity and character of the Jewish prophets, and emphasized the clarity, consistency, and public character of the prophecies themselves. They appealed to criteria extrinsic to any specific instance of prophecy and fulfillment, resting their case on claims of fact established through historical research, logical argument, and conventional suppositions about human behavior.[75] The validation of revelation was the task of reason.

The seminal religious thinkers of Europe would have joyfully abandoned the whole enterprise. Gottfried Lessing published the famous *Wolfenbüttel Fragments* (1774–1777) of Hermann Reimarus largely for the reason that he thought they destroyed the proofs from miracle and prophecy; F. D. E. Schleiermacher considered the issue an embarrassing distraction; and Samuel Taylor Coleridge complained in his *Aids to Reflection* that he was weary even of the word "evidences."[76] But European conservatives held adamantly to the prophetic proof, and no theologian argued more passionately for it than the Lutheran Ernst W. Hengstenberg (1802–1869) in Berlin, whose *Christology of the Old Testament* (1829–1835) exalted the prophecy-fulfillment scheme as an essential proof for the infallibility of Scripture.[77] It was therefore revealing that Hengstenberg's three-volume work was the only book of German theology that was translated and reprinted in the Old South immediately after its publication in Europe. Reuel Keith of the Episcopal seminary in Virginia prepared an English translation in 1836, and the book not only received favorable citations in Southern denominational journals but also found a place in seminary reading lists.[78]

The entrenchment of the evidential tradition in Southern intellectual life was assured by the proliferation of college and university courses on "Christian Evidences." Transylvania instituted one of the earliest in 1798, with Paley's *Evidences of Christianity* as the text. The Presbyterians began a similar course at Hampden-Sidney in 1825, using texts by Paley and Butler. At LaGrange College in Tennessee the faculty added readings from Archibald Alexander, a noted Princeton theologian of Southern background. Oakland College in Mississippi had courses in both Natural Theology and the Evidences; Oglethorpe University in Georgia used Alexander's *Evidences*, while the Associate Reformed Presbyterians at Erskine College in South Carolina were satisfied with Butler's *Analogy*. The Baptists initiated courses on the evidences at Wake Forest in 1838 (using Butler), at Mercer in 1840, Furman in 1852, Mississippi College in 1854, and shortly thereafter at the women's college in Greenville, South Carolina. Students at the Methodists' Randolph-Macon read Paley before breakfast on Monday mornings; Robert Paine, well on the way to a Methodist bishopric, taught the evidential course at LaGrange College in Alabama, while at Emory College Ignatius Few and A. B. Longstreet both assumed responsibility for the course on the "Evidences of Natural and Revealed Religion." The Lutherans overcame any lingering suspicions of rational theology that they may have inherited from the sixteenth century and introduced the evidential tradition to Roanoke College in 1853.

The state schools did not lag behind. South Carolina College began its course in 1831, after a period of neglect during Thomas Cooper's tenure as president. The trustees in 1835 offered the chair to the state's eminent Methodist, William Capers. When he declined, the post went to the Episcopalian Stephen Elliott, who held it until he became Bishop of Georgia in 1840, whereupon the Presbyterian James Henley Thornwell succeeded him. The College of Charleston offered lectures on the evidences as early as 1828; the first president of the University of Alabama, Alva Woods, a Baptist clergyman, taught the standard course there; Longstreet took that responsibility at the University of Mississippi; Richard Johnson at the University of Georgia. By the time that Louisiana State University finally introduced the course in 1860, almost every major school in the South, and most minor ones, had courses on Christian Evidences, usually requiring that students read Paley and Butler.[79]

During the forties the Southern lay theologian and philosopher George Frederick Holmes complained in the Methodist *Quarterly Review* that Paley's proofs undercut the uncertainty that should be ingredient in a free Christian decision for faithfulness, but the evidential theology held its own in the South throughout the nineteenth century, as a staple not only of college courses but of Sunday sermons as well.[80] Was there a revelation in the Bible? "The question," said the clergy, was "simply as to reasonable proof."[81]

4. *Interpreting the Word: Rational Hermeneutics*

The third task assigned to reason was the interpretation of revelation. The clergy acknowledged that the exegesis of Scripture required the exercise of human understanding. Given their confidence in the infallibility and perspicacity of the Bible, the acknowledgment seemed inconsequential. They did not anticipate that interpretation would require any excessive intrusion from the side of reason, and they criticized "rationalists" who bent the texts to fit their own preconceptions. But the orthodox clergy were not entirely conscious of the extent to which an underlying, barely visible rationalism governed their own reading of Scripture. They thought that they simply allowed the Biblical text to speak to them in its original purity, but in fact they were participants in a portentous transition in the interpretation and application of the Bible.

The clergy repeated the seventeenth-century orthodox insistence on the infallibility and inspiration of Scripture, but they did not think that Biblical inspiration could be equated with a mechanical process of dictation in which the ancient writers were merely passive instruments of the Spirit.[82] The Biblical writers used their own powers. That point was crucial for the nineteenth-century clergy; to the sixteenth-century reformers it would have been true but trivial, hardly requiring detailed defense.[83] And in that difference one can trace a changing consciousness within orthodoxy.

Implicit in the orthodox position was the assumption that the intentions, experiences, and idiosyncrasies of a human author informed the nature of the Biblical text. It therefore was important to discern those intentions. One understood the meaning of a text by discovering the intentions of the author, even if this meant, as it occasionally did, penetrating behind the apparent surface meaning of the text to find the deeper intended meaning. The respectable town clergy deplored allegorical interpretation, for they associated it with the fanciful allegorizing of the frontier exhorters. The doctrine of a "double sense" was "detestable." There was only one true sense to every word, which the interpreter discovered by investigating the grammar, the historical context, and the subject matter; only thus might he uncover the author's intentions. "The real sense" of the text, wrote the Richmond Methodist Leroy M. Lee in 1852, is "that which is intended" by the writer. But to say that was to presuppose the possibility of a distinction between the apparent and the real meaning, and in that possibility lay the seeds for a subtle rationalizing of the text, for Lee agreed that philosophical criteria of interpretation were in some sense inevitable: "The principles of interpreting what we hear or read, are instinctive, they belong to our rational nature."[84]

Hans Frei has shown that by the early nineteenth century European scholars were defending a variety of positions on the interpretation of Scripture. One group claimed that the "meaning" of a narrative was its reference to a state of affairs in space and time. Within this group were supernaturalists who believed the Biblical narratives to be literally true, "naturalists" who tried to explain the stories, especially the miracles, as natural occurrences, and rationalists who considered the Biblical accounts intentionally deceptive. A second group believed that the meaning of a narrative consisted of abstract ideas consciously stated in story form: the so-called Neologians in Germany argued that the miracle stories, for example, were deliberate allegories intended to communicate ideal truths and that the writers of Scripture had simply "accommodated" themselves to the mentality of their contemporaries. The third group were the "mythophiles" who proposed that the Biblical narratives embodied ideal truths in the form of mythical stories that reflected a distinct stage in the development of human consciousness. The Biblical writers, in this view, habitually and unselfconsciously expressed their thoughts in mythical categories.[85]

Even the interpreters who read the narratives as literal accounts of spatial and temporal events differed among themselves about the principles of Biblical interpretation. The followers of Johann August Ernesti (1707–1781) in Leipzig argued that exegesis was simply a determination of grammatical meaning, which preceded any theological or historical judgment about the truth of the subject matter. As an exegete, they said, the interpreter should be concerned only with what was written, not with what was true. The disciples of Johann Semler (1725–1791) in Halle, on the other hand, believed that the general rules of intelligibility implicit in a process of interpretation should extend to the subject matter as well as the words, so that part of the interpreter's responsibility was to evaluate the text according to universal criteria of reason and truth.[86]

The Southern town clergy stood firmly with the supernaturalists, often expressing their distaste for such seminal figures of rationalistic, naturalistic, and mythical criticism as G. L. Bauer, Wilhelm DeWette, and above all David Friedrich Strauss. Semler had an equally poor reputation.[87] The Southerners were willing to doubt the authenticity of certain Biblical passages that the critics had called into question; even R. L. Dabney admitted that the last line of the Lord's Prayer in Matthew 6:13 was a later addition to the text.[88] But the ministers tried to bypass most of the troublesome issues by holding fast to the procedures of "grammatico-historical" criticism as they had been expounded by Ernesti. Moses Stuart at Andover Seminary effectively introduced Americans to Ernesti in 1827 by translating his *Elements of Interpretation*, along with an appendix by some of Ernesti's disciples, including K. A. G. Kiel. At Columbia Seminary George Howe used Stuart's translation as the text in his course on Biblical literature. At Southern Baptist Theological Seminary Basil Manly's course promulgated Kiel's version of the Leipzig hermeneutic. And throughout the antebellum period the clergy advertised their allegiance to the "grammatical" method, especially as it was used by Stuart.[89] In practice, however, Stuart and other conservative American Biblical commentators supplemented a purely grammatical-historical interpretation with a rudimentary historical criticism of the kind advocated by Semler.[90]

The most revealing test case was the creation narrative in Genesis. The problem was time: while the Biblical account, as interpreted in conservative circles, suggested that the creation of the earth had occurred six thousand years ago, the geologists spoke of immense changes over a vast, indefinite period. Efforts to reconcile the two descriptions were, if anything, ingenious, and two solutions commanded widespread ministerial assent. Encouraged by Benjamin Silliman at Yale and Hugh Miller in Scotland, some of the ministers argued that each of the seven "days" in the creation story was a geological period of indefinite length. The solution commended itself not only to a small party of English geologists but also to the German neo-pietist Albert Knapp of the first "Tübingen School." Moses Stuart offered a telling criticism when he pointed out, in accordance with Ernesti's principles of interpretation, that the Hebrew word for "day" meant in its grammatical and historical context exactly what it seemed to mean: a twenty-four-hour day. Nevertheless one Southern Methodist claimed as late as 1857 that his fellow churchmen "generally admitted" the theory of Miller and Silliman to be true.[91]

Other scientists and clergymen solved the problem by positing an immense period between the time that Genesis called "the beginning" and the concluding six days of creation, which were understood as merely the final stage in the creation of the species. Between the phrase "in the beginning" and the clause "God created the heaven and the earth," they assumed, millions of years may have passed. Ralston claimed that this was the theory "adopted generally by Christian geologists" and "most intelligent Christians of the present day." The geologists William Buckland and Adam Sedgwick were among its English proponents; in Germany it had the support of Siegmund Jakob Baumgarten at Halle, a devotee of the pietistic philosophical orthodoxy associated with the name of his predecessor Christian Wolff; and most important for Americans, this interpretation carried the imprimatur of Thomas Chalmers (1780–1847) in Scotland, whose Natural Theology and Miraculous and Internal Evidences of the Christian Revelation had enormous influence on Southern Presbyterians. The American Edward Hitchcock, professor of chemistry and natural history at Amherst, popularized the theory in his *Religion of Geology* (1851).[92]

The Southern pastors could therefore appeal to the scientists as guardians of Scriptural infallibility, but as the condition of their guardianship the geologists demanded a subtle rationalizing of the text, which the ministers began to interpret in accordance with the latest findings of nineteenth-century science. Relatively modern notions of geological time became interpretive clues for understanding the "real" meaning of Genesis, which was hidden behind its merely apparent meaning. An astute critic, Moses Stuart, for example, could see precisely what was happening: the clergy were imposing a nineteenth-century world-view on ancient Jewish literature. Natural science was becoming an implicit norm for Biblical interpretation. During the fifties there were signs that some quite conventional Southern clergymen were adopting the "accommodation" theory of the eighteenth-century German Neologians to reconcile science and Scripture: the Biblical writers, so it was claimed, had accommodated themselves to the mentality of their own era by using language intelligible to their contemporaries.[93] The implication was that the nineteenth-century exegete was obliged to penetrate beneath the culturally conditioned language of Scripture to its timeless truth. But this was exactly what the liberals had said all along.

So entrenched was the drive toward reasonableness that even the ostensible critics of natural theology could not avoid the rational orthodox logic. Alexander Campbell (1788–1866) maintained that "the Bible, the whole Bible, and nothing but the Bible" was the basis of Christian fellowship, and he denied that natural reason could, of its own power, even originate "spiritual notions" of God, the soul, or immortality. But Campbell also believed that the Biblical revelation opened our eyes to the fact that all of nature attested and displayed the attributes of God. Indeed he insisted that reason was to confirm and interpret the Scripture in exactly the same manner that the orthodox rationalists had suggested.[94] There was a consensus among the elite clergy that the threefold function of reason—preparation, validation, and interpretation—protected and enhanced the Biblical Word. The "reasonableness of Christianity" was an omnipresent theme in the fashionable churches of the Southern towns.

5. The Catholic Critics: The New Thomists

In 1852 the scholarly Episcopal Bishop of North Carolina, L. Sullivan Ives, was converted to Catholicism. Inspired by the Anglo-Catholic movement in England and by emerging high-church traditions in America, Episcopal clergymen and theological students had been converting regularly since 1841, but no defection so shook the American Episcopal Church as that of Ives, a prominent bishop. There was great interest in his *apologia pro vita sua* when it appeared in 1853 with the title: *The Trials of a Mind in its Progress to Catholicism.* There Ives revealed that he was not attracted primarily by Catholic ritual, sacramentalism, or sacerdotal traditions. He simply could not tolerate the absence of an infallible authority: "Of doubt and confusion I had had enough. My mind reached forth for a distinct and infallible response." His own book was filled with historical argumentation designed to demonstrate the universal authority of the Church, but his goal was to transcend the need to argue.

Protestants, he said, supposed that every believer must be "reasonable."

> How could I believe . . . that a God of wisdom could justify his own avowed designs of special mercy to the poor and helpless by leaving them a party to this merciless scheme of attaining a knowledge of his will through their individual minds and judgments? [95]

But if Ives hoped to escape such argumentation, he must have been disappointed, for the Catholic clergy were fully committed to a pattern of argument analogous to the logic of Protestant rational orthodoxy.

The Roman Catholic pastors in the Southern coastal cities and the border states were the products of a Continental "textbook theology" that propagated scholastic arguments in categories that had crystallized as early as the second century. The dominant personalities in the antebellum Southern Catholic Church were, in the main, emigrants from France and Ireland who had studied theology at Issy, Orleans, and Clermont, or at St. Patrick's, Carlow, or at the Propaganda in Rome. In the European seminaries they had been taught an eclectic theology, preponderantly Thomist, systematized and simplified in Latin manuals that still managed to reflect, albeit blandly, the high Thomist estimation of rationality.

On the surface they seemed quite unlike their Protestant antagonists. In an 1826 reply to criticisms from the Episcopal rector in Augusta, Georgia, the Catholic bishop in Charleston, John England (1786–1842), criticized the Protestant infatuation with "enlightened reason," and two years later he charged that the region's ministers had arraigned divine truth before reason's "tribunal."

> If man was to reject the doctrine, unless it was sanctioned by his own reason, the office of Christ would not be that of a teacher, but of a propounder; and man would be placed over Christ, as the judge who was to decide whether what the Saviour propounded was true; so that man would in fact believe doctrines solely upon the authority of his own reason, and not upon the authority of his revealing teacher; and in this case it would be an absurdity for man to believe any mystery.[96]

England was a formidable critic. Before coming to Charleston in 1820 he was president and professor of philosophy at St. Mary's Seminary in Ireland. He opposed the concordat that gave the Irish government veto power over the selection of Catholic bishops, however, and his appointment to South Carolina was alleged to be a punishment for his political sins. The decision provoked the complaint that his "profound learning" and "theological accomplishments" were now destined to fall on barren soil. But England flourished in Charleston. He joined the Literary and Philosophical Society, built a diocesan seminary, campaigned for classical learning and literature, and founded the weekly *United States Catholic Miscellany* (1822), which became known as "the doctrinal voice of the Church in the United States."[97] An extraordinary administrator whose innovations anticipated the decisions of the Second Vatican Council, a man whose reflections on Church-State relations foreshadowed progressive Catholic opinion in the twentieth century, England spoke with authority.

He not only criticized the Protestant effort to find in reason a "sanction" for revealed truth, but he also argued against the common view that reason was the interpreter of Scripture. Authority, he said, lay in the infallible teaching office of the Church, so it was a mistake merely to correlate reason and Scripture, as if there were no other authoritative basis for theology. The Church preceded the Scriptures; it exercised its teaching office before they were written; they proceeded from the life of the Church. If one admitted that the Church could err, then one would also have to acknowledge that the Bible, the creation of the Church, was equally susceptible to error. It followed logically that the Church, not human reason, was the authoritative interpreter of Scripture, and that the primary duty of the faithful was to believe. "Faith is, then, the belief upon the authority of God, of what reason cannot by its own force discover."[98]

England thus seemed to counterpose reason and authority in a clear contrast to rational orthodoxy; however, he also believed in the unity of truth: "for God, who is the source of truth, cannot contradict by revelation what he teaches us by our reason, the usual aid which he has bestowed on us for the discovery of truth."[99] Of the theological options open to the orthodox Catholic theologians, he chose the one that clearly accorded the highest status to reason. Catholic theology was in a state of ferment in the early nineteenth century, and the European theologians advanced at least five conflicting proposals about the relation between faith and reason. To locate the American priests within this broader European context is to recognize their kinship with the orthodox Protestants.

One group of European clergy, influenced by the publication in 1802 of *Le Génie du Christianisme* by René de François Chateaubriand (1768–1848), held to Christianity on aesthetic and affective rather than on rational grounds. Catholicism was for them a supernatural and divine religion because it was supremely beautiful and poetic. A second group, influenced by Immanuel Kant's strictures against the pretensions of pure reason, decided that natural reason could not produce persuasive proofs for either the existence of God or the reality of a supernatural revelation. In France the Abbé Louis-Eugene Bautain (1796–1867) taught that revealed truth had to validate itself through its own inherent luminosity, and he refused, until Rome compelled him, to accept the traditional apologetic arguments. In Germany Georg Hermes (1775–1831), a professor of Dogmatic Theology at Münster and Bonn, wrote a famous *Introduction to Catholic Christian Theology* (1819–1829), in which he advanced a purely moral defense of faith: Christianity was true insofar as it was requisite for living a moral life. Once again Rome came to the rescue of rationality when Pope Gregory XVI condemned "Hermesianism" shortly after its founder died.

The third group of European Catholics found in the papacy itself a counterweight against reason. Like the sentimentalists and the Kantians, the French "traditionalists" also distrusted a "rational" Christianity. Joseph de Maistre (d. 1821), Vicomte Louis de Bonald (d. 1840), and the young Abbé Felicité de Lammenais (1782–1860) urged upon the Church a suprarational authoritarianism according to which true religion would rest upon the visible authority of the Church and its tradition. Rational "evidences" in their view were either superfluous or peripheral. The Catholic Tübingen School developed the fourth option, which was more open to rational considerations. Johann Adam Moehler (1796–1838) cautioned the French Catholic Kantians against excessive skepticism. Human nature required "proofs," he said. But Moehler also disliked "external fortifications," and he tried to reinterpret the older evidential tradition by juxtaposing it with a doctrine of creation and incarnation in which the whole history of religion and the organic interrelationships of persons in society were viewed as prefigurations and expressions of a supernatural presence in the Church.[100]

The Southern Catholic clergy were largely untouched by these reconsiderations of rationality among the younger European theologians. In this they were not alone, for despite Kantian and Romantic revisionism within the Church an earlier form of neo-scholastic theology held sway in the Sulpician and Jesuit seminaries where most of the European clergy learned theology. As seminary students the Americans had read such texts as Louis Abelly's *Medulla Theologia* (1650), Louis Gabriel de Bonald's *Speculum sapientiae divinae* (1616), Louis Bailly's *Theologia Dogmatica et Moralis ad Usum Seminariorum* (1787), and similar products of the seventeenth century neo-scholastic revival. The lectures of Giovanni Perrone (1794–1876), the most prominent theologian of the Collegio Romano and the patriarch of the "Roman School" of theology, ensured the continued authority of neo-scholastic thought throughout the nineteenth century.

The neo-scholastic manuals taught that the purpose of theology was to prove, confirm, and elucidate Catholic dogma, and they justified their description by appealing to the decision of the Fifth Lateran Council: "verum vero repugnare non potest" (truth cannot contradict truth).[101] The manuals displayed a common logical procedure. The theologian should begin, they taught, with the *praeambula fidei*, a set of natural, rationally demonstrable truths that served as the prelude to the actual articles of faith. The *praeambula* included convictions about the existence and attributes of God, spirituality and immortality of the soul, and natural law. In demonstrating the attributes of God, the theologian could prove that a supernatural revelation was not only within the capacity of an infinite intelligence but was also the most plausible course of action for a benevolent deity.

One could expect to find "evidentia credibilitatis" accompanying the revelation, and rational persons were under no obligation to accept a revelation as divine in the absence of such proofs. The evidences were familiar: miracles, fulfilled prophecies, the efficacy of Christian teaching, the successful dissemination of Christian truth despite powerful opposition. The revelation, thus validated, was an indispensable "auxiliary" to natural theology, providing access to the Christian mysteries, which were above reason but not unreasonable since they were not internally contradictory. The manuals relied heavily on Aquinas, and they castigated the "enemies of human reason" who called into question the Thomist suppositions.[102]

The Southern Catholic clergy were therefore not content simply to appeal to the authority of the Church; they wanted to demonstrate it. They believed that natural theology could vindicate Catholic faith. As a student at St. Patrick's, Carlow, John England had learned his theology from Bailly's *Theologia Dogmatica et Moralis*.[103] His major apologetic work, *The Calumnies of Blanco White* (1826–1828), an answer to an apostate Spanish priest of Irish descent who was living in England, was simply an elaboration of the textbook theology in the European seminaries. England took the traditional evidences of revelation and used them to demonstrate the exclusive authority of the Church. Anyone who found Paley persuasive, he said, should be comfortable with Rome, for the Church's doctrines were supported by "the very same evidence" that Paley had adduced to establish the truth of Christianity.[104]

England believed that he was obliged to prove the infallibility of the Church: "as man is a reasonable being, and must have sufficient motive for his assent or belief, he is not required to believe without evidence." Assent to truths that were "above reason" might well be an appropriate response to the testimony of credible witnesses, but "we would then require evidence that such a witness gave such a testimony, and our evidence would be the sure foundation of our faith. Our faith would then be rational." So England tried to present an accumulation of witnesses, prophecies, miraculous events, and historical circumstances that "united in one tribunal possess all the force of a natural infallibility concentrated to a point."[105]

He was typical of the Catholic clergy who wrote and taught theology in the Old South. In 1791 Bishop John Carroll founded St. Mary's in Baltimore, the first important American Catholic seminary. He negotiated with Jacques André Emery, the superior of the Society of the Priests of St. Sulpice, who sent four priests to begin instruction. The Sulpicians had originated in 1642 in response to the seminary legislation of the Council of Trent, and their schools were cautious and traditional. Theological instruction consisted largely of recitations from the textbooks of d'Abelly, de Bonald, de Collet, Francis de Tolet, and similar representatives of the neo-scholastic revival.[106] The same methods prevailed at St. Mary's, and by 1815 Carroll, as archbishop of Baltimore, had ordained over thirty priests who had studied there. Equally important, the seminary became a prototype for other Sulpician schools in the South.

Benedict Joseph Flaget (1763–1850), educated at Sulpician seminaries in Issy and Clermont, taught at St. Mary's before being named in 1810 to the new see of Bardstown, Kentucky, where he established St. Joseph's College and St. Thomas Seminary. The Kentucky school became a second center for the propagation of neo-scholasticism as well as a platform for aspiring theologians. (Flaget complained that his professors were intoxicated with the "foolish ambition of acquiring a name.")[107] To St. Thomas he brought Francis Patrick Kenrick (1796–1863), who had learned his theology at the Urban College of Propaganda in Rome—the center of the "Roman School" of theology. After teaching for ten years, Kenrick moved on in 1831 to episcopal administration in Philadelphia, but his *Theologia Dogmatica* (1840) documented his continuing fidelity to neo-scholastic argumentation.

Among the graduates of St. Thomas Seminary were the most important neo-scholastic theologians in the Old South. John McGill (1804–1872), the son of an Irish immigrant merchant in Philadelphia, studied theology at St. Thomas and at St. Mary's, Baltimore, and served parishes in Lexington and Louisville before becoming Bishop of Richmond in 1850. At Louisville, McGill demonstrated his commitment to the traditional apologetic by collaborating with Martin Spalding on a lecture series covering the *General Evidences of Catholicity* (1847), a prelude to a larger work published after the Civil War.[108]

Spalding (1810–1872) was also an alumnus of St. Thomas; he had, in addition, studied four years at the Urban College in Rome. In 1834 he packed a thousand books in his trunks and returned to Bardstown as pastor of the cathedral and instructor in the seminary. He soon decided that the books were not as useful in a Kentucky mission as they had been in the cultivated Italian capitol, but they illustrated his immersion in the theology of the Roman School. Although Giovanni Perrone was away from the college during Spalding's tenure as a student, his lectures, published in nine volumes between 1835 and 1842, continued to shape theological instruction in Rome. The neo-scholastic tradition counted heavily with Spalding. In his lectures with McGill on the evidences of Catholicity he insisted that since Jesus required all persons to embrace the true religion, the "proofs" for its authenticity had to be plain enough to persuade any sincere inquirer.[109]

The inspiration for the lectures was the publication of Nicholas Wiseman's *Twelve Lectures on the Connection between Science and Revealed Religion*. A professor of Oriental languages and the Rector of the English College in Rome, Wiseman tried to apply the old proofs within a modern style of argument. Although Spalding's lectures, less complicated than Wiseman's, were largely a cataloguing of the evidences, he began and ended with historical arguments designed to show that the Roman Catholic Church had not only fulfilled the apostolic commission to "baptize all nations" more successfully than the Protestants but had also endured trials that would have destroyed any other community. He developed a defense of miracles, arguing that "the system in favor of which they are wrought must be true and divine," but for him the question of miracles was purely historical; their reality had to be established like any other historical facts. So he adduced testimonies, adjudged the truthful character of the witnesses, and concluded that the concurrence of testimonies among reliable witnesses in diverse times and places should be persuasive to any open-minded person. The Church's catholicity, unity, and antiquity, moreover, testified to its authority and its collegial procedures defied errors: "the great body of Pastors, especially the bishops," in union with the Pope, would never "go astray from the true faith."[110] From the time in 1836 when he reprinted Bossuet's *Exposition of Catholic Doctrine* in the *Catholic Advocate* to the publication in 1855 of his *Miscellanies*, Spalding evinced a fondness for historical apologetic, usually developed in long, critical book reviews. In 1844 he published his own history of the Protestant Reformation.

His historical consciousness distinguished him from the Roman theologians who had trained him, and it prompted his admiration for Frederick von Schlegel, a German Romantic who found in history the confirmation of his belief in an all-ruling Providence. Spalding believed that the historical evidence was sufficient to convict the Protestants of undue concessions to "private judgment and individual reason." Instead of reasoning "from heaven to earth," he said, they reason "from earth to heaven" and consequently reject the authoritative Church.[111] Yet insofar as Spalding inserted his historical description into the polemical molds that he had learned at the Roman seminary, he himself was not simply resting on the authority of the Church, the course advocated by some European traditionalists. To advance evidences for its authority was *ipso facto* to appeal to another source of authority.

At the time he wrote his evidential treatise, such subtlety was a luxury Spalding could not afford. Appointed as a vicar-general at Louisville in 1844, he moved to a growing city with a mushrooming Catholic population. By the time he became Bishop of Louisville in 1848 the city had almost 43,000 inhabitants, and within two years it would become the eleventh largest city in the United States. It was also a city with an oppressive anti-Catholic sensibility among the older Protestant families, and the leading newspaper fanned a nativist animus that resulted in the "Bloody Monday" violence in the summer of 1855. Spalding was almost forced to take every occasion to defend the Church. Even his reverential biography of Bishop Flaget, published in 1852, began with a section on the "striking evidences going to prove the divine origin and character of the Catholic Church."[112]

The Roman Catholic Church in the South experienced its share of inner tensions. The Irish clergy, with England in the lead, maintained a clamor against the French Sulpicians who trained most of the bishops and occupied most major bishoprics. There were also minor theological difficulties. England's reservations about papal infallibility drew the fire of Orestes Brownson, the former transcendentalist who had appointed himself as the protector of Catholic orthodoxy in America.[113] Yet the neo-scholastic apologetic cut across the parties within the Church, and it marked the public debates with Protestants. Both sides agreed, in the words of Patrick Neison Lynch (1817–1882), a noted professor at the Seminary of John the Baptist in Charleston and later the third Bishop of Charleston and a special commissioner of the Confederacy to Pope Pius IX, that "we cannot be called upon to believe any proposition not sustained by adequate proof."[114] The Protestant theologians had no monopoly on the appeal to reason.

CHAPTER FIVE

SCOTTISH PHILOSOPHY AND
SOUTHERN THEOLOGY

In 1857 James Henley Thornwell, professor of Didactic and Polemical Theology at the Presbyterian Seminary in Columbia, delivered the school's annual Inaugural Address. He had surrendered the presidency of South Carolina College in order to assume the theological chair, and everyone there knew that he had come to save the school. "Things had reached a crisis," he wrote later, "and something was to be done or the seminary virtually abandoned."[1] He stood before a grateful and expectant audience that had gathered to hear a man who was described by the historian George Bancroft as "the most learned of the learned."[2]

Thornwell did not have the appearance of a fire-eating polemicist who could save endangered theological schools. He was a small man with diminutive limbs, stooped shoulders, and a flat and sunken chest. He weighed only a hundred pounds. Yet his promise had been manifest since his youth, when two wealthy Southern gentlemen, impressed by Thornwell's intellect, had financed his education at South Carolina College, from which he graduated at the top of his class. Neither his parents nor his patrons were Presbyterians, but Thornwell liked the logical clarity of the Westminster Confession and joined the Church in 1832. Deciding on the ministry, he journeyed to Andover Seminary in 1834 but found it too liberal. He left within a year and went to Harvard to learn German and Hebrew. But having confirmed his opinion that Cambridge Unitarians were little better than overt infidels, Thornwell returned with relief to the South, where he preached for a time in small churches. Filled with ambition and "love of human approbation," he soon began a rise to regional fame.[3] In 1837 Thornwell became a professor of philosophy at South Carolina College, and within three years he ascended to the pulpit of the fashionable Presbyterian Church in Columbia. An omnivorous reader and commanding personality, he entertained himself by memorizing Shakespearean dramas and smoking expensive cigars. But in his more serious moments Thornwell developed the philosophical defense of orthodoxy, always in violent antagonism to "the spirit of the times."[4]

His inaugural address in 1857 was a polemic against transcendentalists, deists, and liberals of every kind, but it was also an apologetic for the rationalism of orthodoxy. Thornwell observed that theology was a positive science grounded in observation and induction, consisting of facts "arranged and classified according to the necessary laws of the human mind." The theologian stood on divine revelation, but philosophy helped him maintain his balance. "We must meet rationalists on their own chosen ground," Thornwell told his audience.

> The great work of seminaries and theological professors now
> is to meet the altered aspects of infidelity; and not only to
> vindicate the external evidences of Christianity, but the in-
> ternal, by showing the complete harmony of sound philosophy
> and theology.[5]

His auditors must have agreed with Thornwell's contention that philosophy could be neither ignored nor proscribed, for his lecture was a grand success. The faculty assured him that its publication would advance the cause of "theological science."[6]

The allusions in his inaugural address to the "laws of the mind" revealed that for Thornwell, as for most other Protestant gentlemen clergy, the philosophy that could best advance theological science was the Common Sense Realism of the eighteenth-century Scottish universities. The Scottish philosophy permeated American intellectual life in the early nineteenth century, partly because of its applicability to both epistemological and ethical problems and partly because of its flexibility. Realism was not so much a set of conclusions as it was a way of thinking that could commend itself to a variety of thinkers. Its themes appeared throughout the spectrum of early antebellum theologies. At Harvard Levi Hedge and James Walker used Scottish methods to undergird liberal Christianity; at Yale Nathaniel William Taylor used them to ameliorate the harsher features of Calvinism; and at Princeton Charles Hodge found them useful in fortifying an unbending orthodoxy.[7] So the Southern denominational theologians, whose divisions were as deep as those of the Northern university faculties, were also able to unite in their confidence that Realism could solve the pressing dilemmas of both epistemology and ethics, and thereby to demonstrate the congruity between thought and behavior and prove the reasonableness of faith.

1. Knowing

Their ideal of a rational orthodoxy required that the clergy overcome the enlightenment critique of religion; this meant, above all, a continuing conflict with David Hume, the "champion of infidelity."[8] In his treatise on human nature Hume had cast into doubt the central assumptions of rational orthodoxy: the unity of truth, a rational soul, an orderly world, an ordering God. The Scottish philosophy provided a refutation of Hume, a critical interpretation of the British empirical philosophy, and a positive proposal about the nature of knowledge. The epistemology suited the needs of the clerical theologians. In the work of Thomas Reid they had a defense of the reliability of knowledge, which enabled them to proceed with natural theology. In the writings of Reid's successors they had, in addition, a recognition of the limits of knowledge, which permitted them to insist on the need for revelation. And in both Reid and his successors they found a method—the "method of consciousness"—that allowed them to describe theology as an inductive science.

Thomas Reid (1710–1796) was a parish minister at New-Machar when he read Hume's treatise. The book compelled him to call into question all of "the principles commonly received with regard to human understanding," and much of his subsequent career was spent in attempts to expose the errors of Hume's "sceptical system." In 1752 he became a regent at King's College, Aberdeen, and a member of the Aberdeen Philosophical Society, and shortly before he left to become Adam Smith's successor in moral philosophy at Glasgow, Reid completed his *Inquiry into the Human Mind on the Principles of Common Sense* (1764), in which he argued that Hume's erroneous conclusions came from John Locke's false premises.[9]

In his *Essay on Human Understanding* (1690), Locke had

CHAPTER FIVE: SCOTTISH PHILOSOPHY 113

grounded knowledge in sensory experience, and to this analysis, when properly qualified, Reid had no objection. But as Reid interpreted his essay, Locke had also said that the mind did not directly perceive the chairs, trees, and bodies of the real world; knowledge of these objects was, rather, mediated through perceptions, which Locke called "ideas." To perceive an object was to have an "idea" of it—an idea that presumably represented the object with accuracy and clearness. This meant, Reid thought, that according to Locke's epistemology "ideas in the mind are the only immediate objects of thought."[10] But then how could Locke be certain, he asked, that the ideas were transparent to external reality? Locke's "ideas" were supposed to be routes of access to the real world, but they were also barriers interpositioned between the world and the self. They were supposedly mediators in the complex negotiations between the knower and the intended objects of knowledge, but how could one assess the trustworthiness of the mediation?

Reid believed that the subsequent history of British philosophy exposed the instability of the Lockean scheme, which began to crack apart when the Bishop of Cloyne, George Berkeley, expanded upon its underlying assumptions. Berkeley demonstrated to Reid's satisfaction that Locke had no good reason to posit the existence of a material substance underlying the qualities perceived in the world. As Berkeley observed, Locke had no direct access to a material substratum standing behind his perceptions; the Lockean experienced visible things merely as "ideas," collections of sensible qualities. But ideas were mental realities, so why not acknowledge that according to Locke's own principles reality was constituted solely of mental perceptions and perceiving spirits? Recognizing that the mind perceived nothing but its own ideas, the astute critic should also recognize that ideas existed only in the mind. It followed that being and perception were synonymous: to be was to be perceived. Berkeley thus pushed Locke's representative epistemology to its logical idealistic conclusion, Reid thought. The world was neither more nor less than a collection of minds and their ideas. For a time Reid shared Berkeley's confidence that such an empirical idealism truly depicted reality and protected both philosophy and faith from the encroachments of materialism, for Berkeley's system required the existence of a supreme Spirit who literally held the world in mind. But Hume shattered Reid's confidence.

Hume observed that a mind which "knew" only its own perceptions had no certain knowledge of any objective realities. As Reid
understood him, Hume brought to full expression the skepticism
implicit in Locke's epistemology. Hume's treatise first suggested
that all conceptions devoid of corresponding sensory impressions
were illusory. Thus he was forced, for example, to abandon any
notion of a substantial spiritual self, because the introspective
search for a self uncovered only a bundle of fleeting impressions
but no spiritual subject. One could never see or touch or hear one's
"self." Moreover no sensory impressions could validate our belief
in causation, which could be analyzed simply into successive impressions of precedence and contiguity. One could never see, hear,
or touch "causality." Hume's world, as Reid viewed it, consisted
of distinct and unconnected perceptions. In that world there was no
place for two of the cardinal assumptions of traditional natural
theology: causality and a substantial soul. When the senses were
silent, Hume was silent.

Hume went even further, though, and recognized that sense impressions were themselves unverifiable. No sensation could verify
its own veracity, and the mind could not rise above its impressions
and examine them from afar. Perhaps all was illusion. Reid believed that Hume had destroyed the cosmos: "Upon this hypothesis,
the whole universe about me, bodies and spirits, sun, moon, stars,
and earth, friends and relatives, all things without exception, which
I imagined to have a permanent existence, whether I thought of
them or not, vanish at once."[11] The problem, as Reid perceived it,
was not only that Hume had left no reason "to believe any one thing
rather than its contrary," but that he had reached this illogical state
of affairs through impeccable logic. Hume's reasoning was just but
his premise was false, and Locke had supplied the premise. Reid
may well have misinterpreted the intellectual relationships among
the British empiricists, and many historians of philosophy also argue that he misinterpreted Hume, but his interpretation remained
standard throughout the nineteenth century, and among most of
the clerical intellectuals his answer to Hume was authoritative.

Reid believed that a critical analysis of Lockean "ideas" would
restore the world that Hume had stolen. Locke had failed, he
thought, to demonstrate that the objects of perception were simply
"ideas in men's minds." Locke's essay implied that every percep-

tion had a double object—an "idea" and a reality that it supposedly represented. But Reid saw no evidence for the dichotomy, which multiplied entities unnecessarily. A simpler alternative, truer to experience, was to define an "idea" as a mental act, not a mental object. To have an idea of a tree was to perceive the tree, not a mental image that mirrored the tree. By defining ideas as objects of perception, Reid thought, the English empiricists had imprisoned the mind within its own sensations, permitting it to have immediate knowledge of nothing but the flux of its sensory impressions. He wanted to put it back into direct contact with the world.[12]

The evidence for his alternative, he said, could be derived from a detailed introspective examination of mental activity. Such an investigation was the task of "consciousness," which Reid defined as the faculty of discerning "the operations of our own minds." He acknowledged that the discernment was difficult.

> To do this requires a degree of attention to what passes in our own minds, and a talent of distinguishing things that differ, which is not to be expected in the vulgar, and is even rarely found in philosophers; so that the progress made in a just analysis of the operations of our senses has been very slow.[13]

Reid's philosophical method, his appeal to consciousness, became a hallmark of the Scottish school.

Reid thought that consciousness contradicted Locke's "ideal system" by exposing the clear difference between internal sensations and the perceptions of real objects. Berkeley had said that our senses gave us knowledge only of our own sensations; to touch a table, for instance, was simply to know a sensation, a feeling, of resistance and hardness. Reid disagreed. He believed that the experience of touching a table had at least two necessary features, both of them immediately present to consciousness: a *perception* of a dense, thick object and a *sensation* of resistance. The one could neither be derived from nor identified with the other. Sensations, in fact, were utterly unlike the qualities that produced them. Real objects could be perceived to have length, thickness, figure, weight, and extension; sensations had no such qualities. The sensation of resistance from a table was distinguishable from the perception of dense material cohesion in the table itself. The sensation of pain from a pin-prick was other than the perception of figure and extension in the pin.[14] A careful description of consciousness failed to confirm the Lockean epistemology.

The consciousness revealed further that atomic units of sensation were not, as Locke had thought, the elemental building blocks of knowledge. The Lockean sense data were, rather, abstractions from the complex mixture of sensations, perceptions, and judgments that constituted a cognitive act. To speak of unitary "sensations" was to abstract and isolate certain discrete elements from an original experience that was richer and more concrete than the abstractions could possibly suggest. In particular, consciousness revealed that a "natural and original judgment" accompanied our perceptions of the world.[15] Certain judgments about existence, causation, and other relations were implicit within every experience; indeed, apart from those judgments one could hardly speak of a coherent "experience."

One goal of the Scottish philosophy was to discern the underlying presuppositions of all experience, the "first principles" of the mind. Reid believed that no one could consistently reject ideas that were implicitly presupposed in every cognitive experience, because their truth would be silently assumed even in the act of negating them. Therefore no one could deny the reality of selfhood, or of causality, or of the world. Hume complained that whenever he went in search of a "self" he could find only fleeting impressions; Reid responded by pointing out that Hume silently assumed the reality of a self capable of experiencing impressions. Reid believed that every sensation necessarily implied the existence of a sensing self; every impression presupposed the existence of a cause sufficient to produce it; and every perception contained within it a judgment of existence: "I cannot see without seeing something." Anyone who attended to consciousness could discover axiomatic assumptions, or "beliefs," that could not be doubted by any reasonable person. These regulative and constitutive principles of the mind were the universal conditions of any meaningful experience. Reid found a plethora of them, including even a universal predisposition to speak truthfully, and thus exposed himself to ridicule, but clearly he was thinking along lines that Immanuel Kant would later explore with greater sophistication.[16]

Reid thought that the common-sense principles were not amenable to logical demonstration, because they were axiomatic and therefore would have to be presupposed even in any attempt to demonstrate their existence. He did, though, confirm the deliverances of consciousness with an appeal to the principles of contradiction and universality. One could verify a "natural judgment" if it was impossible to deny it without self-contradiction. And one could find further verification when a principle was embedded in the structure of all languages: the distinction between verbs and nominal objects, for instance, reflected a universal tendency to presuppose the existence of an active subject and its passive object and thereby certified the existence of a self in relation to a world. With such arguments Reid tried to reconstruct knowledge, and in his own judgment he had restored the credibility of both philosophy and religion.[17]

"Reid's Philosophy of the Mind I prefer to all other works on Metaphysics," wrote a Mississippi Methodist minister in 1852.[18] But the philosophically inclined clergy were more likely to have learned their common-sense philosophy from Reid's disciple at Edinburgh, Dugald Stewart (1753–1828), whose *Elements of the Philosophy of the Human Mind* (1792) appeared in several American editions. Stewart believed that Reid had removed the rubbish of the old systems and laid the foundations for a new one, and he proposed to complete the superstructure. In fact he merely reworded most of Reid's arguments, correcting him only on peripheral matters, though he was far more responsible and creative than some of Reid's followers, notably James Oswald and James Beattie, who were capable of little more than ridiculing their opponents. Stewart's popularity was due to his ability to make Reid seem scientific and serviceable. In using the method of consciousness, he said, philosophers were following the inductive procedures of Francis Bacon and transforming their discipline into a science. In keeping with their inductive method, therefore, they should abandon all speculation about hidden substances and essences and concentrate entirely on the observable properties of both mind and matter in order to discover "laws" or "principles." By abandoning the search for an underlying substance, Stewart believed that he could discard some of the traditional problems of metaphysics, including the debate between materialists and idealists. The philosopher needed to know only the laws of phenomena, not their essences, in order to create a "body of science" that enabled the mind to master "the practical arts of life." Stewart never lost a chance to point out the utility of philosophy, which could, he said, teach young minds to think, formulate rules of investigation, and facilitate education and reform. His *Elements* moved easily from abstractions to trivialities: a refined discussion of the nature of general categories shaded gradually into a discussion of political rhetoric, an explication of the association of ideas suddenly became a proposal for better rules to improve memory.[19]

In his desire to concentrate on the laws of phenomena and to ignore questions about substances, Stewart was led to speak of "the existence of a region . . . into which philosophy is not permitted to enter."[20] Sir William Hamilton, who transmitted the Scottish ideas into the mid-nineteenth century, trying to combine them with Kantian philosophy, made a similar kind of agnosticism one of the cornerstones of his thought. A professor of logic and metaphysics at Edinburgh from 1836 until his death in 1856, Hamilton popularized Kant's epistemology for the English-speaking world, even if in a distorted manner. He defended Reid from his detractors and viewed himself as a Realist, but he connected Stewart's disregard for essences with Kant's claim that reason could not grasp the innermost essence of things. In becoming known, Hamilton said, an object was always relative to our human faculties, so knowledge was always partial, fragmentary, and imperfect. The ultimate nature of the universe was unknowable, and a finite mind could never comprehend the Infinite. The speculative reason always encountered insuperable antinomies when it sought the Absolute. Hence Hamilton's celebrated epigram: "A learned ignorance is . . . the end of philosophy, as it is the beginning of theology."[21] That was exactly what the Southern clergy wanted to hear.

2. *Believing*

An early stimulus for the propagation of Scottish philosophy in America came from John Witherspoon, the president of Princeton from 1768 to 1794. Throughout the late eighteenth century his students flooded the South, where they formed academies, colleges, and seminaries that became centers for the diffusion of Scottish thought. At Augusta Academy in Virginia the pupils of William

Graham, a Princeton graduate, copied and studied Witherspoon's manuscript lectures, and two of them, John Holt Rice and Conrad Speece, later served with other Princeton graduates on the faculty of Hampden-Sidney College. In North Carolina the Princetonian David Caldwell began in 1767 a backwoods school that introduced over fifty ministerial graduates to the Scottish ideas. There also Samuel McCorkle, another of Witherspoon's students, started an academy that trained at least forty-five more clergymen. And their numbers increased: the Princeton-trained clergy, joined by their own students, carried the Scottish message to Transylvania and Centre College in Kentucky; to Martin Academy, Tusculum, Davidson, and Blount in Tennessee; to Moses Waddel's influential academy in South Carolina; to Franklin College in Georgia; and to scores of other short-lived educational ventures.[22]

The influence of the Scottish school expanded well beyond the reach of Witherspoon. The theological lectures in the Presbyterian seminaries were full of Realist suppositions: Thornwell lectured on them at Columbia, R. J. Breckinridge at Danville, and R. L. Dabney at Union. The Southern colleges, private and public, offered a required course in moral philosophy that introduced Scottish notions to every student in the region. In 1822 one of the most eminent figures in American Methodism, Nathan Bangs, recommended the Scottish philosophy as an antidote to "the errors of Locke," and as head of the Church's Publishing House he issued a complete set of the works of Thomas Reid. In a preface to the edition, Bangs insisted that Reid stood "at the head of those metaphysical philosophers who adorned the last century." His commendation was a close approximation to an official Methodist stamp of approval, and within a year book agents were ordering the new edition: even in the back-country of Wilkinson, Mississippi, a Methodist pastor wrote Bangs asking for six sets of Reid's *Works* to sell along with Wesley's sermons and Adam Clarke's commentaries.[23]

The clerical gentlemen adopted the Scottish philosophy as a natural corollary to theology.[24] As early as 1831 Thomas Cooper in South Carolina complained that the Scottish philosophers "are favorites with the clergy (and of course wrong)," but his objections were to no avail.[25] In 1857 the Southern Methodist *Quarterly Review* spoke for Protestant clergymen of all denominations in describing Dugald Stewart as "the Prince of Scotch Metaphysicians" and praising William Hamilton as "the most illustrious philosopher of the age."[26] But the clergy used Realist ideas for differing purposes. Some merely appealed to the authority of "consciousness" for doctrines that they considered self-evident; both sides in a theological debate could base conflicting claims on the deliverances of consciousness. Some found confirmation for the philosophical concepts presupposed in their theology: the reality of the world, the self, the will, causation, the reliability of knowledge, the uniformity of the laws of nature, and the capacity of the mind to receive truth. But the Scottish influence was often more thoroughgoing than such piecemeal descriptions might suggest.

In the works of James Thornwell and John Leadley Dagg one sees how thoroughly the Scottish methods and language could pervade a theological system. For both men, philosophy furnished the methods used to defend orthodoxy; in Dagg's theological manual the Scottish ideas infiltrated even the contents of doctrine. Thornwell used Realism to demonstrate the possibility and necessity of theology; Dagg used it to show the meaning and truth of theological assertions.

In 1850 Thornwell told a friend that "the man who has pondered, and is prepared to answer aright the question, What can we know? is the only man who is competently furnished against the temptations" of skeptical rationalism.[27] At South Carolina College Robert Henry had introduced Thornwell to Dugald Stewart's writings, which he read before moving on to the study of William Hamilton. He liked the Scottish thinkers because he believed that they had threaded their way between the double temptations to which philosophers were prone: sensationalism and idealism.

Thornwell thought that the Lockean sensationalists failed to distinguish the mind's reception and collation of sense data from genuine knowledge, which was constituted not only of sensory processes but also of judgments, comparisons, and beliefs. The idealists, on the other hand, had swung to the opposite extreme. In reacting against the empiricist notion of the mind as a passive sensorium, the idealists at their boldest had attributed all knowledge to the spontaneous creativity of the mind. The German idealists, especially, had become "rampant ontologists" presuming to unfold "the grounds of universal Being from the principles of pure reason." The empiricists opened the door to Hume, who had rightly seen that an unqualified sensationalism precluded any assertions about a supersensuous divine reality. The idealists believed that reason could solve all the mysteries of existence and thus make a special revelation unnecessary.[28]

Thornwell considered the possibility that Immanuel Kant had opened the middle way between the extremes. He studied Kant's *Critique of Pure Reason* and agreed with him that the forms of space and time, as well as the categories of causality and substance, were innate structures of thinking. But he decided that Kant had erred in defining the categories and forms of cognition as mere regulative principles of thought. Certainly it was true, Thornwell believed, following Hamilton's lead, that the mind could grasp only phenomena: "All knowledge is and must be relative in its nature, and phenomenal in its objects." And the perception of phenomena required, as Kant had said, the operation of inherent structures of the mind. But to know phenomenal realities, said Thornwell, was to have an objective knowledge of the world. Just as there were forms of cognition adapting the mind to understand its environment, so also were there "conditions in the thing known, which render it capable of being apprehended by the mind." The mental categories corresponded to objective realities in the external world. Consciousness seemed to indicate as much, for a conscious act of cognition not only had an object but also contained within itself an indubitable belief in the reality of its object. The categorial principles of thought were therefore "guarantees for the objective realities to which they conduct us."[29]

The Scottish tradition offered the middle way between sensationalism and idealism and therefore provided a prolegomenon to natural theology and a preparation for revealed theology. Unlike the Lockeans, the Scottish philosophers recognized that primal tendencies in the mind made knowledge possible, but unlike the idealists, they also saw that these inherent principles were merely the conditions of knowing rather than the sources of truth.

The theological implications were clear. In certifying the reliability of knowledge, the Scottish philosophy supported a natural theology in which scientific investigation of the created order disclosed the existence and nature of the Creator. Assured of the veracity of his belief in causation and the validity of his perceptions, the philosopher-theologian could "see God in the operation of his hands. He is mirrored in his works."[30] Reid and Stewart thus bolstered Thornwell's confidence in the reliability of natural theology. But Hamilton reassured him of the necessity for revelation. Like Hamilton, he argued that the constitution of the mind imposed limits on the cognitive faculties, which inevitably erred whenever they attempted to "apply the laws of finite thought to what is confessedly beyond them." Human consciousness was constrained to use finite and phenomenal experience in its efforts to arrive at theological truth, and this meant that reason could never fully apprehend God's nature. "Of the infinite, we know that it is, though we do not know what it is." A "law of our being" compelled us to walk by faith more than by sight while in this "sublunary state."[31] Revelation was necessary. Scottish Realism demonstrated for Thornwell both the possibility and the ultimate insufficiency of natural theology; it accommodated the claims of both faith and reason.

Having found a philosophical justification for a religion of nature and of revelation, Thornwell could argue that the doctrine of justification was the "principle of unity" in an adequate theological system precisely because it was the central theme in "both . . . Natural and Revealed Religion." The pertinent question in both was: "How shall a man be just with God?" Reason inevitably asked the question whenever it reflected religiously; revelation answered it. In sustaining the claims of both reason and revelation, philosophy therefore protected the central principle of Christian theology.[32]

At first glance John Leadley Dagg (1794–1884) seemed an unlikely philosopher. He proposed to write his *Manual of Theology* (1857) by going "straight to Scripture," and he cautioned his readers about the need to restrain philosophy within due bounds.[33] But from beginning to end his discussion of Christian doctrine made extensive use of Scottish methods and conclusions. A Baptist minister, Dagg served churches in Virginia from 1817 to 1825, when he moved to the Fifth Baptist Church in Philadelphia. But he soon returned South, first as the principal of a Baptist women's school in Tuscaloosa and then in 1843 as the professor of theology at Mercer University in Georgia. He departed for Mercer with great fanfare. The University of Alabama awarded him an honorary doctorate as he left, and within two years he was named to the presidency of Mercer. But after a successful eleven-year tenure, Dagg was suddenly unable to maintain harmony among the faculty, and in 1856 the trustees requested his resignation. At the time, he had not written a single book, but when he was sixty-three he published his *Manual of Theology*, the first of several treatises that helped to form Southern Baptist doctrine. His *Treatise on Church Order* appeared the next year, followed by a text on the *Elements of Moral Science* (1859) and a presentation of the *Evidences of Christianity* (1868). Dagg earned a considerable reputation as an "orthodox and traditional" theologian, and his manual became a standard text in the Southern Baptist Theological Seminary.[34]

Dagg began his book with the explanation that the study of theology was a duty because the obligation to seek truth belonged "to the constitution of human nature." Implicit in his explanation were three assumptions: first, that the writing of theology presupposed a general philosophical view of the self; second, that the pursuit of theological truth was one instance of the wider search for truth in general; and third, that theological statements could therefore be subsumed within the broader class of metaphysical statements, even though they may have originated from a source higher than reason. It seemed that theology, then, should be subject to the same kinds of warrants that justified any other intellectual enterprise. And indeed the Scottish philosophy furnished Dagg with one of his main criteria of theological truth. He accepted the Scottish notion that a moral and religious "principle" was, along with other principles, ingredient in human nature. Such a principle, he said, required suitable influences for its development and perfection; and "the adaptedness of a doctrine to produce this effect" could be taken "as a proof of its truth and divine origin."[35]

Dagg organized his treatise according to the traditional topics of Protestant orthodoxy—God, sin, Christ, the Holy Spirit, grace, and eschatology—but he introduced each topic by specifying the "duty" to which it corresponded: to love God, to believe in Christ, to repent, or to live and walk in the Spirit. He acknowledged that his method of presentation defined "the articles of faith, to a great extent, from the inward exercises of piety."[36] But he insisted that his pattern of organization followed logically from his criterion of truth. If a moral and religious principle, requiring growth and nurture, was innate within the self, and if a doctrine was true insofar as it nurtured the religious principle, then the theologian would naturally define the doctrines with an eye to their effect on piety. Dagg was saying, in effect, that the truth of a theological system could be determined, at least in part, by its commensurability with piety, defined as the development of an innate religious principle. In other words: the Scottish description of human nature provided a criterion of theological truth.

"The Author of the Bible is the maker of the world, and the author of all truth; and his works and his word must harmonize, for Truth is always consistent." Dagg had confidence in the congruity between divine revelation and Scottish Realism, and he frequently used a method of analogy in which philosophy furnished the contents of the older Christian doctrines. God's ways of governing the world, for instance, were analogous to "the established order of sequence" discovered by philosophers in physical events; the mystery of God's mode of omnipresence was analogous to the mystery of the mind's mode of presence in the human body; and God's knowledge of the world was similar to the activity of the Scottish "consciousness."

> We obtain knowledge of our own mental operations by means of consciousness; and, as this is without any process of reasoning, and not by our bodily senses, or the testimony of others, it may give us the best possible conception of God's mode of knowledge. All things which he knows are before his mind as immediately and completely as the states and operations of our minds are before our consciousness. . . .[37]

Dagg naturally believed that a God so amenable to analogical description had revealed himself "in universal Nature," including both the moral and religious feelings and the external natural order. Reason could therefore establish not only God's existence but also a number of his attributes, including his unity, spirituality, omnipresence, and immutability. Natural religion, however insufficient by itself, taught "the fundamental truths on which all religion is based."[38]

Dagg found the Scottish ideas equally useful in defending a Calvinist anthropology: the Scottish description of mental process confirmed his belief in the bondage of the will. "Do human volitions occur as effects of antecedent causes, in an established order of sequence?" The Scottish discovery of mental "laws" suggested an affirmative answer:

> Impressions on the organs of sense produce their appropriate sensations in the mind according to fixed laws. Perceptions follow, and judgments, and trains of reasoning, all of which ...conform to fixed laws.... The science of mental philosophy proceeds on the supposition that such laws exist.[39]

It followed that volition, too, occurred within a chain of causes and effects, and that the Methodist claims on behalf of human freedom were unscientific. Yet "consciousness" also testified that all men and women were sufficiently free to be morally responsible, and the "common sense of mankind" taught that it was their duty to repent.[40] So the Scottish philosophy also justified evangelism and religious exhortation.

Dagg was received as an orthodox Baptist theologian, and his manual never created the slightest controversy. As a seminary text it was a formative book in Southern Baptist churches. Yet both in theory and in practice Dagg intermingled theology and philosophy, reason and revelation, and in that respect he was typical of his orthodox allies. Southern religious conservatives often claimed to be devotees purely and simply of Scripture, but their self-perception was inaccurate. As the articulate theologians well knew, religious conservatism in the Old South was always as much a matter of philosophical as of Biblical considerations.

In 1856 the Presbyterian John Bocock complained about "the flippant vogue of the modern philosophy of consciousness." In its rightful place, he said, the consciousness could provide sound, clear, reliable knowledge, but Bocock suggested that the method was intrinsically unreliable: "one man's consciousness will tell him one thing, and another's will tell him another thing. Men will ever find *their own* doctrines in their consciousness."[41] With a similar kind of criticism, though far more penetrating, John Stuart Mill had subverted the hegemony of the Scottish philosophy in British thought. The criticism did not do justice to the nuances of the Realist tradition, but the creative thinkers of the mid-nineteenth century were in any case eager to abandon the static and formal categories of the eighteenth century. Yet even after the Civil War Reid and Stewart were honored names in the Old South—and elsewhere in America. The most eminent Northern proponent of Common-Sense, James McCosh of Princeton, did not publish his major work until 1875; the most notable Southern Realist, John L. Giradeau, employed the Scottish ideas during the 1890s to undergird a conservative theology at Columbia Seminary. By that time many American theologians viewed the Scottish philosophy as an anachronistic relic, but for half a century Realism had been the reliable handmaiden of Southern theology, and (to this topic we now turn) the foundation of Southern ethical thought.

CHAPTER SIX

THE MORALISTS

In 1855 Thornwell published his *Discourses on Truth*, a treatise in moral philosophy designed to prove that rational beings were morally responsible not only for their acts but also for their opinions: truth was a duty.[1] The book illustrated the penchant of antebellum American theologians for equating ethical and theological categories. Irrationality was immoral, error was ethically suspect, and heterodoxy implied moral culpability. But in writing the book Thornwell was also expressing the consensus that moral philosophy was a branch of theology. One reviewer described his discourses as "a high example of those noble efforts which are made to conjoin, nay to identify the teachings of a true philosophy with the Word of God; the result to which every valid theory must inevitably come."[2]

Because moral philosophy was a form of natural theology, Thornwell planned to establish the ground of moral obligation solely by means of philosophical description. He believed that the moral philosopher should describe, elucidate, and explain the moral convictions that people actually held, and that a sufficiently thorough description would display "the constitutive and regulative principles" of human nature. The foundation of ethics was divine command, but only insofar as the will of God was "expressed in the constitution of the human mind." Morality was not dependent on Biblical revelation, which merely validated and enforced the conclusions of a sound moral philosophy, and ethics was not the prescription of authoritative rules but a dissection of consciousness that would, in revealing the constitution of human nature, uncover the natural law.[3] So theological ethics also depended on Scottish philosophy.

Moral philosophy occupied an exalted position in the intellectual life of the Old South. Practically every college had a required course on the subject, usually taught by the president and fashioned to preserve the values of Victorian culture. The courses were ethical in the broadest sense, embracing mental philosophy, political theory, social decorum, religion, and civil duties. They transmitted the culture's values to each new generation of students, trying to make inherited moral expectations seem plausible and persuasive. Nineteenth-century moral philosophy was therefore not simply a churchly activity; its locus was as much the university and philosophical society as the pulpit. But of twenty prominent antebellum Southern moralists, sixteen were clergymen who subsumed their ethical reflections under a theological umbrella.[4] For these men an acceptable moral philosophy had to serve at least three purposes: it had to demonstrate the rationality and immutability of morality, undergird piety, and make sense of Southern society.

The Catholic clergy learned their moral theology from the scholastic handbooks, the so-called *Institutiones morales*, that developed out of the conciliar legislation at Trent and tried to resolve particular "cases of conscience" in the light of natural law and revealed dogma. The manuals, written by the same neo-Thomists who furnished the theological textbooks—Abelly, Bailly, Alphonsus Ligouri, and others—ranged in tone from an uncompromising rigorism to an easygoing laxity. (The text used by John England in seminary was eventually condemned by Rome for being excessively scrupulous.) But the *Theologia Moralis* (1841–1843) of Francis Kenrick, who became archbishop of Baltimore in 1851, praised the mediating position established by Ligouri's classic *Medulla Theologiae Moralis* (1748), and Kenrick's text became standard for Catholic clergy. The *United States Catholic Miscellany* testified in 1843 to its instant authority. By that time John England had already applied the neo-scholastic methods in his published letters on domestic slavery (1840), in which he cited Aristotle and Aquinas while arguing that in a sinful world slavery was compatible with natural law, so long as the slave was justly acquired and humanely treated by the master.[5]

The Protestant preachers had no uniformly authoritative tradition of moral philosophy, but they found a ready substitute by way of the Scottish universities. The Scottish ethic outdistanced every rival: it made piety seem scientific and science seem pious, and it coincided perfectly with the social vision of the town pastors and their aspiring congregations.

1. *Sense and Sensibility*

In drawing on the language and logic of the Scottish tradition, the Southern clergy became entangled in an old debate about the rationality of ethics. Their moral theology bore the imprint of the earlier division in British thought between "rationalists" and "sentimentalists." By the early nineteenth century the once sharp line between the two parties had begun to fade, partly because the popularity of utilitarian ethics made some of the old problems seem unimportant and partly because the Scottish ethicists had arrived at a synthesis between the older schools. But the conflict nevertheless stood in the background of much of the ministerial moralizing in the Old South.

The rationalist tradition originated in the late seventeenth century in reaction against such ethical "voluntarists" as Thomas Hobbes and René Descartes, who derived morality from either arbitrary divine commands or prudential human decisions. The Cambridge Platonists stood in the forefront of the movement: in 1688 Ralph Cudworth argued in his *Treatise Concerning Eternal and Immutable Morality* that even God's will was subject to regulation by the eternal rational essences within his nature, and he used Platonic arguments to show that immutable moral truths, reflecting the divine wisdom, were accessible through an intellectual insight into "the truth and reality of things."[6]

In 1705 Samuel Clarke, the prince of English clerical rationalists, joined in the crusade against Hobbes, and his essay *On Natural Religion* developed and refined the new vocabulary. Clarke thought that morality was rooted in necessary and eternal "relations" that directed even the divine will. God's primal relationship to the world entailed a network of relations: creator to creature, superior to inferior, governor to governed, self to selves, and countless others. Clarke concluded that virtue was "fitting" behavior, which he defined as activity in accordance with the actual relations and proportions of Being. Morality was therefore the child of the "understanding," which had the task of discerning the fitting decision in any particular situation.

> By this Understanding, or Knowledge of the natural and necessary relations, fitnesses, and proportions of things, the Wills

... of all intelligent Beings are constantly directed, and must
needs be determined to act accordingly.[7]

Ethical obligation was implicit in moral knowledge: to know was
to be obliged, because to disregard or disobey a moral insight was
to contradict the nature of things and fall into absurdity, a fate any
rational creature would avoid. Clarke thus assimilated ethics to
logic and geometry and established a new moral language. The
governing conceptions in a rationalist ethic—understanding, reason, relations, the fitting, the nature of things—pointed to an ontological order to which the rational self was to conform.

There was another way to react against ethical authoritarianism, however, and in 1699 Anthony Ashley Cooper, Earl of Shaftesbury, wrote an *Inquiry Concerning Virtue* that located the virtuous
in "sound affections" that were directed toward the good of the
broadest possible social system. Shaftesbury wanted to prove that
a proper balance of passions, maintained through a "moral sense"
that delighted in harmony and beauty, would produce both private
and public good, benefiting self and society.[8] When Francis Hutcheson defended and expanded Shaftesbury's ideas in his *Inquiry into
the Original of our Ideas of Beauty and Virtue* (1725), he securely
established the "sentimentalist" school of moral theory. The book
brought Hutcheson an invitation to the philosophy chair at Glasgow, but it also provoked the Glasgow Presbytery to bring charges
of heterodoxy against him. He attracted the approval of the university and the suspicions of the presbytery by arguing for the existence of a "moral sense" antecedent to self-regarding motives and
independent of revelation. As Locke had defined perception as
the mind's grasp of ideas stimulated by external objects, Hutcheson described the moral sense as a power of receiving and enter-
taining "agreeable or disagreeable ideas of actions." But he denied
that virtue arose from reason, which he viewed as merely sagacity
in pursuing an end. The moral sense, rather, was an instinctive
approbation of benevolent activity, an affectionate admiration for
whatever promoted the public good. Hutcheson tried to demonstrate the existence of the moral sense by showing that prudential
calculation was not capable of producing the moral feelings—
reverence, admiration, pity, benevolence, gratitude, or shame—
that characterized human nature, and that morality could not arise

simply from law and commandment, because when moral agents made judgments about the goodness of the law, they appealed implicitly to an antecedent standard of evaluation.[9] Like Clarke, Hutcheson helped to create a new ethical vocabulary, but his categories—sensibility, feeling, affection, intention, sense, disposition —pointed not to an external ontological order but to an economy internal to human nature.

In the early eighteenth century the differences between rationalists and sentimentalists seemed insuperable. The English clergyman William Wollaston spoke for the rationalists when he insisted that moral thought should consist entirely in discerning the abstract relations of things and not in any description of human nature. But as early as 1726 Joseph Butler came to believe that each of the methods enforced the other, and in his writings on the "conscience" he began to work out the mediating position that would prevail among the American moral philosophers.[10] More than any other moralist, Butler was responsible for the exaltation of conscience in nineteenth-century ethical theory. The concept had roots in ancient philosophy, but Butler's analysis was so influential that one Southern textbook described him as the first man ever to recognize the supremacy of the conscience among the affections and principles of human nature.[11]

Butler described the self as a system of internal relations, including instincts and propensions, but he disagreed with Shaftesbury's attempt to ground moral obligation in the passions. He found within the self not only "propensions to do good" but also "a faculty that approves them," a "principle of reflection" that he called conscience. The ability of the conscience to stand in judgment over the lesser impulses demonstrated its superiority within the self's internal economy; judgment implied a claim to direction and superintendence; the "might" of the conscience implied its "right" to hold sway within the self. Butler hoped that such a notion could transcend the dispute between sentimentalists and rationalists, and he was willing to label the conscience either as "moral reason" or as "moral sense," because he thought that it included both a sentiment of the understanding and a perception of the heart.[12]

After Hume reasserted the sentimentalist position, Richard Price, a nonconformist English clergyman with great influence in America, responded in his *Review of the Chief Questions and Dif-*

ficulties of Morals (1757). Price posed the issues in the older terms: was a moral judgment a feeling and emotion or an accurate perception into the nature of things? He answered as a rationalist, but he made it clear that the issues were changing. He began his essay with a polemic against Locke's empiricism, hoping to defend the rational quality of moral judgments by showing that "understanding" was a richer and more complex process than empiricists had ever imagined. To understand, he argued, was not merely to reflect on sensory data: the understanding could stand in judgment over the senses, pronounce them mistaken, compare them to one another, and rise above them to make judgments of meaning. The process of understanding therefore presupposed categories that transcended sensory experience. Even to distinguish a stone from a tree, Price would have said, was to employ general categories—essence, space, solidity, power, number, identity, causation—that were not given in the sensory experiences. The understanding "knew" how to compare and contrast particular configurations of sense qualities, and this knowledge had to be prior to the sensory experience itself, which otherwise would have been merely an indistinguishable blur. Price therefore distinguished between the "power of reasoning," which merely investigated relations between known objects, and an "understanding" that gave rise to "new original ideas," including the ideas of right and wrong. Such moral notions could not be derived from a "sense," he said, for they were completely unlike any sensory experience. Every moral sensibility, moreover, presupposed a prior rational discernment; a moral feeling—a desire or an affection—could arise only after one understood "the nature of the thing" that evoked the feeling. One desired happiness because one knew what it meant to be happy; one felt approbation when one antecedently recognized an act to "fit" the realities of a situation.[13] Moral feelings were themselves "rational." Price dealt with ethics as a branch of epistemology; his criticism of Locke provided the categories for his ethics.

By the time the Scottish philosophers turned their attention to moral thought, the way was already prepared for a synthesis between rationalist and sentimentalist themes. Thomas Reid easily formed an alliance with Price; his discussion of the moral sense occurred not within his essay on instinct or as part of his analysis of desire but rather as a part of his treatise on "rational principles of action," much of which was a polemic against Hume's contention that moral approbation was "only a certain feeling" and that reason could determine only means but not ends. Reid believed that Locke's theory of ideas had led to Hume's ethical fallacies. Locke drove a wedge between sensations and the external world; Hume detached the moral sense from ethical realities. To Reid it seemed that both men failed to recognize the quality of judgment implicit in every kind of "sensory" experience:

> When Mr. Hume derives moral distinctions from a moral sense, I agree with him in words, but we differ about the meaning of the word *sense*. Every power to which the name of a sense has been given, is a power of judging of the objects of that sense, and has been accounted such in all ages; the moral sense, therefore, is the power of judging in morals. But Mr. Hume will have the moral sense to be only a power of feeling, without judging: this I take to be an abuse of a word.

A moral "sensation" was a complex mental act that included both feelings and judgments, and in most instances the feeling was the consequence of a logically prior judgment.[14]

Reid followed Butler in identifying the moral sense as the "conscience," a power both active and intellectual. As an active power it infused every virtuous act with a proper intention; Reid shared the sentimentalists' interest in the subjective state of moral agents: "Every action," he said, "takes its determination from the motive that produces it." But as an intellectual power the conscience formed intuitive rational "conceptions" of objective moral qualities. Reid even believed that a rational conception of justice or injustice was a sufficient ground of moral obligation: he agreed with Price that to understand the concept of justice was to recognize its obligatory quality.[15] In its original intellectual setting, the Scottish "moral sense" was a concept designed to reassert the rationality of moral judgments without abandoning the notion of an ethical "sensibility."

Reid tried to confirm his views through a description of human nature that would reveal the axiomatic presuppositions of moral judgment: the result was a "rational synthesis" between the sentimentalist and rationalist traditions. When Dugald Stewart published his *Philosophy of the Active and Moral Powers of Man* (1828), he continued the same program, drawing on the ideas of Butler, Reid, and Price. Because it surrendered neither reason nor sensibility, the synthesis appealed to the Southern clergy. It preserved the scientific status of ethics and yet coincided with introspective forms of piety. It united head and heart. And that was exactly what the clerical gentlemen wanted to do.

2. *The Science of Ethics*

When John Witherspoon began lecturing on moral philosophy at Princeton in 1768, he took for granted Hutcheson's dictum that the principles of duty had to be drawn from the study of human nature, but he saw "no occasion to join Mr. Hutcheson, or any other, in their opposition to such as make reason the principle of virtuous conduct." The truth, he said, probably lay in an eclectic merger of Clarke's "reason" and Hutcheson's "affection."[16] Such an eclectic ethic became standard after Francis Wayland, the president of Brown University, published his *Elements of Moral Science* (1835), the most famous of the ethical handbooks and the model for Southern moralists, who disliked Wayland's views on slavery but found his theoretical discussions attractive. Basil Manly made the pilgrimage to Providence to see Wayland: "I find him a great deal more satisfactory than any man I meet on all the points about which I wish to inquire."[17] Most of the Southern textbooks in moral thought were therefore revisions or expansions of Wayland, who had combined the rationalist interest in the "relations of things" with the sentimentalist language about motive and feeling. In a moral decision, he argued, the intellect discerned the relations, and the conscience, which had both an impulsive and discriminating power, created an intuitive awareness of the obligations arising out of those relations.[18]

The Southern clergy admired Wayland because he gave them an alternative to utilitarianism. Uniformly they bemoaned the prevalence of utilitarian doctrines in America. The utilitarians, they thought, had popularized an ethical relativism, ignored the inner sources of the moral life, and failed to undergird the social order. Although Hume and Jeremy Bentham received ample criticism for their secular versions of utilitarian doctrine, no ethicist was subject to greater scorn than William Paley, whose *Principles of Moral and Political Philosophy* (1785) had been a popular textbook in American colleges. No clerical writing on ethics was complete without a polemic against Paley. He was "unsafe for young scholars," he was "poison"; his book was "rotten from beginning to end," it was even "immoral"; his ideas were "sophistic" and "defective"; to apply to them the honorific title of "philosophy" was an "egregious misnomer."[19]

Paley had insisted that divine commands were providentially congruent with the general welfare of mankind and that virtue consisted in activity aimed at procuring a divine reward. By arguing that conscience was an acquired, not a natural, faculty; by designating actions as right merely because they were commanded; and by identifying divine command and human happiness, Paley had succumbed—so it was charged—to relativism. His ethic admitted of no intrinsic difference between virtue and vice, permitted no distinction between expediency and right, and allowed no ethical value to survive transient conceptions of what was useful for society. By transferring moral quality from the intention of the agent to the consequences of the act, he made morality a matter of purely external calculation. And by equating morality and pleasure, he encouraged an "eager and restless struggle for wealth, honor, and power."[20] Paley stood accused of crimes against ethics, piety, and society.

The source of his error was clear to James H. Thornwell: "Human consciousness is a territory which he never entered." Paley had failed to see that moral philosophy was also mental philosophy. All systems of thought, including moral science, wrote Henry Bidleman Bascom in his *Lecture on Moral Science* (1833), must emanate from "the sublime study of the human mind," and his maxim indicated the regular procedure of the Southern moralists, who tried to discover the ground of moral obligation by describing and distinguishing the modes of moral consciousness.[21]

R. H. Rivers exhibited the method in his *Elements of Moral*

Philosophy (1859). He was a protégé of the Methodist Bishop Robert Paine, who for sixteen years as the president and professor of moral philosophy at LaGrange College in Alabama had led his students through the works of the eminent Scottish figures. Rivers idolized Paine, sought his counsel about education, served under him on the faculty, and eventually wrote the official episcopal biography.[22] By that time Rivers had also begun to ascend the ecclesiastical ladder. In 1843 he accepted the presidency of a "school for young ladies" in Athens, Alabama; within five years Centenary College in Louisiana offered him a salary of $1500 to become vice-president and professor of moral science. Rivers accepted the offer and soon moved into the president's chair, but he became dissatisfied and, despite entreaties, resigned in 1853. He was head of Wesleyan University in Alabama when he published his text in moral philosophy. With its vindication of slavery, its Southern "nationalism," and its orthodoxy on religious and social issues, the book became a required text in the course of study for neophyte Methodist ministers.[23]

Rivers's analysis of consciousness revealed the existence of moral feelings that were unlike all other perceptions, memories, intellections, sensibilities, appetites, propensities, desires, and affections. The feeling of remorse, for instance, was neither a purely intellectual discrimination nor simply an undiscriminating sensibility. It could even be distinguished from such closely related feelings as regret or sorrow. It was a unique moral feeling.[24] By isolating and describing such modes of moral consciousness, the Southern ethicists hoped to exhibit the reality of conscience as an original moral power. The existence of a conscience, wrote John Dagg in his *Elements of Moral Science* (1859), was "demonstrated by our consciousness of its operations."[25] Distinctive moral feelings could have emerged only from a distinctive moral faculty.

The concept of "conscience" enabled the clergy to show that a propensity to make moral distinctions was ingredient in human nature; that duty rather than utility was the criterion of moral propriety; that there was a point of contact with God, an internal "natural revelation"; and that there was "a foundation laid in nature" for the distinction between right and wrong.[26] But it also had implications for talking about the rationality of ethics: their interpretation of the conscience permitted the ministers to argue that moral philosophy was a "science of duty" that investigated the "laws of morality" through rational methods.[27] Ethics had a status equivalent to that of any physical science.

The Southern moralists taught that ethical judgments were intuitive but not irrational. They agreed that an instinctive "feeling of approbation immediately arises on seeing a benevolent action, and a feeling of disapprobation on seeing an intention of doing harm."[28] Yet they refused to define an ethical judgment as simply a spontaneous moral sensation. Such a view, wrote Dagg, allowed no place for reasoning in the ascertaining of duty and therefore annihilated the "science" of morality.[29] Nineteenth-century American moralists were generally of two opinions: one group described the conscience as a separate faculty, distinct from reason, another conceived of it as a peculiar operation of reason.[30] But both insisted on its rationality. Even in asserting the priority of moral feeling, Dagg denied that one could separate conscience from intellect as if it were a separate compartment.

> The impulse of conscience is never contrary to our moral judgment. If there is a primary impulse of conscience, antecedent to the exercise of moral judgment, it consists in an elementary benevolent affection, which is not directed to any definite result until our relations to other things begin to be understood. It is then directed in its exercise by moral judgment, formed on the knowledge of these relations.[31]

The various possibilities could be located along a spectrum: some moralists claimed that the understanding guided and regulated an antecedent moral feeling;[32] others said that the feeling originated "in concert with" an "intellectual" perception of right and wrong;[33] still others argued that the moral feeling was subsequent to "a judgment of the understanding, or rational perception of the moral quality of an act."[34] But even if moral sensibility was grounded in primitive and spontaneous feeling, a moral judgment was by definition a rational act. As Robert L. Dabney told his students at Union Seminary in Virginia: "Wherever reason is, there, and there only, are moral judgments."[35] The notion of conscience, as it was transmitted through the writings of Butler and the Scottish thinkers, ensured that ethics could be considered a rational enterprise.

3. *A Moral Sense and a Warm Heart*

The Southern moralists valued the "scientific" aura of moral philosophy, but they also found in the idea of a "moral sense" and the
closely related emphasis on motive and intention a philosophical
vocabulary that shaded into the language of piety. The conscience
lay in close proximity to the warm heart. The Scottish synthesis
therefore commended itself to churchmen because it coincided at
so many points with the special accent on inwardness in the two
major streams of Southern Protestant piety: Puritanism and Wes-
leyanism. Moral philosophy was not only an instance of the rationality of religious thought but also an instrument in the pat-
terning of piety. However much it may have functioned for later
generations as a surrogate for faith, moral science in the Old South
was no substitute for Christian belief and piety. The ethical textbooks were anchored securely within the history of Southern spirituality, and the clergy advocated the Scottish synthesis because it
confirmed their Puritan and Wesleyan convictions.

Puritanism originated in the sixteenth century as a movement
of "divers godly and Learned" who wanted to reform the Church
of England "according to the pure Word of God."[36] The earliest
Puritans were reformers, first of the Church but of themselves and
their fellowmen as well. Their criterion of reform was Scripture,
in which they found explicit and indispensable directives for struc-
turing the Church and its worship. Throughout the sixteenth century they struggled to sweep away ceremonial accretions and traditional practices, but during the long battle with the established
Church many of them decided that the first step in reform had to
be the inculcation of piety. Without entirely abandoning their aspirations to become architects of a new ecclesiastical order, they
labored increasingly as physicians of the soul.

Puritan pastors were adept at diagnosing spiritual pride and
fleshly temptation; they were cartographers of the inner life, coun-
seling godly souls who yearned to be "undoubtedly sure" of their
salvation.[37] As a consequence they eventually began to believe that
all true religious experience followed broad patterns that could be
discerned through careful introspection. In the seventeenth century
New England Puritan churches required of their members a credible narration of "conversion," a convincing exhibition that the

seeds of saving faith had been planted. Every Church member was expected to have a certain introspective expertise: an ability to follow the progress of the soul as it moved by degrees from the first stages of faith toward a full trust marked by assurance of salvation.[38]

Puritan ideals could be found even in seventeenth-century Virginia, but they pervaded the Southern churches only during the eighteenth-century Great Awakening. The "New Side" Presbyterians from New Jersey and Pennsylvania who carried the revival to the upper South during the 1740s, reaping the harvests sown by the itinerant Anglican evangelist George Whitefield, had derived their accent on inward experience from Puritan sources. They stood in marked contrast to the "Old Side" Presbyterians, largely of Scotch-Irish origin, who preferred creedal subscription and orderly Church government over revivalist fervor. The "Old Side" preachers never effectively penetrated the Southern frontier; they left it to the revivalists. And although the Southern Presbyterians eventually withdrew their support from the turbulent camp meeting revivals of the early nineteenth century, they never abandoned their introspective Puritan piety.

After Presbyterian enthusiasm peaked, the Southern revival continued through the activities of the "Separate Baptists" who had come into existence during the New England awakening. Some of the regenerate folk within Northern Congregationalist churches had decided that they could not abide their more stolid and flat-footed companions, and they formed separatist congregations to cultivate inward piety. In the process some of them decided that such external forms as infant baptism subverted the purity of the Church. In 1755 a group of these Baptist "Separates" migrated to Guilford County, North Carolina, and the South has never been the same. They joined in the Southern awakening, soon outnumbered or infiltrated smaller Baptist groups, and permanently stamped the piety of Southern Baptists with a New England Puritan imprint.

The Methodist circuit riders followed in the footsteps of the Baptist farmer-preachers. As an extension of the English Wesleyan revival, the Methodist awakening in the South originated in 1772 as the pious exercises of a society within the Anglican establishment. But by 1784 their zeal propelled the American Wesleyans out of the Church of England, and they soon became one of the largest Southern denominations. Despite their distaste for Calvinist doctrine, they had much in common with the older Puritans, and among the first books printed by the Methodist publishing agency were classics of Puritan piety by Richard Baxter and Joseph Alleine. The Methodist *Quarterly Review* described Baxter's devotional writings as being "beyond the reach of criticism."[39]

For puritanic Baptists and Presbyterians and for Wesleyan Methodists the central moment in the revival, the experience of conversion, was neither a new revelation from God nor a mystical absorption into the divine, but an experience of forgiveness, an undeserved gift, deeply felt and described in highly personal terms. But their "rebirth" also entailed responsibilities; it initiated a process of personal growth designed to impose control over such passions as anger, lust, pride, and fear, and to elicit the more positive virtues of love and compassion. Religious experience was supposed to come to fruition in ethical behavior. Hence a comparison of Puritan and Wesleyan piety on the topics of assurance, holiness, and order broadens the context for understanding Southern moral philosophy.

Like the Puritans, the Wesleyans yearned for assurance of salvation. Wesley had worried profusely about his own inability to maintain his trust and confidence in a merciful God. But the mainline Puritans believed that sanctified dispositions and behavior provided the only usable clues for the believer seeking to obtain "sound evidence of a good estate."[40] Although Wesley valued such "indirect evidence," he thought that it was not comparable to the immediate and direct "Witness of the Spirit." Perched on the boundary of ecclesiastical disorder, the mainline Puritans remained suspicious of those fervent souls who claimed that the immediate witness of the Spirit evidenced the presence of justifying faith.[41] Firmly entrenched within the structures of High Church Anglicanism, Wesley felt free to seek experiences of spiritual immediacy. Thomas Ralston acknowledged that the Southern Methodists were still subject to ridicule for holding to the Witness of the Spirit, but Bishop George Pierce of Georgia nevertheless asserted that it was the most characteristic Methodist teaching.[42] Both the Wesleyan and the Puritan theologians argued that there were "degrees" of true faith and thus distinguished themselves from Continental Lutheran pietists, but the Puritans believed that even a strong faith was mingled with unbelief and doubt, so that the quest for assurance always proceeded in the face of inner struggle. The Wesleyans agreed that a weak faith was a genuine faith, but they taught that the Witness of the Spirit brought liberation from all doubt, fear, and sorrow.[43] The differences were clear, but so were the similarities. Both groups shared a common preoccupation with inwardness and introspection. Both believed that the quality of inner experience could be a signpost along the way to assurance.

Like the Puritans, moreover, the Wesleyans believed that a process of "sanctification" followed the gift of pardon. Christian life was a gradual growth in holiness, an upward movement, sustained by divine grace, that led the believer through ascending levels and stages toward perfection. Both groups spoke of it as a process of "mortification" and "vivification," a struggle to overcome the self and to love other people as a demonstration of love for Christ. The difference lay in the Wesleyan confidence that perfection was attainable in this life. During the process of sanctification, Wesley wrote, the seeds of holiness gradually matured to a point of ripeness; then in an instant the heart was cleansed of sin and "filled with pure love to God and man." Christian perfection, an unremitting disposition of love, was the goal of faith. Wesley taught that faith was subordinate to love; it served as a means for the restoration of love. Because the Scripture commanded the Christian to "be perfect," and because God's grace was sufficient for every task, Wesley argued, a disposition of perfect love was a realistic goal of Christian piety. Even a minor transgression of the law was not a blot on the perfection of the sanctified Christian so long as love was the "sole principle" reigning in the heart.[44] After 1825 American Methodists, particularly in New York and New England, increasingly sought the "blessing of perfect love" and thus helped spark a holiness revival complete with millennial expectations and reforming fervor. Southern Methodists were more subdued, though a few, including the influential Lovick Pierce in Georgia, adopted the views of the Northern holiness advocates.[45] In any case, the Southern Methodists, like their Northern counterparts, routinely searched their hearts for the sign that the Spirit was working in them the grace of perfect love, the gift of pure motivation.[46] Baptists and Presbyterians, meanwhile, were searching their hearts with equal ardor, even if their expectations were more modest.

Like the Puritans, finally, the Wesleyans assumed that the expression of religious feeling followed standard patterns, indeed that thought patterned feeling. Both groups expounded a calculus of the emotions. It seemed reasonable that if God had conferred salvation "according to a certain plan," the permutations of inward experience should reflect that order and no other. But the theologians disagreed about the components of the pattern, or, as George Pierce expressed it, "the order in which they are experienced by the Christian." Methodists believed that the Christian life began with a subjective feeling of "conviction" and guilt, which led to contrition and reformation, the two components of "repentance." Then came the trust and confidence of faith, accompanied by pardon and the experience of "regeneration," or conversion. The order was climaxed by the process of sanctification, leading ideally to perfect love.[47] According to the Calvinistic Puritan traditions, however, Christian experience began with pardon and regeneration; faith came next, then repentance, and finally the process of sanctification.[48] Each scheme was amenable to meticulous refinement, and even allies disagreed among themselves about the minutiae, but all assumed that religious feeling displayed a standard pattern. Order was a motif of Protestant piety.

Among the goals of piety, therefore, were introspective watchfulness, purity of intention, strenuous inner discipline, and self-control. William Warren Sweet once defined Southern churches as "moral courts." Their jurisdiction extended not only to external behavior but also to internal feeling. The churches tried to enervate the forces of disorder within and without the self; their members faced sanctions not only for intemperate and immoral behavior but also for unrepented feelings of anger or hostility, for excessive and disproportionate exuberance, and similar deviations. Ministers urged their congregations to examine themselves, to "probe the soul to the very center."[49] And antebellum letters and diaries were filled with reports of "the watch over [the] heart," in which Southern Christians discovered time and again that they were indolent, sensual, anxious, impatient, deceitful, rebellious, and cold.[50]

Because they conceived of the process of sanctification as requiring strenuous discipline, inner commitment, and self-control, the town pastors felt a perpetual discomfort with the turbulence of conflicting passions, a sense of unease in the presence of unstructured feeling. The unpredictability of feeling defied the regulation and control that sanctification was expected to produce. Sensing that passional impulses were threats to the internal stability that marked the sanctified believer, the clergy called, in the words of the Methodist Thomas Ralston, for "a violent warfare on the impulses of our nature." Impulse, wrote the Presbyterian Thomas Smyth, should be "absolutely under the control of reason."[51] Piety presupposed self-control.

Moral philosophy in the Old South, therefore, repeated the older themes of piety; it recast the traditional Protestant demand for introspection, pure motivation, and self-control into new scientific forms. The descriptions in the moral textbooks of right willing, pure intention, moral sensibility, and harmony among the faculties translated the language of the prayer meeting into the jargon of a philosophical science. The intention was not to abandon the prayer meeting but to confirm its insights, to illustrate in ethics as in epistemology the unity of truth. An ethic founded in a moral sense was the philosophical counterpart to a piety of inwardness and introspection.

A few Americans in the Northern colleges expounded an ethic in which consequences were more important than motives, but the influence among Southerners of Wayland and of Archibald Alexander at Princeton confirmed their preference for an ethic in which right intentions and obedience to moral law were the primary considerations. Rivers's *Elements of Moral Philosophy* illustrated the congruence between the new philosophy and the old piety. The moral law, he argued, was a revelation not only of God's will but also of his eternal Reason; obligation to obey the law was therefore an axiom, a "first truth," for which no higher reason could be given. And virtue consisted simply in obedience, which Rivers called "right willing." A moral agent was virtuous when he willed to obey the law in every thought and action; an act was virtuous insofar as it was performed out of an intention to obey moral law. The presence of other motives did not compromise the ethical quality of the act so long as the primary motive was simply to obey, but consequences were secondary. A beneficial act performed out of self-interest was not virtuous.

> An action conforming externally to moral obligation, but which does not conform to obligation in the intention, is not a virtuous action, because it lacks the main element of virtue, viz., conformity to moral obligation in the intention.[52]

An ethical act was one performed with the intent of obeying the divine law revealed in Scripture, the natural law revealed in creation, a just civil law, or even the laws of human health and hygiene.[53] The intention to obey "law" was the mark of a moral person.

The course of moral culture, therefore, was identical with the prescriptions of piety: the moral person would attend assiduously to the inner life, the domain of motivation. Only through introspection could one certify purity of intention.

> Subject yourself to frequent and rigid self-examination. Go into your own heart and search its inmost recesses. . . . Be willing to know the whole truth, to see the entire character, however unpalatable the truth and however deformed the character.[54]

Since morality consisted of "right" willing, moreover, the will had to be "rational, not arbitrary"; volition was subject to the understanding. An ethical act was a decision by a solitary, rational will. Introspection therefore was a search for rationality as well as purity of heart.[55] Moral science incorporated the ideal of reasonableness within the techniques of introspective piety.

The ethic also provided a scientific justification for the traditional Protestant suspicion of the self's impulsive vitalities. Moral philosophy rested on "mental philosophy," or the "philosophy of mind," which was essentially a classification, ordering, and interpretation of the mind's "powers and susceptibilities."[56] By analyzing the self as a harmony of intellect, sensibility, and affections, Rivers defined a person as a complex balance of "powers," an uneasy equilibrium of conflicting forces and counterforces. A person was a hierarchy of capacities, ideally superintended by reason, and the goal was neither to eliminate the appetites and passions nor to indulge them but to maintain their proper subordination to rational governance. Self-government, wrote Rivers, always implied "the control of the appetites and passions."[57]

"In a perfectly virtuous mind," wrote John Dagg in his text on moral science, "the impulses are so adjusted as to operate in harmony." The problem of self-government was then analogous to the social problem of Southern society: the lower impulses could best attain their object when they acted in "subordination to the higher."[58] The intentions of the moral philosophers coalesced in a series of linguistic images: regulation, control, discipline, proportion.[59] Mental philosophy therefore certified the goals of piety by demonstrating that the religious duty of maintaining internal control had the sanction of a dispassionate, scientific psychology. No less an authority than Thomas Reid had argued on philosophical grounds that the "human constitution" required the passions to be always "under the dominion of reason," and Dugald Stewart had defined the ethical ideal as balance and proportion among the faculties.[60] When combined with the distrust of impulse that had grown out of the religious culture, that yearning for balance easily turned into an attempt to impose order on a recalcitrant self. "Life has all got into disorder with me," wrote one minister in his diary. "I must try to systematize it more."[61] His private dilemma reflected a cultural ideal, particularly suited to the respectable middle classes in the Southern towns.

The clergy were sensitive to the interrelations between internal control and social order. It was not only that "complete subjection of the appetites, passions, and affections" was essential for "ordinary respectability."[62] The ministers believed that internal discipline undergirded social order, and much of the legalism in Southern religion developed out of a fear of exciting uncontrollable passions. Theaters and novels were suspect because they threw the passions out of proper balance; horse racing engrossed the heart and so diminished "intellectual culture"; drunkenness released destructive impulses.[63] A doctrine of the passions could even be called into service in defense of slavery, as it was taken for granted that black "servants," unlike their "better disciplined masters," were unable "to control their feelings."[64] Philosophy, piety, and social policy converged in the demand for control.

4. Relations

The British tradition of moral philosophy also furnished the Southern moralists with the dominant theme of their social ethic: the category of "relation." The purpose of moral science, Rivers argued, was "to exhibit man in his relations" to his fellow-creatures, the law, and God.[65] First elaborated by Samuel Clarke but later taken up into the Scottish synthesis, the category seemed tailor-made for Southern society, and especially for the classes whom the town pastors wanted to address.

Jasper Adams (1793–1841) introduced his *Elements of Moral Philosophy* (1837) with the observation that moral science had two objects: to form and cultivate the "sense" of duty and to determine the obligations implicit in "the various situations and relations of life."[66] Adams's own career had led him through a series of those relations. The son of a New England Congregationalist farmer, he graduated from Brown in 1815. Though he soon joined the Episcopal Church, Adams studied theology at Andover and after teaching natural philosophy for a time at Brown applied in 1820 for ordination into the priesthood. Most of his years as a minister he spent in the South. In 1824 Adams became president of Charleston College, a post he occupied for twelve years. He was a tolerant and inquisitive man who employed many of his mornings studying German Biblical criticism with the Unitarian pastor, Samuel Gilman.[67] But his religious and social predispositions were conservative: as a churchman he approved of the English Oxford Movement and its quest for medieval spirituality, and as a social philosopher he admired Edmund Burke's strictures against social turmoil and revolution. Like other Southern moral philosophers, he found in the category of "relations" the organizing principle of an ethic for upwardly mobile, competitive people.

The standard outline of the Southern moral textbooks was taken from the tripartite division of duties in Samuel Clarke's *On Natural Religion*. His arrangement of the "duties"—to God, ourselves, our fellow-creatures—was adopted even by moralists who did not share his intellectualist slant on ethics, and Francis Wayland's use of the schema helped make it standard in America. The point of the outline was to assert that duties were grounded in the relations that structured society: Creator and creature, ruler and ruled, husband

and wife, parent and child, master and servant, rich and poor. The category of relation could easily become a cipher for "office, birth, knowledge, wealth, and other distinctions known and acknowledged among men," to which Jasper Adams accorded the sanction of providence on the grounds that no community had ever existed without them.[68]

The antebellum South has been characterized as a "traditional" society, quasi-aristocratic and hierarchical, supported by a precapitalist, subsistence manorial economy. In such a society, deference was valued higher than egalitarian informality, respect for tradition and family counterbalanced the drive for efficient productivity, and "the best people" were expected to exercise authority. The structures of leadership and influence were patriarchal; the master—of both the home and the plantation—was the dominant social figure, exercising his prerogatives largely in face-to-face relationships rather than through impersonal structures and in local rather than centralized institutions. Such a society was not unaware of moral values, but within a slave economy benevolence assumed the form of paternalism, personal honor ranked above utilitarian considerations, and loyalty to other individuals superseded attachment to abstract ethical ideals.[69] Southerners may have been more committed to efficient economic productivity, competition, and progress than such a depiction of the society would suggest, but certainly chattel slavery, plantation economics, and racial tensions profoundly shaped the region's culture and distinguished it from the rest of the nation.[70]

Within such a society a social ethic based on the sanctity of relations could easily be used as a justification for "traditional" cultural values. The ethical texts addressed themselves to persons defined by their location in society: they outlined the duties of rulers, citizens, husbands, wives, masters, and servants, not of persons as representatives of an abstract cosmopolitan "humanity." They exalted the family as the fundamental human institution and the husband as head of the family. They sanctified privilege and existing prerogatives, qualifying and limiting the egalitarian rhetoric of the eighteenth century. In the Southern lexicon, the concept of "relation" stood in contrast to "philanthropy," the insidious fallacy that all persons could be "equally exalted in social and political condition."[71] I have "but little sympathy," grumbled Rivers, "with the lady who marries her father's coach-man."[72] And of course the defense of slavery in the Southern manuals conceptually defined an entire class of the population as permanent serfs, fully dependent on patriarchal owners.[73] The idea of "relation" could serve in a myriad of ways to bolster the traditionalist social arrangements of Southern society.

But there was another side to the Southern moral philosophy, which, after all, was merely an adaptation of themes that were popular both in Europe and in the North. In calling for the suppression of impulse the clerical moralists tried to impose uniformity, regularity, and rational order on the self. Their call for the "systematic arrangement of time" and their support for temperance reflected a Victorian appreciation of time-thrift, time-accounting, and self-discipline.[74] And the doctrine of relations could also set limits to deference and hierarchy: because all persons were separated from and near to God by an "equal distance," wrote Adams, the various social classes met in the Church "on something like equal terms." The divine-human relation intersected the various other relations of human society; worship therefore served, he thought, "to inspire the humbler ranks with a sense of their rights."[75]

The moralists used relational concepts to push toward generality and abstraction in moral thought and to promulgate universal norms that contradicted traditional cultural values. They argued that the "relations of mutual dependence and reciprocity" in society required loyalty to such abstract values as truthfulness and justice rather than simply faithfulness to superiors and comrades within the social hierarchy. In describing the relations between ruler and ruled they exalted talent and accomplishment above heredity and "breeding" and glorified active, informed citizenship. Indeed the doctrine of relations could, in theory, mitigate even the rigors of the master-slave relationship. "Your fellow-man may be your slave, and owned as property," wrote Rivers, "but the right of ownership is greatly modified by the fact that he is your fellow-man."[76] A universal and ideal relation qualified the concrete and real one. Such a teaching could subvert as well as serve traditional social arrangements—and do both at the same time.

The clergy sensed that they were not addressing primarily a plantation aristocracy or the unreflecting masses, but men and women who were unsure of the prerogatives and duties attendant on their station in society. The professional elites received special attention: the ethical handbooks often contained lengthy admonitions to physicians, lawyers, merchants, journalists, teachers, and clergymen.[77] The ministers thus designated themselves as the moral specialists within an urban society marked by emerging economic and professional specialization. At the same time, they presented themselves as the mediating group in a culture sensitive to gradations of class and status but unsure about the boundaries. Adams urged the Southern pastors to take advantage of their social location:

> The spiritual functions of the clergy bring them into friendly and confidential relations with every class of mankind, from the humblest to the highest, and this peculiarity in the nature of their office gives them constant facilities for rendering themselves useful to every grade of society, by promoting peace [and] giving instruction and advice....[78]

Seen in this light, the handbooks in moral philosophy illustrate the aspirations of the urban clerical elite, who strove for exactly such a position of leadership and influence.

5. A Theological Ethic

In reflecting on social order, the ministers returned repeatedly to such themes of British moral philosophy as rationality, sensibility, intention, and relations. But they combined these philosophical themes with the images and doctrines of the Christian tradition. Theology and philosophy merged to form a vision of social order. Thomas Smyth of Charleston, for example, expounded to his fashionable Presbyterian congregation a theological ethic that generated discussion in Southern journals, Northern newspapers, and scholarly European reviews, and he made ample use of the philosophical traditions. His ethic exemplified the three dominant philosophical tendencies that marked the Southern moral textbooks: he accepted the Scottish synthesis, defined morality as purity of motive, and incorporated the image of "relation" into a social vision that was overtly conservative but implicitly subversive of agrarian values. But Smyth inserted his moral notions into a Reformed theology that subtly altered their force and meaning. He justified his injunctions theologically by appealing to the time-honored doctrines of divine sovereignty and human sinfulness. Detached from piety, he said, ethics was without positive significance.[79]

Smyth shared the widespread disillusionment with Paley, whose individualistic utilitarianism he denounced as mere "expediency," unbefitting the Christian ethical life.[80] He was more favorably impressed with Wayland, whose *Limits of Human Responsibility* (1838) he described as a responsible statement, devoid of reformist fanaticism. Like Wayland, he tried to bring the theory of a moral sense into harmony with the concept of relation. But a moral sense, for Smyth, was inseparable from a regenerate heart, and a "relation" was a way of speaking about divine providence.

An appraisal of rebellion and guilt suggested to Smyth that the precondition of ethical activity was the regeneration of the will. That explained his interest in the motives, rather than the consequences, of ethical behavior. The prerequisite for moral life was purification of the will through piety, self-denial, and the repudiation of "all that constitutes our naturally sinful self." The first imperative was the rebirth in each person of the capacity for selfless obedience. Preoccupied with the purity of intention that marked the regenerate life, Smyth was theologically predisposed toward the Scottish accent on motivation. A purely motivated obedience was the criterion of right. "Resigning his own will," the ethical man would "lay himself upon the altar of duty," entirely unsullied by self-regarding motives.[81]

Smyth was familiar with the Kantian ethic of Francis Lieber, Professor of History and Political Economy at South Carolina College, whose two-volume *Manual of Political Ethics* he read sometime before 1848, and he also studied the works of Thomas Reid. But duty was not simply a formal philosophical category for Smyth; the shape and content of the dutiful life came from Christ, who was the object, model, and measure of duty. According to Smyth's "pyramid of duty," only an ethical intention grounded in selfless love for Christ was intrinsically praiseworthy. "In fact, so important is this principle of Order in Duty, that duty ceases to be duty, and becomes disobedience, when not rendered in the order in which it is required." Obedience to Christ was of necessity the center of every ethical act. Jesus himself demonstrated the pattern of that obedience by submission to the divine will, self-denial, and concern for the downtrodden.[82]

Smyth deplored most nineteenth-century reform movements because they seemed to suggest that "all the tares of depravity could be at once and completely eradicated by the devices of man's wisdom and man's philanthropy." To modify corrupt social institutions with the hope of transforming character was to confuse the effect of corruption with its cause. Instead, Smyth, with most other Southern Protestants, believed that social reform must proceed by individual reformation. The Church would change the social order only by gradually transforming sinful persons into good, virtuous, peaceful citizens and neighbors.[83] Therefore the internal volition of the isolated individual was the center of interest.

Smyth thought that only the theological illiteracy of the Northern reformers could explain their propensity for "absurd and extravagant theories." One of their main errors was their failure to recognize the providential status of society's relations.

> God himself being a God of order, everything that is must be established with certain relations, consequences, and if capable of them, rights and obligations. These are founded in nature and are necessary and inflexible. We are therefore required to observe this order, and to act in accordance with these relations, subject to inevitable retribution.[84]

He thought that the temptation of the reformer was to overlook the normative status of the existing world order and its established relations. Not only the revealed Word but also the mysterious providence of God imposed an obligation of obedience. To flout the providential order was to disobey the divine will, and the dreadful error of the worldly philanthropist lay precisely in his fatal attempt "to turn back the course of eternal providence."[85]

Presumptuous social experiments would always fail, "ever . . . held in check by the fortuities and complications still beyond" the control and understanding of mere mortals. But failure was not so serious as disobedience, and disharmony with providence was "as truly disobedient" as transgression of the law.

This order of divine providence affects also our position, circumstances, and sphere of duty, as much as the duty itself. . . . Duty therefore requires us to accept God's arrangements, to acquiesce in them, to act in harmony with them, and not to fall behind or to go beyond them, until in the use of proper means, God opens or shuts the door.[86]

The danger ever existed that reform masked a vain and insidious amendment of the providential relations of being.

Because of his convictions about sin and providence, or, differently stated, about motives and relations, Smyth repudiated pacifism, socialism, the public school movement, universal manhood suffrage, and feminism; for similar reasons he defended slavery. In 1861, he alluded to his natural antipathy to slavery, which had been overcome only by the Biblical testimony that bondage was a "providentially ordered system of labor."[87] His earliest public involvement with the issue, in 1836, consisted simply of a plea that slavery be considered a civil institution, outside the purview of ecclesiastical authority.[88] Smyth's initial reluctance to affirm the slave system, and his conviction that slavery was evil, brought angry responses from its ardent apologists, especially after the publication in 1851 of his book on the *Unity of the Human Races*. He wrote the book to defend the Biblical account of creation after Agassiz of Harvard had suggested the hypothesis of a multiple origin for the races. Smyth charged that the covert motive for the attack on Genesis was often a desire to degrade the African in order to justify barbaric treatment, and he explicitly acknowledged that the Genesis account made "every man a brother," thus evoking criticism even from the New York *Democratic Review*.[89]

Actually, however, Smyth's opposition to abolition was never subject to serious question, even though he never owned slaves himself. When he toured the British Isles in 1846, the secretary of the Scottish Anti-Slavery Society described him with good reason as a "suspected person."[90] Although Smyth publicly stated at the first great meeting of the Evangelical Alliance in London in 1847 that slavery was an evil, he viewed abolitionism as "secret satanic fanaticism."[91] He wrote little, however, until February, 1861, when he produced several articles that were reprinted in the *New York Journal of Commerce*; his defense of the institution occupied the front page of three issues. He lay the groundwork for the series by arguing that the abolitionists, like the pacifists and the economic reformers, had overlooked human sinfulness and divine sovereignty. The first article, he said,

> proved that slavery is a part of the original curse pronounced on the earth, on man, on woman, and is therefore to be classed among the evils incident to a sinful nature in a sin-polluted world, and a providential remedial agency for accomplishing wise and beneficent results. . . .[92]

One could hope and work for "progressive amelioration" within the system, remembering, however, that the slave economy was part of a universal "preparatory system of Providence" in which trials, temptations, and difficulties were essential and right. To this Smyth added a series of arguments about the curse of Ham, the Mosaic Code, and slaveholding by Old Testament patriarchs. "The Bible and Slavery," he concluded, "go hand in hand."[93] By 1861 Smyth was a zealous apologist for slavery.

A social conservatism grounded in Calvinist theology, however, could have unsettling implications in an agrarian and traditionalist society. Because of his religious and ethical convictions, Smyth was more at home in a competitive mercantile world than in a deferential plantation culture. He spoke out on behalf of economic progress and encouraged his urban congregation to strive for success within the commercial order; he became a dedicated champion of Southern businessmen during an era in which they generally lacked the prestige of planters, politicians, and military officers. It must have been comforting to Charleston merchants when Smyth observed in 1858 that the commercial classes surpassed their agrarian colleagues in charity and public-spirited benevolence. Smyth occasionally criticized the "rapacious spirit of modern commerce," but he also insisted that "the most diligent pursuit of business is not only not inconsistent with spiritual business, but is congenial with it and greatly profited by it."[94] Carefully distinguishing between hazardous speculation and legitimate enterprise, Smyth assured the industrious merchant of temporal blessings. Diligence, honesty, and piety would invariably "secure measurable success." "Riches and wealth are spoken of in the Bible as if their bestowal were one of the ways in which God prospers and blesses His people."[95] Wealth was a sign of God's favor as well as a divinely ordained opportunity for generous benevolence.

Smyth then supplemented this rudimentary Gospel of Wealth with a strenuous Protestant ethic. He proclaimed that laboring men and women should rejoice in their labor since self-denying work was itself a Scriptural injunction. Refusing to be satisfied with a "Lazy South," Smyth taught his congregation that industry was a religious duty and that prudence and economy were Christian virtues.[96] In calling for an inner-worldly asceticism, in connecting rewards with labor, and in exalting the intrinsic value of self-discipline connected with work, Smyth spoke to and for the urban mercantile South.

Smyth did not fully accept the popular Southern doctrine of the "spirituality of the Church," according to which the Church, as an order of grace, was permitted no official involvement in the social reform of the state, an order merely of justice. On occasion he suggested that Christianity was truly interested in men and women "merely that it may prepare them for the world to come," while civil government guided them "in all things that regard this present life." But he argued more frequently that the Christian faith had "the most vitally important relations" to civil polity and social justice, even suggesting that the diffusion of righteousness in social relations might hasten the millennium, a claim often made by the Northern reformers whom he disliked.[97]

In fact the Southern churches never truly abstained from social comment; their self-described isolation was merely a protective gesture during the slavery controversy. Indeed their heavy intellectual investment in moral philosophy ensured that the gentlemen clergy would continue to address the concrete issues of Southern society, whether as apologists for existing social and political arrangements, as unwitting critics of the traditional South, or, on occasion, as cautious spokesmen for human values.

CHAPTER SEVEN

SEALS OF THE COVENANT

"No single topic has, in this country, been more fruitful of controversies and books than baptism."[1] With that judgment, expressed in an 1854 edition of the Southern Methodist *Quarterly Review*, few ministers could have disagreed. During the first half of the nineteenth century the Southern clergy wrote hundreds of sermons, meditations, and polemical treatises on the sacraments, with special attention to the proper mode, subjects, and efficacy of baptism. Yet the flood of repetitive arguments did not diminish the interest in sacramental matters. A popular fictional romance written in 1856 as an easily digested polemic on baptismal practice went through twenty-six printings in two years.[2] Surely the topic would not have been so "fruitful" had it been divorced from the desire of competitive churches to dramatize their differences in order to attract members. Yet the confrontations over sacramental practice also revealed broader theological commitments and exposed half-conscious philosophical presuppositions.

"Men's views of baptism correspond to their theological doctrines, sound or unsound," claimed one Virginia Methodist pastor in 1854.[3] And indeed the imagery of their sacramental writings serves to locate the Southern clergy within a specific tradition of historic Protestant thought: the "covenant theology." Covenantalism was a complex of doctrines and images and metaphors that had emerged in the sixteenth and seventeenth centuries in response to a variety of practical and pastoral issues. How can I be assured of salvation? Why should I perform good deeds? Of what use is baptism if salvation depends on an eternal decree or a faithful voluntary decision? How can corporeal elements and visible actions either convey or confirm spiritual life and grace? To such questions about assurance, ethics, and sacraments, a large company of Protestants on the Continent and in England responded with the claim that God had initiated with his creatures a covenant relationship with apparently mutual obligations. God was obliged to save men and women who fulfilled the covenant condition of faithful discipleship; they were obliged to lead lives of faith and obedience; and sacraments were necessary as visible pledges of covenantal fidelity. Largely through its prominence in Puritan theology, the covenantal metaphor became one of the powerful images of early American religious life. As late as the Civil War Southern Protestants still viewed themselves as a covenanted people and believed that the Christian sacraments were the covenantal seals.[4]

Southern sacramental writings also exposed a prime presupposition of the region's articulate clergy, namely, the autonomy and priority of "spirit," understood as a philosophical as well as religious category. The South's Reformed and Wesleyan theologians took for granted a series of dichotomies: matter and spirit, flesh and spirit, Word and Spirit, internality and externality. The duality was partly an inheritance from sixteenth century Continental humanism, filtered through Reformed theology and piety. Martin Luther had insisted that the Spirit revealed itself in and through external sacramental elements and the external words of Scripture; but the Swiss Reformed theologians, influenced by Renaissance humanism, believed that the Spirit acted directly on the minds of men and women, enabling them to use the sacrament rightly and to interpret the Scripture properly. They distinguished the corporeal means from the spiritual meaning; in effect, they divided the world into spiritual and material spheres which could rarely intersect, and then they located Christian existence solely in the realm of the Spirit.

By the seventeenth century the English Puritans, who took most of their cues about theology from the Continental Reformed theologians, were arguing that all external religious aids were secondary and subordinate to inward spirituality. Sacraments were effective only for the soul wherein the Spirit dwelt; the internal illumination of the Spirit necessarily preceded any true understanding of the external words of Scripture; and the Church took on reality and substance only where the Spirit had poured out its gifts.[5] Such ideas permeated the Southern churches, and the revivalistic demand for spiritual immediacy tended to reflect and to confirm them. The Southern clergy took from their past a covenantal theology and a dualistic philosophy: nowhere was either more evident than in the sacramental debates.

1. *The Covenantal Condition*

Early Christian references to baptismal "sealing" suggested connotations ranging from the branding of slaves to the ratification of public documents with an official stamp; the image of the covenantal seal had a long and complex history.[6] But the Southern theologians drew their understanding of the covenant from sixteenth- and seventeenth-century sources, and the relevant starting point is the teaching of Ulrich Zwingli, pastor of the Great Minster in Zurich after 1519, who used the doctrine of the covenant to defend infant baptism against the criticisms of Swiss Anabaptists. Zwingli elaborated the metaphor in terms that persisted throughout the early nineteenth century. He defined baptism as a covenantal sign or seal, the latter term coming from Romans 4:11, where Paul called circumcision "a seal of the righteousness of faith." According to Genesis 17:1–4, God had entered into covenant with Abraham and his seed and thus with the whole people of Israel. The sign of the covenant was circumcision, which signified Abraham's duty to lead his offspring to God, and Zwingli saw in that sign a proleptic demand and justification for infant baptism. Christians, he said, were also under covenant with God, and their new covenant was in substance continuous with the covenant of Abraham, since both pointed in different ways to the same Christ. Baptism, in turn, according to Colossians 2:11–12, was the Christian analogue of circumcision. Therefore God's command that Abraham's children be circumcised was sufficient reason for Christians to baptize their children. Since children were included in the covenant with their parents, there was no reason to deprive them of the sign of that which they already possessed.[7]

Sixteenth- and seventeenth-century Reformed confessions documented the increasing emphasis on the definition of sacraments as covenant seals. But it was not always clear what the definition meant. Did sacraments seal by certifying God's covenant promise? Or did they testify to the faith and covenant membership of the baptized? The question was especially troublesome in the Church of England, where covenantal doctrines seemed to conflict with an older sacramental tradition embedded in the Prayer Book. In 1552 Archbishop Thomas Cranmer removed from the Book of Common Prayer the assertion that infants were "saved from perishing" by baptism, and the Thirty-Nine Articles of 1536 made no reference to the older doctrine of baptismal regeneration. But the liturgy still referred to baptized infants as "regenerate," so that Anglican standards were amenable to a variety of interpretations.

During the following three centuries the doctrine of baptismal regeneration repeatedly divided the English clergy. It was involved in the seventeenth-century divisions between Calvinists and Arminians, between Puritans and traditionalists, and even among Puritan reformers. It reappeared in eighteenth-century conflicts between latitudinarians and high churchmen and in nineteenth-century disputes between the Oxford Tractarians and their evangelical critics. Some English theologians said that the sacrament was a conditional pledge to the faithful that they would experience rebirth as adults if they kept the covenant conditions; others believed that infant baptism immediately conferred regeneration, and a few of them explained sacramental rebirth by pointing out that the sacrament sealed an "absolute" covenant. The metaphor seemed infinitely malleable when applied to sacramental matters, so that controversies over baptism and the Lord's Supper maintained the interest in covenantal themes well into the nineteenth century.[8]

The association between sacramental and covenantal language was so deeply entrenched in the Old South that it shaped the baptismal theology of even the Episcopal high-church movement. When John Stark Ravenscroft (1772–1830) set out to confirm the sacramental feeling of Southern Episcopalianism, he did so by redefining the covenant. Ravenscroft was the son of a prosperous and genteel Virginia physician. He studied law at William and Mary, spent a few years as a gentleman farmer, and then became interested in religion, meeting for a time with a group of Republican Methodists. But their low views of ministerial authority disturbed him so much that he joined the Episcopal Church and by 1817 received ordination. After serving parishes in Mecklenburg County, Ravenscroft moved to the city as an assistant to Bishop Richard Channing Moore in Richmond. There he confirmed his belief that the success of the Church depended on its ability to convert the intellectual and influential classes and "with the aid of their example to build up congregations and parishes as opportunity might offer."[9] But Ravenscroft was also persuaded that social standing would be of no avail in the long run apart from a proper understanding of the Church as "the authorized source of agency between heaven and earth," and that required a redefinition of the covenant.[10]

High-church Episcopalians were active in the eighteenth century, but the consecration of John Henry Hobart as Bishop of New York in 1811 signaled the resurgence of an organized effort to assert the authority of the Church by reaffirming the necessity of a threefold ministry of bishops, priests, and deacons, standing in an unbroken apostolic succession, charged with responsibility for sacrament and liturgy. By 1822, when Hobart founded General Theological Seminary in New York, the conflict between high churchmen and their evangelical opponents within the denomination was underway, and Ravenscroft became one of Hobart's outspoken disciples. As Bishop of North Carolina after 1823, he used every opportunity to "bring our clergy to view" baptism more correctly, even to the point of withholding his official consent to the episcopal consecration of his friend William Meade, to whom he attributed a faulty understanding of Church and Sacrament.[11] Under his oversight North Carolina became a haven for high-church Episcopal clergy.

Southern Episcopalians had debated the sacramental issues in their *Theological Repertory* throughout 1820, and in the summer Ravenscroft found an occasion to expound his own views. When an earnest laywoman wrote him seeking guidance about the relationship between sacraments and rebirth, he responded in a lengthy letter that distinguished two meanings of "regeneration." The word could refer to the partial restoration of our capacity for spiritual improvement, but it also could refer to "our change in outward condition when we become openly and visibly parties to the new covenant." In this sense, regeneration occurred "in baptism," which by introducing them into the visible Church transformed infants, the heirs of sin, into "heirs of the promise."[12]

Like most earlier English and American theologians, Ravenscroft believed that the covenant was conditional. When clergy spoke of covenantal "conditions," however, they usually had in mind the requirement that men and women respond to God with faith and repentance. But according to Ravenscroft baptism itself fulfilled the condition: there was "no promise," he said, "but to the baptised believer."[13] By introducing infants into the Church and thus into the covenant, baptism brought regeneration, not simply according to a "judgment of charity" but "absolutely and virtually flowing from the promise."[14] When Ravenscroft expressed his ideas in public, the Presbyterian John Holt Rice charged that he had restricted the sovereignty of God by precluding any divine decision to extend saving grace beyond the boundaries of the visible Church. Ravenscroft responded by referring to the covenant. We do not speculate, he said, on God's "uncovenanted mercy." We venture to speak only of the revealed promise and its conditions:

> Is there any revealed means of obtaining an interest in the covenant ratified in the blood of Christ, other than by the application of its seal in the sacrament of baptism?[15]

The Church, he explained, originated in the covenant with Abraham, so Church and covenant were inextricably joined. There was no Church apart from the covenant; no covenant outside the Church.[16]

Ravenscroft did not intend to imply that every baptized person would remain within the covenant; he had no use for a Calvinist doctrine of indefectible grace.[17] Baptismal regeneration was real and effective, but infants could fall away from grace as they matured. In fact, repentance and conversion were simply the means through which the baptized sinner who had abused the grace of regeneration could be brought again into favor; such a "conversion," however, was a matter of free decision, accomplished by a will that had been empowered through the means of grace available in the Church.[18] Conversion was an appendage to the baptismal covenant.

Ravenscroft believed that religion was "throughout a reasonable service" and that the doctrine of baptismal regeneration was as reasonable as any other.[19] If his sacramental doctrine was irrational, he implied, then "the whole frame and polity of the Church" was in question, because sacerdotal power was inseparable from sacramental grace; the status of the minister rested on his sacramental office, which clearly elevated him above the laity. Ravenscroft's revered authorities were Edmund Law and George Bull, churchmen of the eighteenth century who also had combined sacramental and sacerdotal themes.[20]

He had influential allies, including Bishop James Kemp (1764–

1827) of Maryland and later Nicholas Hamner Cobbs (1795–1861), who in 1844 became the first Episcopal bishop of Alabama. Richard Channing Moore in Richmond joined Ravenscroft in affirming the doctrine of baptismal regeneration, though Moore insisted that baptismal grace be supplemented by a later conversion experience.[21] But Ravenscroft's journal entries took on a pessimistic cast as early as 1823, and the formation of a revitalized Episcopal Seminary at Alexandria, Virginia, in that year signaled the failure of high-church aspirations, for its founders and faculty became the leading figures in the "evangelical" wing of the Southern Episcopalians.[22] The school's first dean and professor of Biblical criticism was Reuel Keith (1792–1842), a graduate of Middlebury College in Vermont who had studied theology at Andover. Keith's sacramental views prompted Ravenscroft to observe that he knew no more of the Church than a horse.[23] The seminary's professor of systematic theology was William Holland Wilmer (1782–1827), a native of Maryland, educated at Washington College, whose *Episcopal Manual* (1815), the earliest formal presentation of the Church's doctrine in the South, defined baptism as a sign and seal of the covenant, not the fulfilment of its conditions. Wilmer explicitly denied that the sacrament effected regeneration.[24] Ravenscroft appealed to the authority of George Bull in trying to persuade him to change his mind, but Wilmer retorted that Bull was only a "fallible man," and he demanded Scriptural evidence that regeneration was bestowed by baptism.[25] Wilmer's opposition was a serious impediment. Four times president of the House of Clerical and Lay Deputies, president of William and Mary after 1826, he was a prominent antagonist. Ravenscroft had good reason to be pessimistic.

Ravenscroft's most powerful foe was William Meade (1789–1862), a Princeton graduate who for twenty years hold the top episcopal post in Virginia. Wholeheartedly committed to ministerial "improvement," Meade was one of the founders of the seminary at Alexandria, and he wrote extensively on pastoral, theological, historical, and sacramental topics, always in defense of the "evangelical" position. He could cite the writings of Richard Hooker, the Elizabethan apologist revered by the high-church party, but he also felt free to draw on the sacramental writings of John Calvin, who was anathema to the high churchmen.

Fearful that it would lead to superstition, Meade was wary of Ravenscroft's language about baptismal regeneration. Like Wilmer, he defined baptism as the seal of the covenant, a promise to believers and their children, and he warned against so identifying the seal with the covenant as to make baptism indispensable. Meade believed that the sacrament introduced infants into the Church and remitted their original sin, but he refused to say that baptism was "necessary to salvation." He preferred to speak of it as a "conditional" seal; it was a promise that the Spirit would embrace and nurture the baptized child. But even baptized children could grow up to resist the Spirit, so the efficacy of the sacrament depended finally on continuation in faith and repentance.[26] For Meade, therefore, as for other Episcopal evangelicals, the doctrines of sin and atonement, forgiveness and sanctification, faith and rebirth were more compelling than the ecclesiasticism, sacramentalism, and sacerdotalism of the high-church party.

After 1833 the English Oxford Movement offered renewed hope and encouragement to the American high churchmen. John Keble's sermons and devotional poetry, Edward Bouverie Pusey's treatises on baptismal regeneration, and John Henry Newman's Catholic interpretations of Anglican history and doctrine were better received in America than even in England.[27] But by 1840 an evangelical counterattack blocked the progress of Oxford sentiments, especially in the South. The Church in Virginia officially disclaimed all sympathy with what Meade called the "heretical opinions and Romanistic tendencies" of the Oxford theologians.[28] Even Bishop James Hervey Otey (1800–1863) of Tennessee, whose "Three Sermons" on the Church in 1843 persuaded his opponents that he was "laboring under an absolute monomania with regard to the [apostolic] succession," disapproved of Newman's activities.[29] When Bishop L. Sullivan Ives of North Carolina "defected" to Catholicism in 1852, he inadvertently helped to ensure that Southern Episcopalianism would retain its "evangelical" character throughout the nineteenth century.

In Ravenscroft's ideal church, sacramental consciousness and social status complemented each other. To the influential Lutheran pastors in the Southern coastal towns, however, it often seemed that sacramental traditionalism obstructed the effort to reach "men of wealth, of character, and of piety."[30] Many of the ministers in the two major Southern synods believed that the older sacramental doctrines of their denomination were either irrelevant or scandalous. Martin Luther had proclaimed that baptism as a Word and Work of God was a true sacrament even in the absence of faith, and he criticized any separation of the divine promise from its external sign. He believed that God was active in and through the tangible and visible element and could even speak of God as being "in and with" the water of baptism, blessing and sanctifying it as a means of grace and the bearer of His glory.[31] The Lutheran Augsburg Confession (1530) therefore claimed that baptism was necessary for salvation, and it condemned the Swiss Anabaptists for saying that children could be saved without the sacrament. But Luther's sentiments seemed a bit strong in the nineteenth-century South.

The Lutheran clergy in South Carolina cherished their reputation as moderate men, and they established close relationships with German Reformed congregations that were utterly opposed to traditional Lutheran sacramentalism. In North Carolina the clergy pledged in 1816 to accept the Augsburg Confession but then decided to allow latitude in interpreting the standards.[32] The interests of the leading Carolina Lutherans were manifest in their argument for a new Theological Seminary of the Evangelical Lutheran Synod of South Carolina and Adjacent States, established in 1830 and then moved in 1834 to Lexington, South Carolina.

> An enlightened age requires an intelligent ministry. . . . In order to enable our ministers to be useful in the present enlightened age, they must be qualified to show that religion is adapted to the most cultivated intellect, and draw arguments in its defence from the schools of philosophy, and the speculations of genius, as from a knowledge of the original languages of the Scriptures.[33]

To ministers intent on reaching an enlightened age, it seemed eccentric to dwell on the sacraments. John Bachman in Charleston repudiated the doctrine of baptismal regeneration, defined the sacrament only as a symbol and evidence of faith, and retained "the ordinance" of infant baptism largely for historical reasons. The seminary's ranking theologian, Ernest Lewis Hazelius, felt that sacramentalism was an obsession with divisive minutiae.[34]

To the Lutheran pastor in New Market, Virginia, however, concessions to the modern religious spirit seemed unnecessary and unfaithful. Paul Henkel (1754–1825) viewed with distaste such innovations as the substitution of modern English liturgies for the older German services, and his printing press, which he had operated since 1806, provided him the means to publicize his dissatisfaction.[35] Henkel did not fasten onto sacramental issues as the symbol of repristination. His own sacramental theology, as expressed in his *Catechism* (1811), was open to several interpretations. But in 1818 his son, David Henkel (1795–1831), began to complain about the lax sacramental doctrine of the North Carolina Synod, which in the following year summoned him to answer the charges that he had attributed salvation solely to the agency of baptism and refused Church fellowship to anyone who disagreed.[36] The North Carolinians adjudged him guilty of error, so in 1820 the Henkels met with a handful of clerical and lay delegates and formed the Tennessee Synod, which became the bastion of Lutheran confessionalism in the South.

David Henkel argued that if the substance of baptism was the Word—the promise of "spirit and life"—then the sacrament must be a means of regeneration, for the Word was saving, whether as preached or as proclaimed in the sacrament. In ratifying the covenant, a seal guaranteed the fruition of its promises. Most Southern Protestants would have agreed that the sacrament was a "visible Word," replete with doctrinal meaning and designed to move the mind and emotions through its symbolism. But Henkel believed that baptism was an efficacious Word that embraced even infants unable to comprehend it, though they later could resist it and fall from grace. A Word was not simply addressed to the understanding.[37]

When Henkel died in 1831 he seemed out of touch with his age. The future of Lutheranism appeared to belong to the "American Lutherans," led by Samuel Schmucker at Gettysburg Seminary in Pennsylvania, who wanted to revise or abandon the standard Lutheran sacramental doctrines. Schmucker denounced confessionalism, defended revivalist piety, and recommended revisions in the old formulas. But during the forties his proposals clashed with the rising tide of confessionalism, brought by a wave of immigrants from Germany. The newcomers settled mainly in the Midwest—

one group formed the Missouri Synod—but to the disciples of David Henkel their success seemed to vindicate the Tennessee position. In 1851 The Henkel Press triumphantly printed the first English translation of the *Christian Book of Concord*, the authoritative collection of Lutheran confessions. John Bachman continued to view the confessional movement as retrograde, even unscriptural, and he helped hold back the tide within the South. But after the Civil War it washed over the Lutheranism of the Carolinas.[38]

2. The Conditional Covenant

High-church Episcopalians and confessional Lutherans represented a minority voice within the Old South. To most Southern clergy their sacramental doctrine seemed eccentric, even superstitious. Alexander Campbell attracted attention when he preached that the aim of baptism was "remission of sins," but Campbell conceived of the sacrament as simply a formal sign expressing the attitude of God toward faithful adults and deriving its value from faith.[39] In the opinion of the Reformed and Wesleyan theologians who made the major inroads into the Southern town churches, the sacrament was no covenantal condition but rather the seal to a conditional covenant. The distinction came out of the seventeenth century, when Continental and English Reformed theologians had distinguished between a conditional covenant, binding on all persons, requiring repentance and faith, and an absolute covenant, intended solely for the elect, promising them the grace sufficient to perform the required conditions. By the beginning of the eighteenth century, theologians of all kinds—Calvinists and their critics—were speaking with highly diverse intentions of "covenantal conditions." And by the nineteenth, the Methodists and Presbyterians of the Old South had decided that the primary function of sacraments was to seal a conditional covenant, but they disagreed about what that meant.

The Methodist patriarch, John Wesley, had affirmed both baptismal regeneration and the need for conversion as a conscious adult experience of rebirth. Repeatedly he referred to the sacrament as the "ordinary means" of regeneration, a means to infuse a principle of grace and wash away the guilt of original sin. Baptism for

Wesley was the entrance to the covenant and the doorway to the Church; it was the means through which God usually bestowed the grace of salvation. Yet Wesley also believed that the grace of baptism could be lost, and he felt himself to be addressing men and women who were tempted to rely too heavily on the mere outward sacrament, without bringing to completion the principle that baptism implanted. Therefore he could also call upon the baptized to be "born again" and remind them that an outer ceremony performed in their past was not the rebirth that they were now required to seek. Wesley was both a sacramentalist and an evangelist—a combination that his American disciples found difficult to duplicate.[40] Even his protégé Richard Watson in England permitted the covenant metaphor to overshadow the doctrine of sacramental regeneration, and when the American Methodists looked to England for an authoritative word, they decided to reprint, not Wesley's baptismal writings, but rather Watson's work on "The Nature, Subjects, and Mode of Christian Baptism."[41]

In practice the revivalist enthusiasm of the early Methodists in the South overwhelmed their sacramental structures. Only in the early nineteenth century did they really begin to think of themselves as a Church rather than a "society," and therefore at first they did not always treat the sacrament even as the doorway to Church membership. They preferred to think of fellowship in the Church as the terminus of a rigorous probationary period and thus as the result of inner experience, faithfulness, and self-discipline. By 1840 the Methodist *Discipline* referred merely to the "dedication" of children in baptism, implying that the sacrament was a parental pledge rather than an effective rite.[42]

To the town pastors who began writing sacramental treatises during the late 1840s and early 1850s, however, a merely symbolic doctrine of baptism seemed unduly vulnerable to Baptist criticism. They wanted to prove that the sacrament had "consequences of the deepest, broadest, highest, and most enduring character."[43] At the same time, they did not want to be associated with the current reassertion of baptismal regeneration in the Church of England. On this point Wesley was an embarrassment, especially when critics of Southern Methodism cited his sacramental views. In reply the Methodist clergy either denied that Wesley had ever believed in sacramental rebirth or they claimed that he had renounced the dogma as his insight deepened.[44] Thomas Summers in Nashville appealed to universal experience and observation to prove that the sacramentalism erroneously attributed to Wesley was a "simple absurdity."[45]

The Methodist alternative was to define baptism as the seal to a universal but conditional covenant. The Wesleyans established its universality by documenting with Biblical texts the assertion that Christ's vicarious death was unlimited in scope: he died for all. Every infant was therefore within the covenant. Reformed theologians insisted that only the children of the faithful could be accounted participants in the covenant from birth, but the Wesleyans claimed that because the atonement established the covenant and because "all children sustained the same relation to the death of Christ," therefore all stood within the covenant and had the right to receive its baptismal seal.[46] Baptism was not the entrance to the covenant; on that issue Leonidas Rosser of Fredericksburg, Virginia, expressed the Methodist consensus:

> Baptism, as in the case of circumcision, was added as a seal after the covenant of grace was made with man, not to give efficacy to the covenant . . . but as confirmatory of it. Thus, children are not baptized in order that they may be brought into covenant with God, for they are already recognized by God as his children, and embraced in his covenant, by virtue of the atonement.[47]

Baptists charged that the Wesleyan argument undercut the doctrine of original sin and obviated any need for a redeemer.[48] The Methodists replied that the universality of original sin, though real and tragic, had been overcome through a universal atonement. Though born in sin, infants were at the moment of birth born also into forgiveness. In fact, baptism signified that the guilt of original sin was unconditionally forgiven, so that an infant, incapable of either faith or repentance, was nevertheless in a "state of justification." The sacrament did not convey salvation, but when administered to infants it formally recognized and celebrated their prior release from condemnation.[49]

The covenant, however, was conditional; its benefits were contingent; so the efficacy of the sacrament was also conditional. As they grew to maturity, children invariably fell from their initial state of justification, nullifying the covenantal arrangement. Only through repentance and faith could they hope to redeem the divine pledge of forgiveness and salvation. In the baptismal washing God pledged himself to grant "all the blessings of the covenant of grace," but only on the condition of faith and repentance.[50] Summers described the conditions in terms characteristic of rational orthodoxy. In baptism, he said, we pledge to renounce our sinfulness, to obey, and "to believe the whole revelation" of God. "And that we may do so rationally it binds us to search the Scriptures . . . to canvass the evidences of Christianity."[51]

The Methodist sacramental theologians believed, however, that baptism was not simply a pledge but also a "means" of grace that helped to produce the qualities it symbolized. The sacrament was the entrance into the Church and so the ordinance of initiation into the midst of other salutary influences: the Word, prayer, and exhortation. Baptism placed the infant "in a relation which secures for it the ordinary blessings of the cross." And the vivid symbolism of the sacrament was designed to "assist" the unregenerate in the quest for grace.[52] Rosser cited John Calvin, usually the target of unabated Methodist criticism, to support his claim that baptism was "an assistance and support to faith," not merely a pledge of obedience.[53] Yet in discussing the effect of baptism the Wesleyans revealed the extent to which the rationalism of orthodoxy had permeated their sacramental piety. Summers was typical in offering psychological interpretations of baptismal efficacy.

> Whatever is suggestive of holy thoughts and emotions—whatever brings the beauty of holiness before the mind—whatever impresses us with its necessity and points out the mode of its attainment, must minister to our sanctification. Baptism does all this.[54]

By producing an inward comprehension of doctrinal truths, by moving the mind and heart, the sacrament was an effective means of grace.

Summers called baptism "a saving ordinance"; James L. Chapman in Memphis went so far as to say that in God's "ordinary plan" of salvation the Christian had to be "born of water" as well as of the Spirit. He refused to consign unbaptized infants to damnation, but he denied that the condition of the covenant was merely belief.

Only the person who believed "as a baptized person" would ordinarily be saved.[55] Other Methodists disagreed; Chapman and Rosser came under attack from pastors within the denomination who wanted to safeguard the conviction that "religion is of the heart, independent of all outward ceremonies."[56] But Summers received the open approval and support of the South's Methodist editors and bishops.[57] The ranking clergy were ready for some outward ceremony.

As the conversionist spirituality of the Wesleyans stood in tension with their sacramental heritage, so the Reformed doctrine of election created sacramental problems for the Presbyterians. Although the defense of infant baptism occupied the attention of major figures in American Presbyterianism, they were hard-pressed to integrate sacramental piety fully into a theology of predestination.[58] In his *Lectures on Paedobaptism* (1834), Samuel J. Cassels of Washington, Georgia, complained that baptism was too often regarded as "a loose appendage to our church." Typically he tried to rectify the problem by explaining the sacrament's covenantal nature.[59] Many ministers ignored the issue; even the *Southern Presbyterian Review* acknowledged that "the intellectual power of their system" led most of the denomination's clergy to elevate the pulpit over the sacramental liturgy.[60] And in their descriptions of baptism they often transformed the sacramental font into another kind of pulpit.

The classical expounders of Reformed sacramental theology, Ulrich Zwingli and John Calvin, had disagreed about baptism. Zwingli described it as a sign of obligation and a pledge of obedience, but Calvin thought that God's promise of salvation rather than any human pledge of obedience was the substance of the sacrament. He believed that baptism was primarily a divine gift designed to incorporate persons into the Church and to reveal God's merciful intentions toward them. Therefore Calvin taught that the sacrament strengthened faith and helped sanctify the life of the Christian; it was an instrument through which God effectively performed what the sacrament symbolized, but only for the elect. Calvin never truly harmonized his sacramental feeling and his predestinarian theology.[61] The Southern Presbyterians, moreover, were not quite "Calvinist" and not quite "Zwinglian"; the covenant permitted them to stand somewhere in between.

As a divine seal, they argued, baptism ratified God's covenant promise: it certified that the divine mediatorial activity symbolized by the visible sign had actually taken place, and it bound God to fulfill his promise of salvation. But since only the elect were destined for salvation, the Reformed pastors had to admit that God was not obliged to save all who were baptized. The covenant required true faith, and God fulfilled his promise when he saved the truly faithful, who were synonymous with the elect. For the elect the sacramental promise was as good as the deed; the visible confirmation of a divine promise was synonymous with its fulfillment —a point that led both Wesleyans and Baptists occasionally to accuse the Presbyterians of teaching a covert form of baptismal regeneration. But for the reprobate the baptismal seal was fruitless. Presbyterians denied that the sacrament conferred saving grace, or removed the stain of original sin, or justified the baptized infant, just as they denied that baptism was necessary for salvation.[62]

Some refused even to say that baptism conferred Church membership. The Puritans who had composed the standard Reformed creed, the Westminster Confession (1647), had assumed that baptism admitted members into the visible Church.[63] The topic, however, was not fully clarified, and later Richard Baxter argued that the children of Christians were in some sense members before baptism.[64] By the nineteenth century most Southern Presbyterian clergy believed that "the children of believing parents" were included in the covenant and therefore "born in the gospel church" prior to baptism.[65] The sacrament was "a recognition of membership," wrote one minister, who added that even adults joined the Church before being baptized.[66]

Baptism was only as effective as the covenant that it sealed, but any accent on the power of the covenant became an oblique affirmation of the potency of its seal, and the Presbyterians had confidence in the covenant. Like their Puritan predecessors they still supposed that God usually cast the line of election through the loins of godly parents.[67] The Baptists accused them of trying to "make religion hereditary," of suggesting that salvation was a natural inheritance.[68] When pressed, no Reformed theologian would have seriously entertained such a thought. Yet the Presbyterians did observe that genuine piety seemed to flow in familial streams.[69] The Synod of Georgia reminded its members that God was "covenant-keeping" with faithful families. In one congregation, the synod reported, every child who had received "the seal of the covenant" eventually "shared in the saving influences of the Holy Spirit."[70]

The sacrament ratified and guaranteed the privileges of covenant-membership; it entitled the children of the faithful to the means of grace by which the elect among them would experience God's effectual calling. And the Presbyterian clergy were persuaded that churchly nurture "generally" produced happy effects.[71] But they thought that baptism came to fruition only through pious nurture; the pulpit was the extension of the baptismal rite. George D. Armstrong (1813–1899) of Norfolk, Virginia, discovered the metaphor that expressed the sacramental rationalism of the Reformed pastors. A graduate of Princeton and Union Theological Seminary, one time professor of chemistry at Washington College in Lexington, and pastor of Norfolk's First Presbyterian Church for over forty years, Armstrong became widely known through his defense of slavery and his description of the sacrament. In his *Doctrine of Baptism* (1857) he explained that baptism sealed the right of Church membership—a commonplace notion. But then he developed an extended analogy between the Church and the academy. The visible Church, from its first institution, he said, "possessed the character of a school." Under the Old Testament dispensation the Church of Abraham was a school in which disciples were "trained," and God had commanded the patriarch to enter his "scholars" into the academy "in earliest childhood." The New Testament had brought no essential change, so Armstrong interpreted Jesus's Great Commission in Matthew 28:19 with the aid of pedagogical imagery: "Go ye, therefore, and . . . make scholars of all nations."[72] Only by exercising their right to education, government, and discipline within the Church could the baptized infants of faithful parents realize the efficacy of the sacrament.[73] Learning was the completion of the liturgy.

3. A Sign of Faith

Infant baptism was "irrational," and it therefore threatened to "injure the credit of religion with the reflecting men of the world."[74]

So wrote Robert Boyté Crawford Howell, an urban Baptist preacher who spent most of his career at the elegant Gothic First Baptist Church in Nashville, where he preached for over twenty years to some of the town's leading citizens. His prestige ensured his frequent selection as president of the Southern Baptist Convention. But Howell also wanted his denomination to partake of a certain prestige; he yearned to attract the "reflecting" portion of the community. The son of a yeoman farmer, he identified himself with the "planter" tradition, which he sought to redefine within a town environment. Howell believed that the pressing demand of the times was the creation of an urbane generation of Baptist preachers who would be acceptable in the towns and cities. He helped to form a Tennessee Baptist Conference for Ministerial Improvement that would send the Church's future leaders to the University of Nashville to be polished and refined, and he campaigned for a Southern seminary to complete their theological education. His pride in the rationality of Baptist practice and his confidence in its appeal to the respectable classes expressed his broader ambitions for the denomination.[75]

Howell was hardly typical of the antebellum Southern Baptist preacher, but his sacramental polemic summarized a consensus that had been standard for three centuries. Apart from their rhetoric about reasonableness, Howell's treatises consisted of time-honored Biblical argumentation. Methodists and Presbyterians read 1 Corinthians 7:14, discovered that infants were there designated as being holy, and concluded that they deserved the baptismal seal of holiness; Howell replied that this was no covenantal holiness, entitling to baptism, but matrimonial holiness, denoting the child as legitimate despite the paganism of one parent. His opponents observed that Acts 2:38–39 contained a promise both to believers and to their children; Howell replied that the promise was simply to send Christ. It did not justify infant baptism. Paedobaptists recalled Christ's desire to have children brought to him; Baptists insisted that Christ called them for a blessing, not for baptism. Paedobaptists pointed out that the apostles baptized entire households; Baptists answered that no text mentioned infants among those families. And then the Baptists observed that Jesus's commission to his followers instructed them first to make disciples and then to baptize, a procedure fitted only for adult believers. The arguments had not changed since the seventeenth century.[76]

The Baptists still insisted, in fact, as English Baptists had insisted in the 1640s, that the doctrine of the covenant was "the hinge on which the whole argument turns."[77] The Baptist movement in America had grown out of the Puritan ferment in England during the reign of James I, a period when theologians were fascinated with the covenant. Baptist theologians had always criticized the sacramental implications of the covenant theme, and the Southern Baptists were no exception. They did not propose to do away with the doctrine of the covenant. Like almost everyone else, they described the relationship between God and his creatures as a "covenant" relation. But while Methodists, Lutherans, and Presbyterians contended that the covenant with Abraham, sealed by circumcision, was identical in substance with the Christian covenant, which therefore required an analogous seal, Baptists always distinguished two covenants. They found in Genesis 17:1 a "covenant of circumcision" in which God promised Abraham temporal blessings for his natural descendants, and in Genesis 12:4 a "covenant of grace," a "new covenant," transacted between the Father and the Son and then simply announced to Abraham. The Abrahamic covenant, sealed with circumcision, had no relevance for first-century Gentiles or nineteenth-century Christians. In basing infant baptism on that covenant, the paedobaptists had confused a national promise to ancient Jews with the promise of salvation.[78]

The Baptists believed that their competitors could not, in any case, sustain the analogy between baptism and circumcision. An abrogated rite, they believed, could not justify a rule binding for Christians. Baptism manifestly did not succeed circumcision, for the two rites were dissimilar: women, for example, were baptized but not circumcised, and circumcision did not, in its symbolism, have anything in common with the baptismal imagery of death, burial, and resurrection. The issue, wrote Howell, touched on the fundamentals of Biblical interpretation: no external institution in the Old Testament could be interpreted as prefiguring any external institution in the New Testament. To forget that rule was to transform the Christian Church into a mere extension of Judaism.[79]

Howell's commentary illustrated the continuing popularity of the ancient method of Biblical interpretation known as "typology." Ever since the first century, Christian exegetes had discovered throughout the Old Testament a variety of events, ceremonies, and individuals ordained by God to foreshadow the Incarnation, and despite their expressed allegiance to a sober grammatical and historical method of interpretation, the Southern clergy still believed that the priests, kings, rites, and laws of the ancient Jews were "types" that prefigured Christ's earthly appearance and revealed him in veiled form to Israel. Sixteenth-century Protestant reformers had often based their sacramental theology on the typological analogy between Jewish circumcision and the Christian sacrament, and similar forms of sacramental typology persisted among the Episcopal, Methodist, Lutheran, and Presbyterian clergy of the Old South.[80] But Howell insisted that Jewish types had only "spiritual" antitypes: circumcision typified regeneration by the Spirit, not baptism by water.[81] Some of his opponents agreed but added that the "spiritual meaning" of Jewish and Christian sacraments was sufficiently similar to establish the analogy between them and justify infant baptism.[82] The Baptists, however, concluded that the Old Testament forms prefigured only "spiritual truths" and had no relevance for the external institutions of Christendom.[83]

The Baptists preferred therefore to call baptism a "sign" of inward spirituality rather than a seal of God's covenant. John Dagg contended that the sacrament was "nowhere in the scriptures called a seal." Baptism was a public pledge, a ceremony of Christian profession. Since the Scripture required profession and appointed baptism for that purpose, the sacrament could be considered indirectly "necessary to salvation." Every disciple was obligated to make a baptismal profession of faith. But the sacrament, or, as the Baptists preferred to call it, the "ordinance," was a sign of fidelity by the believer, not an efficacious divine promise.[84] Baptist theologians denied even that the rite was the entrance into the Church: the "visible saints" within the Church were admitted, as they had been in Puritan New England, through a judgment of the congregation upon their "faith and obedience," and then they were baptized.[85] The "light of piety" was usually so transparent that most members could safely be assumed to have "undergone a saving change" prior to membership; their baptism simply attested to their conversion.[86]

The Southern Baptists held fast to the old Puritan ideal of a pure Church filled with regenerate saints. Within such a vision of the Church, notions of baptismal grace could be considered only subversive distractions.

Arguments over baptism were difficult to resolve because they sprang from differing conceptions of the Church and therefore had immediate practical consequences. The topic of the Church evoked an intense reaction in mid-nineteenth century America. The historian Philip Schaff wrote in 1846 that "the great central theme of the Present, around which all religious and theological movements revolve, is the Church question."[87] His words applied not only to ecclesiastical politics, confessionalism, and sacramentalism in Germany, Catholic liberalism and ultramontanism in France and Italy, and the English Oxford movement, but also to the American Lutherans debating the authority of the confessions; Episcopalians struggling over order and ceremony; Methodists and Baptists debating the locus of governing authority in their denominations; Landmark Baptists expounding "axioms" and "principles" to prove that the only true churches were local institutions that practiced believer's baptism and stood in continuous historical succession since the time of Christ; Presbyterians divided over the function of the eldership and over claims for the *jure divino* status of presbyterial order; and Roman Catholics uncertain about the power of local trustees.[88] The Church struggles cut across denominational lines and pitted revivalists against sacramentalists and traditionalists against innovators and reformers of almost every variety. The American theologian John Williamson Nevin spoke of a "silent war" in "almost every denomination" over the nature of the Church.[89]

4. *The Presence of Christ*

The South's open debates over the Lord's Supper reflected the differing views of the Church. The discussions usually had little to do with traditional sacramental issues: the divisive problem was always admission to the sacrament—a question that referred directly to the nature of the Church. Methodists believed that the Lord's Supper was a meal for the faithful, but, following Wesley's example, they also tended to admit repentant "seekers" to the sacrament in hope that they would find there the grace sufficient for conversion. Episcopalians usually invited their own "orthodox" members; Presbyterians extended an invitation only to the truly faithful and, on occasion, to their older children. By the 1850s most Baptist churches had decided to admit only faithful members of their own congregations. Their policy of "close communion" provoked most of the open debates over the Lord's Supper.[90]

When they did comment on the nature of the sacrament, Wesleyan and Reformed theologians looked upon it either as a "memorial of Christ," the classical Zwinglian doctrine,[91] or as a locus of Christ's "spiritual presence," the view that Calvin had defended[92] But they rarely went into detail—an omission that in itself revealed their indifference to the nuances of sacramental piety and theology. Only after 1846 did the eucharistic issues occupy the attention of any major Southern theologians.

In that year John Williamson Nevin published *The Mystical Presence*, a learned tract that he supplemented with articles on the Church fathers and reformers in the new *Mercersburg Review*. His studies of the Church, Christ, and the sacraments signaled the emergence of a new theological movement, nurtured within the unlikely environs of tiny Mercersburg Seminary in southeast Pennsylvania. Nevin argued that the eternal Logos, the second Person of the Trinity, had taken the human and divine natures into himself in an abiding organic union, and that salvation was the completion of humanity through a mystical union with the Incarnate Christ, who was uniquely present in the actual but supernatural Church. Hence the eucharist was also a mysterious indissoluble union of supernatural grace and visible elements, providing a special communion with Christ, who was spiritually present in both his divine nature and his humanity, including the substance—the "vivific power"—of his flesh.

Nevin's doctrine, clothed in an Hegelian Idealist philosophy, thoroughly provoked his former mentor and colleague at Princeton Seminary, Charles Hodge, who after a two-year silence issued in *The Princeton Review* a refutation in which he exposed allegedly heretical propensities in Nevin's thought. Hodge said that Nevin exaggerated the unity of the two natures in Christ, and he insinuated that Nevin's language about a mystical union covertly substituted a theory of inherent human righteousness in place of the doctrine that God graciously "imputed" Christ's righteousness to the elect believer. Since the two natures in Christ were distinct, Hodge argued, sacramental communion comprehended only the divine life, which alone possessed the divine property of omnipresence. Hodge interpreted the sacrament with spiritualistic categories, concluding finally that to eat and drink of Christ was simply equivalent to having faith in him, a view that Calvin had explicitly denied. Nevin responded by depicting Hodge as an unwitting proponent of sectarian subjectivism, and their debate continued intermittently until the outbreak of the Civil War.[93]

When in 1857 John Adger assumed the chair of Church History at Columbia Seminary, with the duty of lecturing on Church polity and sacramental theology, most Southerners had apparently chosen to ignore the Mercersburg-Princeton debate. *The Southern Presbyterian Review*, which in 1850 printed an article that even opposed the consecration of the bread and wine at the Lord's Supper, failed to review Nevin's *Mystical Presence*.[94] *The Presbyterial Critic*, a journal published in Baltimore by two conservative Southerners, Thomas Peck and Stuart Robinson, suggested that Nevin had been treated unfairly and commended him for focusing attention on the nature of the Church, but the journal also warned that he was "open to suspicion."[95] Adger made certain, however, that his students understood the Northern debate, and in his mind Hodge, not Nevin, was suspect.

Before graduating from Princeton in 1833 Adger had studied under Hodge, whom he believed to be a "great theologian." But Adger was a man of wide-ranging experience and firm convictions. A twelve-year tenure as a missionary to the Armenians had given him an unusual exposure to cultural and religious diversity, and he eventually decided that Hodge never quite comprehended the subtleties of either Church government or sacramental doctrine. Several years of labor in a mission to the slaves in Charleston preceded his appointment to Columbia Seminary, where his classroom responsibilities required close study of Calvin's *Institutes of the Christian Religion*.

He decided to construct his annual lectures from two sources: the *Institutes* and the writings of the disputants at Princeton and Mercersburg. And Adger did not assume a stance of neutrality.

The lectures were in part devoted to rebutting the article in which Hodge had first criticized Nevin's book. When he lectured on the Lord's Supper, Adger openly affirmed and approved Nevin's interpretation of Calvinist doctrine. He drew upon the historical investigations in Nevin's *Mystical Presence* while warning his students that Hodge's analysis of Calvin was "imperfect, partial, and unsatisfactory." And he added that the major voices of Southern Presbyterianism—R. J. Breckinridge at Danville Seminary and James H. Thornwell at Columbia—shared none of Hodge's reservations. Like Nevin, however, Adger recognized that his "high" sacramental views distinguished him from some of the authoritative figures of American Reformed theology, especially from such late eighteenth-century proponents of the "New Divinity" as Samuel Hopkins and Joseph Bellamy and from such nineteenth-century "New School" theologians as Albert Barnes. But Adger also criticized his colleagues in the Old School Presbyterian tradition, and he accused even Jonathan Edwards of falling away from the historic Calvinist position. He fully accepted Nevin's negative judgment on the "Modern Puritan" tradition.[96]

Had he wished, Adger might well have named his fellow Southerner in Richmond, Robert L. Dabney, among the apostates from Calvinist sacramental doctrine. Dabney had close personal and theological relations with Hodge, who urged him to teach at Princeton. But when his colleagues convinced him that his departure would destroy Union Seminary, Dabney remained in Virginia, where after 1853 he used his growing influence to propagate the sacramental doctrine that Nevin and Adger found so distressing.[97] Dabney regularly told his students that Calvin had advanced an "impossible theory" that violated not only the testimony of Scripture but also the "intuitive reason." He believed that Zwingli had been far more emancipated from superstition and prejudice than the other major sixteenth-century reformers, and he shared Zwingli's view of the Lord's Supper as a "commemorative seal," though he did not think that the Zwinglian doctrine sufficiently emphasized the "sealing nature" of the sacraments. In any case, Dabney's sacramental lectures ensured that the fledgling Presbyterian ministers of Virginia were thoroughly cognizant of Calvin's "untenable and unscriptural" aberrations. He accused the Mercersburg School of proposing a species of "modern semi-

Pantheism," and he urged his students to disregard Nevin's notions about a "mystical union," which had led to "gross and extreme" views of the Lord's Supper, as well as other "unscriptural perversions."[98]

In their sacramental lectures, Dabney and Adger presented two divergent Reformed eucharistic doctrines. Recognizing that sacramental thought embodied assumptions about Christ and salvation, they discussed in detail themes that were only implicit in the passing references to the Lord's Supper among most other Southern Protestant theologians. Their differences therefore provide the indices for identifying the most common Southern sacramental doctrines and for discerning the Christology of the rational orthodox theologians.

Adger took the Incarnation as his starting point: there he discovered "the sublime truth of life for us."[99] He believed that Jesus was the fully human embodiment of a fully divine life, and he shared with Nevin a reluctance to overemphasize the distinction between Christ's two natures. Adger did not accept the Roman Catholic and Lutheran doctrine that the divine and human natures interpenetrated one another through a mutual communication of properties (*communicatio idiomatum*), but he did accent the continuity between the humanity and the divinity because he thought that an exaggerated disjunction would diminish sacramental doctrine. Dabney, however, assiduously maintained the distinction, criticizing both Calvin and at least one well-known fellow Southern theologian for the lack of precision in their doctrine. R. J. Breckinridge at Danville warned in 1858 that the divine and human natures of Christ should not be "divided" even "in contemplation." The warning disturbed Dabney. He felt it to be "incautious" and promptly pointed out that the human nature of Christ obviously underwent experiences alien to his divinity. Dabney suggested that even Calvin's Christology, implicit in his sacramental doctrine, insufficiently distinguished the omnipresent divine nature from the finite, fleshly humanity with its "essential attributes of locality and dimension."[100]

When pressed, Dabney would have joined with Adger in affirming the unity of Christ's Person; and both of them believed, with most Southern Protestant theologians, that the mode of unity was the mutual concurrence of both natures in the Person of Christ.

How, then, does one explain the differences of emphasis and why were they sufficiently important to elicit concern? One answer lies in three preceding centuries of Reformed theological development. By the seventeenth century, Reformed dogmaticians had begun to formulate and espouse a rational principle according to which the finite could never comprehend or contain the infinite. By late in the century, the phrase *finitum non capax infiniti* had become an axiom governing Reformed sacramental and Christological doctrine, ensuring that no Calvinist would ever confuse or confound the infinite divine nature of Christ with his finite humanity. It became axiomatic to the seventeenth-century dogmaticians, and also to most theologians within the Church of England, that finite human nature, even the human nature of Christ, could not, despite Lutheran claims to the contrary, embody the infinite divine nature.

Dabney was the heir of this dogmatic tradition, which he derived largely from Turretin in Geneva. But with Nevin's help, Adger discovered the Calvin who antedated the scholastic systematizers. Consequently he recovered something of Calvin's lingering affinities with Catholic humanism. Calvin, too, had refuted Lutheran claims that Christ's human nature embodied the properties of his divinity, and one could argue that the *finitum non capax infiniti* was implicit even in his own theology. But the recent research of doctrinal historians suggests that it was Calvin's seventeenth-century successors (and opponents) who in developing and systematizing the concept distorted Calvin's thought by ignoring the residues of Catholic tradition that he retained.[101] In any case, it became a standard complaint of Southern Lutheran traditionalists that the failure of Reformed and Wesleyan theologians to accept a real corporeal presence of Christ in the Lord's Supper resulted from their application of "reason and the principles of philosophy" to Christological doctrine.[102] Whether they stood with Adger or Dabney, most Southern theologians were inclined to adopt a Reformed, not a Lutheran or Catholic, doctrine of Christ.

Disagreements about the nature of Christ led to disputes over salvation. Having begun with the Incarnation, Adger argued that salvation was the reconstruction of the created self through communion with the incarnate "life" of Christ. Salvation in his view was not merely the result of an arbitrary forensic "imputation" of Christ's righteousness to the elect believer. "There is a legal difficulty which justification removes. But does there not remain a difficulty as to the vital connection? Must there not be some natural tie of life betwixt the Redeemer and his people?"[103] The question was reminiscent of a crucial distinction between the sixteenth-century theologies of Philip Melanchthon, who understood justification solely as imputation, and Calvin, who wanted to speak simultaneously of justification and union with Christ. Adger stood with Calvin. Dabney was closer to Melanchthon; he had no desire to discard the motif of "union with Christ," but for Dabney salvation was, at bottom, God's merciful imputation of righteousness to the unrighteous.[104]

The consequences of their disagreements about Christ and salvation were manifest in their sacramental doctrines. Because he believed that the human and divine natures of Christ were joined in an organic personal union, Adger concluded that the spiritual presence of Christ in the Lord's Supper necessarily included his human nature, which was "the connecting link between his Godhood and our manhood." He therefore insisted that true life for the Christian depended on communion with the flesh of Christ, not simply with his Spirit.

> Others say we do have some kind of communion with Christ but it is spiritual, and not of his flesh and blood; whereas he says, "My flesh is meat indeed," and that we have no life unless we eat that flesh and drink that blood.[105]

Adger denied that sacramental eating was synonymous with faith: "It is rather a consequence of faith."[106] He did not believe that the presence of Christ was corporeal, but Adger could speak, like Calvin, of a real spiritual presence that comprehended both the divine and human natures of Christ and that could not be reduced to a psychological event.

As an orthodox Reformed theologian, Dabney had to affirm that the Lord's Supper was a means of union with Christ. But he defined that union in such a way that eucharistic communion became little more than a didactic message designed to produce an inward comprehension of doctrinal truths with correspondingly appropriate emotional reactions. For Dabney the phrase "union with

Christ" meant simply that the Spirit had operated in the same manner, though with differing degrees of effectiveness, in both Christ and the believer, creating a similar quality of spiritual life in both of them. Christ and the elect shared common graces, affections, and volitions; this common possession constituted their unity, which Dabney carefully described as a "mediate union." But the sacramental consequences were clear.

The Lord's Supper simply designated the divine promise that the elect would experience the blessings of faith and sanctification; it foreshadowed and produced a certain quality of inwardness, and this alone constituted sacramental communion with Christ. Dabney not only denied that the sacramental presence included the human nature of Christ, but he also disavowed the Calvinist teaching about a substantial, though spiritual, union between Christ and the believer in the sacramental rite itself.

> Is the vital union, then, only a secret relationship between Christ and the soul instituted when faith is first exercised and constituted by the indwelling and operation of the Holy Ghost: Or, is it a mysterious yet substantial conjunction of the spiritual substance, soul, to the whole substance of the mediatorial humanity? In a word, does the spiritual vitality propagate itself in a mode strictly analogous to that, in which vegetable vitality is propagated from the stock into the graft, by actual conjunction of substance. Now Calvin answers, emphatically: the union is of the latter kind. His view seems to be, that not only the mediatorial Person, but especially the corporeal part thereof has been established by the incarnation, as a sort of duct through which the inherent spiritual life of God, the fountain, is transmitted to believers, through the mystical union.[107]

Calvin's position seemed to Dabney to be, at best, "overstrained." Dabney thought that the Lord's Supper was a means of grace, but only because it represented and signified to the intelligent believer the "central truths of redemption." The sacramental actions and elements symbolized Christian doctrine for the benefit of the sanctified understanding. Dabney therefore equated eucharistic feeding with faith, the classical Zwinglian position. To feed upon Christ, he said, was to believe in him. Sacramental eating differed in no essential respect from any other faithful act.[108]

It would be saying too much to call John Adger a disciple of Nevin and the Mercersburg School. For years, though, students at Columbia seminary absorbed an interpretation of Calvinist theology that had its roots in the historical research being carried out at Mercersburg. During a period in which many journals boycotted Nevin's writings for fear of his alleged "Romanism," Adger identified himself with the interpretations of Reformed sacramental thought that Nevin had advanced. Students at Union, meanwhile were learning of Calvin's excesses.

The distinctions between Dabney and Adger mark the boundaries within which most Southern theologians remained—not only the Presbyterians but also the Wesleyans, Baptists, Episcopalians, and most of the Lutherans outside the Tennessee Synod. The choice was between Calvin and Zwingli, communion or commemoration, sacramental mystery or didactic message. The lack of attention to the details of the eucharistic tradition indicates that sacramental mystery seemed either suspect or irrelevant, and even among such "sacramentalists" as Adger the duality between spirit and flesh remained a persistent assumption.

The Roman Catholics, in any case, chided the Protestant clergy for having lost their sacramental sensitivities. The Catholics claimed that there were seven sacraments, not simply two, and that they permeated all of existence, from birth to death. Baptism, confirmation, ordination to the priesthood, marriage, the Mass, penance, and extreme unction marked with supernatural grace the milestones of human life. And of course the Catholic theologians were far less inclined than their Protestant counterparts to offer psychological interpretations of sacramental efficacy. They affirmed baptismal regeneration and they insisted that through the miracle of transubstantiation the elements of bread and wine actually became in substance the real body and blood of Christ, who was then sacrificed in the Mass.

Even the Catholic theologians, however, could not ignore the prevailing accent on sacramental "rationality." John England pointed out repeatedly that Catholic baptism did not ensure salvation, at least for adults: sacraments contained and conferred the grace that they signified, but only to men and women with the proper internal dispositions. He acknowledged, moreover, that it was incumbent upon him to prove the reasonableness of transubstantiation. I have, he said, never "known an attempt to defend the doctrine upon the ground of its being a mystery, which would indeed be a silly effort, and no proof." So England proceeded to expound the epistemologies of "modern philosophers" and medieval schoolmen in an effort to show that Catholic sacramental doctrine was really no more mysterious than nineteenth-century chemistry.[109]

It was "illogical and unphilosophical" of Protestants, he said, to charge that the doctrine of transubstantiation contradicted either the senses or the reason. Even modern philosophers, chemists, and geologists denied that the senses could reveal the nature of "substances." Senses could take cognizance only of appearances, and even in "the mineral kingdom and other departments of nature" one substance could take on the appearance of another. Catholics, said England, were merely asserting, in accordance with a typological interpretation of the Old Testament and a literal reading of the New, that the body and blood of Christ could appear in the humble guise of bread and wine, a miracle, to be sure, but one fully consistent with the epistemology of science. And he insisted, moreover, that Protestants erred in saying that Christ's body could not be present in more than one place at the same time. It was, again, "unphilosophic" of them to assume that a body in its "spiritualized" state must be subject to the natural laws of matter. The Protestants, not the Catholics, said England, bore the burden of irrationality, for when they spoke of "eating by faith" or "eating" a symbol, they simply collapsed into unintelligibility.[110]

England's reliance on the persuasive power of dialectic, his appeal to science and philosophy, and his unusual insistence on the "spiritualized" nature of Christ's presence in the Eucharist represented, to some extent, a break with an older sacramental sensibility. He held on to the mysterious, but he could also sound like a man fully convinced about the rationality of mystery.

The Protestant clergy, however, went far beyond John England in their effort to fit sacramental doctrine into the world-view of rational orthodoxy. They valued the sacraments primarily for their pedagogical usefulness. Baptism and the Lord's Supper graphically taught about a covenant-keeping God, and thus symbolized the rationality of divine activity. The ceremonies instructed the mind, purified the passions, and reassured anxious believers. Sacraments were visible words, and words were the instruments of the sanctified reason.

CHAPTER EIGHT

A RATIONAL WORLD:
THEODICY

The early nineteenth century was the era of theodicy in Southern religious thought. By "theodicy" the clergy meant the vindication of God's power, goodness, and rationality, and their preoccupation with the topic was the logical consequence of their whole conception of theology. In defending the justice and benevolence of God, they were asserting that their ideals, aspirations, and moral demands were congruent with the ultimate nature of reality. If God is not benevolent, wrote a Methodist, then our own benevolent efforts are "unconnected with any of his governing purposes."[1] If God was arbitrary or irrational there was no coherent explanation of the world that could evoke the commitments and maintain the behavior that the clergy wished to promote.[2] They were optimistic and confident, free of serious doubts, but their very optimism made them impatient with any theology that seemed unable to explain the seeming irrationality within a supposedly rational order.

Most of the opposition to Calvinism in the eighteenth and early nineteenth centuries could be traced to the feeling that its adherents made God responsible for sin and evil; yet for many the attraction of Calvinism was its reassurance that a rational God was fully in control of his creation. It is far too simple to view the incessant debates between Calvinists and Arminians in the Old South as merely disagreements over revivalist strategy, or as adaptations to a frontier mentality, or as the adjustment of theology to an optimistic democratic ethos. The terms of the debate, after all, were derived from seventeenth-century theologians who never heard of revivalism, never lived on a frontier, and never had the slightest interest in liberal democracy in its American forms. It is closer to the truth, even if it is not the whole truth, to say, as the preachers themselves said, that the dispute between Calvinists and Arminians was compelling because both sides believed it to be of enormous importance that God and the world should be rational.

1. Calvinists and Arminians

The conviction that the Calvinist doctrines of sin and redemption contradicted the benevolence of God provided one of the few strands of continuity among the various forms of eighteenth- and nineteenth-century "Arminianism." The Arminian traditions originated when Jacobus Arminius (1559–1609), a pastor and professor of theology at Leyden in Holland, decided that the "high Calvinism" of the Reformed scholastics inadvertently depicted God as the author of sin. The high Calvinists claimed that God ordained Adam's fall in order to save some persons and to damn others; to his elect he then provided irresistible grace, which he denied to the reprobate. All men and women were totally depraved; election to salvation depended on an unconditional eternal decree; and Christ died only for the elect, who would inevitably persevere in righteousness. Arminius argued that the entire scheme was an affront to the wisdom, justice, and goodness of God. As an alternative, he proposed that God decreed to save all believers and that Christ died for all persons, so that sufficient grace was given to all. Arminius believed that faith was the fruit of grace and that the will had no power to believe unless it was empowered by grace. But he denied that grace was irresistible; the will could resist and continue to sin, and in that case there was no question about where to locate the responsibility for its sinfulness. Arminians insisted that their doctrine vindicated the justice of God, but the Synod of Dort (1618–1619) disagreed and defined Arminianism as a heresy.[3]

In the aftermath of the synod almost any deviation from the newly defined orthodoxy received an "Arminian" label, but by the end of the eighteenth century the designation was being used to refer to three disparate groups: Anglican traditionalists, liberals, and Wesleyans. The Restoration of Charles II to the English throne in 1660 hastened the eclipse of Calvinism in the Church of England. Originally a mark of high-church opposition to Puritanism, Arminian theology became during the Restoration period the standard teaching of most Anglican clergymen. They believed in original sin and divine grace, but they rejected predestination as a slander on God's goodness. While the Dutch theologians occupied themselves with sin, election, atonement, grace, and perseverance, the English Arminians concentrated on the single issue of predestination and its implications for divine and human morality. Archbishop John Tillotson, who rose to eminence after the 1688 revolution, expressed the prevailing sentiment:

> I am as certain that this doctrine [eternal decrees] cannot be of God as I am that God is good and just, because this grates upon the notion that mankind have of goodness and justice. This is that which no good man would do, and therefore it cannot be believed of infinite goodness. If an Apostle, or an angel from heaven teach any doctrine which plainly overthrows the goodness and justice of God, let him be accursed. For every man hath greater assurance that God is good and just than he can have of any subtle speculations about predestination and the decrees of God.[4]

Early English Arminianism was more a mood and temper than a precise set of doctrines, and it soon merged imperceptibly with an easy-going latitudinarian attitude toward doctrine. But even this attenuated Arminian sensibility rested on an unshakable confidence in the benevolence of God.

By the middle of the eighteenth century the label was no longer restricted to the mild-mannered and congenial Arminians of the Restoration period. The connotations of the name became less reputable in the eyes of Anglican traditionalists. In 1740 John Taylor of Norwich, a nonconformist minister, published his *Scripture Doctrine of Original Sin, Proposed to Free and Candid Examination*, in which he concluded that the Bible did not support the traditional doctrine of original sin, a teaching that was incompatible with God's goodness, holiness, and justice. The older Arminians had not questioned original sin; Taylor said that the doctrine of native depravity made God responsible for evil because it implied that he sent his creatures into the world with insuperably sinful inclinations. Taylor acknowledged the ubiquity of sin but denied its heritability; sin was, in his view, a personal act, not a corporate status.[5]

Calvinists delighted in affixing the title of "Arminian" to Taylor's doctrine, but others claimed the name and suggested that Taylor had no right to it.

In particular, John Wesley accused Taylor and his liberal allies of reprehensible errors, none more serious than their views on original sin. But the Wesleyans agreed that the God of Calvin was an arbitrary tyrant. Wesley taught that the Calvinist doctrine of election contradicted God's justice, truth, sincerity, love, and goodness.[6] The Wesleyans believed sin to be inherited but grace to be ubiquitous; hence everyone, they thought, was sufficiently empowered by a "prevenient grace" to turn from sinfulness to faithfulness and obedience. Common to both the liberals and the Wesleyans was the assertion that freely deciding men and women bore the responsibility for sin, and that God's activity conformed to the ideals of benevolence and justice.

In the Old South the term "Arminian" referred primarily, though not exclusively, to the Methodists, who proudly associated themselves with the revolt of Arminius against Calvinism.[7] Most Methodist clergy, even those of minimal learning, tried at least to read the anti-Calvinist writings of John Fletcher, an English contemporary of Wesley. "The young preachers studied the polemical books of Wesley and Fletcher," recalled one Methodist, "and each felt that he had not done his duty unless he had assailed what he believed to be the God-dishonoring doctrine of an unconditional decree."[8] The Southerners thus resumed the English debates, and though the issues ranged from atonement and imputation to freedom and grace, the discussion invariably returned to the morality and rationality of God.

"The substance of the entire controversy," wrote the Methodist Thomas Ralston, was the doctrine of the atonement.[9] Old School Calvinists believed that Christ died only for the elect; a few Calvinist revisionists claimed that he died for all but that only the elect could fulfill the condition of faith; the Arminians said that he died for all and that through grace all had the capacity—Methodists called it "gracious ability"—to believe, repent, and reap the benefits of the cross. Arminians justified their position by pointing out the universal reference of such Scriptural passages as Mark 16:16 and 2 Thessalonians 2:13; Calvinists responded that the passages referred to "all sorts and conditions of men," not all persons, and in turn, appealed to Romans 9–10.[10] But the Arminians also claimed that only a doctrine of gracious ability grounded in a universal atonement could show "that God always acts rationally," while the Calvinists asserted that the Methodists reduced God to a supplicant, unable to save whomever he would.[11]

To the Arminian it seemed that Calvin had failed to explain why God should choose one person and not another; hence the Calvinist deity seemed "arbitrary, capricious, and unreasonable." The Methodists, said Ralston, believed that every act of God was "based on a sufficient and infallible reason"; he evaluated "moral character"; he observed the principles of "reason, equity, and justice."[12] The Calvinist response was to insist that God's reasons were not ours and that he could see "good reasons" when we could see none.[13] The "reason why," said Thornwell, is to be referred wholly to the secret and impenetrable will and wisdom of God.[14] That was the deeper rationality that lay behind the external appearances.

The Methodists disliked any such disjunction between appearance and reality. They were uncomfortable with the Calvinist doctrine that God "imputed" Christ's righteousness to the elect, accounting them righteous despite their fallen nature. They could not accept the assertion that God, in the act of imputation, viewed a sinner as righteous, for this suggested that God was either mistaken or morally undiscriminating: "An all-wise and holy God must view things as they really are. He never can consider one person as having performed an act, and at the same time as not having performed it."[15] An omniscient deity could not look upon a morally disobedient creature as being obedient; the world was no hall of illusions for the all-embracing insight of God. But traditional Calvinists replied that the principle of imputation was "the very keystone which supports the arch of the Christian system."[16] Salvation was possible and reality was trustworthy only if the sinner were not, in the eyes of God, what he seemed to be. In the realm of appearances, confusion and chaos prevailed; in a fallen world, respectability cloaked vicious principles and self-seeking motives paraded in the guise of virtuous activity. Only the doctrine of imputation could, as Thornwell said, "unriddle" the anomalies.[17] Only if God "accounted" us righteous in Christ, despite our lack of just desert, could we repose in the certainty of his benevolence and mercifulness.

Even the convoluted debates over the freedom of the will returned finally to the question of God's morality. The discussion proceeded in the channels that Jonathan Edwards had constructed in the eighteenth century; Southern treatises bristled with allusions to Edwards. "No man would undertake to refute Edwards if he understood him," wrote one Southern Presbyterian in 1854.[18] Edwards had left an inheritance of "difficulties and confusion," replied an Arminian. But even Edwards's critics acknowledged the power of his treatise on the freedom of the will. "With the exception of the *Essais de Theodicée* of Leibnitz," wrote A. T. Bledsoe of Mississippi in 1853, "it is perhaps the greatest effort of the human mind to get rid of the seeming antagonism between the scheme of necessity and the holiness of God."[19]

Edwards had argued that the willing self bore the responsibility for its inevitable misdeeds even though it was enmeshed in a chain of causes. Men and women were unable to choose the motives that elicited their acts, but they were yet free to act (and an act implied consent). Unable to choose indifferently the motives that would excite and attract their wills, they were nevertheless free to do what they willed. Edwards located freedom in the external act, not in the choice itself. But this freedom was sufficient, he thought, to relieve God of any responsibility for human sinfulness.[20] So he tried to reduce the notion of self-determination to absurdity.

Generations of Southern Calvinists rehearsed the Edwardean analysis of motivation in order to prove that the will was powerless to choose the good without the special influence of divine grace but that the reprobate were yet responsible for their decision to capitulate to sinfulness.[21] The Arminians replied that a volition was an original cause and that to speak of "motives" was simply to describe the will in action, "moving" one way or another.[22] But the metaphysical reply was intended to undergird an Arminian doctrine of grace, which in turn verified the benevolence of God:

Here is the dividing line between these two renowned systems of theology. If God has provided a gracious ability for every sinner, by which this soul-destroying moral inability may be counteracted . . . then is Arminianism true: the responsibility is thrown upon the sinner, and "the ways of God are justified to man."[23]

The Calvinists replied that a God without the ability to control the will and conduct of men and women so as to render them holy could not "guarantee the prosperity of the universe for one hour." God's goodness was inseparable from his power; an impotent deity also implied a chaotic world.[24]

Arguments between Calvinists and Arminians doubtless served a variety of functions, depending on where and under what circumstances they were conducted. But the antagonists were also disputing whether one or another historic religious tradition was best able to vindicate a whole system of cultural and religious values. The question was not merely which theology could best secure good behavior in the world, although Arminians did claim that the doctrine of predestination undercut moral responsibility, and Calvinists asserted that Arminian "free will" made human activity seem "unmotivated" and therefore dangerously arbitrary. The question was not only which theology could best satisfy religious needs, though Calvinists accused the Arminians of forgetting that salvation was a merciful gift, and Arminians replied that the Calvinist doctrine of the bondage of the will precluded any meaningful sense of religious decision and commitment.

Was a rational orthodox theology possible? The debates between Calvinists and Arminians cannot be separated from that question. Two observations illustrate their interrelation. First, the clergy treated the rationality and the benevolence of God as overlapping attributes; at times they spoke as if the two were synonymous. Just as they argued, with reference to the moral behavior of men and women, that irrationality was immoral and immorality unreasonable, so also they assumed the inseparability of God's goodness and rationality. Second, their doctrine of divine goodness and rationality formed a link, even the major link, in a chain of assertions that constituted a "world-view": a connected system of ideas that claimed to accommodate all possible experience. In such a world-view there were certain ultimate categories in terms of which everything else was to be explained; one such category was the notion of God's "rationality," which was not simply an isolated affirmation but a linchpin pulling together a great number of ideas. Because God was rational, divine truth was "necessarily capable of systematic reduction," which made theology possible.[25] Because God was rational one could trust in a "plan" of salvation; one could assume that Christian life was orderly; one could be confident that the effort to live reasonably and benevolently was an expression of God's will. Both sides agreed that God must be rational, and each accused the other of compromising his rationality by proposing a distorted view of the plan of salvation. Each side claimed, in other words, that only its version of Protestantism could sustain the world-view that all took for granted.

2. The Reasonableness of Calvinism

The Calvinist defense was compromised by divisions within the ranks over atonement, imputation, and freedom. In the eighteenth century, orthodox Reformed theologians had split into two groups: an "Old Calvinist" faction, interested in practical piety and inclined to interpret traditional dogma so as to support evangelistic appeals, and a "Consistent Calvinist" or "New Divinity" group, occupied with the speculative development of Edwardean ideas.[26] Among the New Divinity proposals was a "governmental" doctrine of the atonement—a theory that had received attention in Europe when a pious Dutch intellectual, Hugo Grotius, published his *Defence of the Catholic Faith Concerning the Satisfaction of Christ*. Grotius offered an alternative to the two major theories of atonement that hitherto had been prominent within the Church, namely that Christ had died either to satisfy the wrath of God or to transform the dispositions of the sinner. He suggested that Christ had in fact died to preserve the integrity of the divine moral order. Having created a consistent moral system, with appropriate sanctions and punishments, God could not simply overlook human transgression without undermining the moral system itself. Pardon without atonement would have abrogated the divine government, which served both to manifest God's glory and to benefit the creation.

During the eighteenth century theologians in both England and America used the governmental metaphor. Jonathan Edwards employed some of the imagery while retaining the essentials of the older satisfaction theory. But Edwards's followers experimented with the new terminology. Traces of it were evident when Samuel Hopkins wrote his *System of Doctrines* (1793); Joseph Bellamy of Bethlehem, Connecticut, drew upon the governmental motifs in his *True Religion Delineated* (1750); and in 1785 Jonathan Edwards, Jr., presented an explicit, detailed governmental theory in his *Three Sermons on the Necessity of the Atonement*. The younger Edwards was replying to religious liberals who insisted that the notion of Christ's purchasing forgiveness made reconciliation a matter of debt and payment rather than free and merciful grace. In his reply he repudiated the notion that the atonement consisted in the literal payment of a debt.[27]

As fully developed by the New Divinity men, the governmental doctrine consisted of the assertion that Christ died to "maintain the authority of divine law," enabling God to pardon sin without undermining moral order. He died for all, but election to salvation was limited, for only the predestined could avail themselves of the benefits of the atonement. Yet for the elect forgiveness was purely a gift: Christ's death did not pay their debts. The atonement satisfied the "public justice" of God, in that it enabled him to maintain appropriate governance over the cosmos while yet exhibiting mercy. But the crucifixion did not satisfy his "distributive justice," which determined the moral and religious accountability of mankind. As the norm of distributive justice, the law continued to demand the punishment of sinners; only the gracious mercy of God could relieve them of the law's demands. The atonement was therefore the preservation of a system of order that harmonized justice and mercy. The governmental theorists offered a theological counterpart to the new scientific consciousness that emerged in the seventeenth century, with its notions of universal reason, omnipresent law, and inexorable regularity.[28]

For a time it seemed that the governmental metaphor was to become a hallmark of American theology; even such antagonists as Nathaniel William Taylor at Yale and Leonard Woods at Andover could agree in their use of the idiom. And governmentalism made inroads into the South, as well, along with other New Divinity ideas. The first president of the South Carolina College, Jonathan Maxcy, was known as a persuasive advocate of the governmental doctrine among his fellow Baptist ministers.[29] The New Divinity secured a firm footing in east Tennessee after 1795 when a Presbyterian minister named Hezekiah Balch journeyed to New England seeking funds for his new Greenville College and happened to read Hopkins's *System of Doctrines*. The Synod of the Carolinas accused Balch of teaching false doctrines—a charge sustained by the General Assembly—but the school's alumni disseminated Hopkinsian precepts throughout the region. After founding Maryville College in 1842, moreover, an energetic colleague of Balch's named Isaac Anderson exposed scores of Tennessee ministers to the New Divinity.[30] Presbyterian traditionalists deplored the innovations, but eastern Tennessee remained a stronghold of New England theology.

At Columbia Seminary in South Carolina, meanwhile, the new professor of Biblical languages, George Howe, created a furor shortly after his arrival in 1830 by introducing the governmental scheme to Presbyterian seminarians. A graduate of Andover, he used as one of his classroom texts the *Theological Lectures* of Leonard Woods and thereby evoked the wrath of his colleague Thomas Goulding. Within four years the situation was critical. Aaron Leland, an uneasy occupant of the chair of theology, complained to his friend Thomas Smyth: "The state of the seminary is bad: we talk of peace but there is no kinship or cordiality. The efforts of Dr. G[oulding] . . . against Br. H[owe] are secret but untiring. The accusation now is heresy."[31] It took a visit from an official Board of Visitors to restore a tenuous harmony and to confirm Howe's orthodoxy, a task undoubtedly facilitated by the ambiguities in Woods's text. But by 1838 the seminary professors felt compelled to pledge themselves to teach that Christ's death did literally satisfy the wrath of God, whatever else it may have accomplished.[32] That pledge signaled the demise of undiluted governmentalism among the leaders of Southern Presbyterianism.

Yet even the traditionalists could not ignore the new idiom, and throughout the early nineteenth century they followed a consistent pattern of first criticizing the governmental doctrine but then appropriating its imagery into their more conventional satisfaction theory. By the 1840s it was a standard practice of Baptist, Methodist, and Presbyterian theologians to affirm a notion of penal satisfaction but then to expound on the idea that the atonement was also necessary to preserve the "moral government" of the cosmos.[33] Southern critics almost uniformly advanced one theme: that the governmental theorists were correct in what they affirmed but mistaken in what they denied. "But [our doctrine] really includes all that theirs claims," wrote R. L. Dabney, "while it embraces the

vital element which they omit, vicarious penal satisfaction."[34] Thus
the Southern clergy exhibited their concern for the order and regularity of a cosmic moral system. Even while struggling against
innovation, they adapted their orthodoxy to coincide with the preconceptions of a post-Newtonian era.

By the time the furor over the New Divinity had diminished, the
Presbyterian Church was in the throes of a new battle over the New
Haven Theology of Nathaniel William Taylor at Yale. Largely in
response to the challenge of Unitarianism, Taylor had devoted
most of his career as a theologian to the problem of theodicy. Channing and the Unitarians broke with orthodoxy because they considered the doctrine of total depravity a slander on the justice and
benevolence of God as well as a libel on the integrity of human
nature: "Other errors we can pass over with comparative indifference," Channing had said in 1819, "but we ask our opponents to
leave us a God worthy of our love and trust, in whom our moral
sentiments may delight."[35] Taylor and his allies at Yale denied
that their form of Calvinism burdened God with the responsibility
for sin. They taught that sin, in a true Calvinist view, consisted in
an act of the will, not in a propensity or property of human nature
underlying volition. Hence guilt was personal, and though all persons inevitably sinned, they had the power to do otherwise, in principle if not in fact. When his fellow Calvinist Bennet Tyler of the
new Theological Institute in Hartford, Connecticut, insisted that
sinful acts flowed from a sinful, morally contaminated nature, Taylor charged that Tyler had made God the author of sin. Throughout New England and the Midwest the older orthodoxy came under
siege by a new generation of churchmen intent on preserving the
benevolent image of God.[36]

The New Haven theologians said that the doctrines of limited
atonement, imputation, and human inability were merely secondary
explanations of Calvinist theology. They were transient conceptual
forms intended to express the deeper Calvinist vision of humankind as fallen, justified by faith through Christ's atonement, and
reborn through the influence of the Spirit. But whenever any secondary explanation seemed no longer compatible with the principles of right reason, the theologian had no choice but to seek other
modes of expression. So the Taylorites preached that the sinner

was able but unwilling to repent; that sinfulness consisted in actions, not in the imputation of Adamic guilt; that regeneration was a voluntary change in the elect, made in response to the moral suasion of the Spirit presenting truth to the mind; and that the atonement was a governmental act, unlimited in scope, permitting God to extend forgiveness while preserving his moral order.[37] Arminians claimed to see little difference between the older and newer varieties of Calvinism, because both assumed that only the elect would avail themselves of divine grace. But when the New Haven doctrines spread among Presbyterians during the early 1830s, they produced a series of heresy trials that helped divide the Church in 1837 into antagonistic New School and Old School factions.

It took time for the Taylorite controversy to penetrate the South. John Holt Rice spoke for many Southerners when in 1829 he told Leonard Woods that he failed to grasp what "brother Taylor" was doing: "I find it hard to understand him. Is the fault in me, or in him?" Some of the more inquisitive Southern Presbyterians were ready to enter the fray, however, and Rice complained the following year that "Evangelical men" were beginning to dispute, "some for *old* orthodoxy, and others for *new* metaphysics." He told Archibald Alexander at Princeton that "the young men" insisted on reading and discussing the new and dangerous "theological systems."[38] Yet when George Baxter succeeded Rice as theological professor at Union Seminary in 1831, the installation ceremony produced evidence of Southern indifference to the North's "angry controversies." William Hill of Winchester, Virginia, used the occasion to rebuke the quarreling Northern Calvinists. "We have stood aloof," he said, "and wondered and grieved at their indiscretion."[39]

By the time the New Haven theology attracted attention in the South it bore a tinge of radicalism that ensured its unpopularity among traditional Presbyterians, for during the 1830s Taylorism became a rallying point for Calvinists intent on revivalism and reform. When the Presbyterians divided in 1837, Taylorite theology had come to be associated with the reforming group that demanded support for interdenominational evangelistic and reform societies, cooperation with Congregationalists on the frontiers, and a crusade against slavery. The New School reformers were by no means uniformly Taylorite in theology or abolitionist in their social views, but the prevailing stereotypes made it difficult for conservative Southerners to judge the New Haven doctrines solely on their theological merits.[40] The new theology did find some supporters in east Tennessee, where Thomas Craighead, founder of the University of Nashville, had prepared the way earlier by teaching that there was a residue of freedom within the self and that "God never was the author of sin, by will or contrivance." When Frederick Ross of Kingsport founded the original *Calvinistic Magazine* in 1827, the journal bore the imprint of the New Haven doctrine, much to the dismay of conservatives. By 1834 W. L. Breckinridge of Kentucky was pointing to Tennessee as a region of apostasy.[41]

Nathan L. Rice complained that "the leaven of New Schoolism" had also tainted the purity of doctrine among Kentucky Presbyterians, but in 1834 the Kentucky Synod adopted the "Western Memorial," accusing the General Assembly of being soft on the New School.[42] Many Presbyterians in Virginia and North Carolina suspected that the theologians were quibbling over semantics—a suspicion voiced openly by Amasa A. Converse of Virginia in the pages of his *Southern Religious Telegraph*. But William Plumer of Richmond founded a new publication, *The Watchman of the South*, to oppose Converse's paper, and Union Seminary presented an unbroken front against theological innovation, even though the faculty divided over the constitutionality of the legislation expelling the New School from the General Assembly in 1837. And the Synod of South Carolina and Georgia resolved that the General Assembly had tolerated "radical errors in essential points of doctrine" when it failed to condemn a prominent Northern New School preacher named Albert Barnes. The faculty of the synodical seminary at Columbia, at first reluctant to pronounce on the controversy, fell into line when the Synod pledged Columbia to Old School fidelity in 1838. The faculty agreed to affirm belief in the imputation of sin and righteousness, the satisfaction theory of atonement, and regeneration as a direct, immediate, and invincible act of the Spirit. New School presbyteries and congregations in the South—a small minority—usually professed themselves to be doctrinal traditionalists who were simply distraught at the Old School disregard for constitutional process at the 1837 assembly. Most Southern Presbyterians responded to Taylorites with the same arguments they were using against the Arminians.[43]

3. *Speculative Theodicy*

"The origin of evil," wrote a Southern clergyman in 1855, "is the darkest problem in the constitution of the universe. . . . It is a broad and fearful chasm intervening between the lustre of man's free agency and the glory of God."[44] Most of the clergy tried to solve the problem by attributing sin to the will; some argued that it was an insoluble mystery;[45] a tiny number argued that sin remained an enigma unless it could be shown that sinfulness was a transient reality soon to be overshadowed by the salvation of the "whole human race."[46] But such "universalist" hopes did not prevail in the South; by 1860 the region contained only 20 of the 664 Universalist churches in America.[47] So a few theologians proposed speculative solutions to the problem of evil, and during the 1850s the Southerners took up the problem with a new intensity.

The New Divinity theologians had proposed one speculative explanation for evil in the world. During the French and Indian wars Joseph Bellamy produced a disquisition on *The Wisdom of God in the Permission of Sin*, an attempt to show that human sinfulness was a necessary means to the highest human good, namely, the knowledge of God's redemptive mercy. Had humankind not been permitted to sin, we would never have known God as redeemer. Bellamy exemplified a tendency among the Edwardeans to discuss theodicy by trying to fathom the purposes of the divine will. The leit-motif of the New Divinity was "divine causality," and the Edwardeans sought to find an explanation for evil by showing that sin issued from a divine plan. One of the motives of Taylor and the New Haven theologians was the desire to revise the assumption of Bellamy and Samuel Hopkins that moral evil was essential to the perfection of the universe. Taylor argued that even God could not prevent sin in a moral system, because divine intervention would contradict moral agency.[48]

In one form or another Taylor's doctrine—or one like it—commanded assent among several Southern theologians during the 1840s. But in the next decade, partly by accident and partly by design, the topic of theodicy came under renewed discussion. One reason was the publication in 1854 of Albert Taylor Bledsoe's *Theodicy; Or, Vindication of the Divine Glory, as Manifested in the Constitution and Government of the Moral World*. Bledsoe

(1809–1877) had spent twenty years trying to solve the problem of evil; his reflections on theodicy were a thread of continuity within a career marked by abrupt changes. The son of a Kentucky newspaper editor, he graduated from West Point in 1830, but his conversations with the academy's Episcopal chaplain, Charles McIlvaine, awakened intellectual and spiritual interests, and after a period of duty in New Mexico, Bledsoe resigned his commission and began to study law in Virginia. By 1833 he was teaching French and mathematics at Kenyon College in Ohio but also studying theology under McIlvaine and William Sparrow, who would eventually move on to a theological post in the Episcopal Seminary in Virginia. Sparrow urged him to find the fallacy in Edwards's treatise on the will, and Bledsoe took up the task with enthusiasm. In 1835 he became a deacon in the Episcopal Church, but he taught for a year at Miami University in Ohio before becoming rector of Grace Church in Sandusky. Influenced by Wesley's interpretations of the Anglican Thirty-Nine Articles, Bledsoe then tried to become a Methodist minister, but to no avail. So he decided to practice law in Illinois and Ohio.[49]

Throughout his odyssey Bledsoe wrestled with Edwards, and in 1845 he published *An Examination of President Edwards' Inquiry into the Freedom of the Will*, which located Edwards's fallacy in his failure to distinguish between will and sensibility. Bledsoe owed his discovery to his reading of Victor Cousin, who had popularized the Scottish philosophical methods in the French universities. The Scottish analysis of consciousness revealed to Bledsoe a clear difference between desires, affections, feelings, and emotions, on the one hand, and volitions, on the other. Edwards, he thought, had confused them; he had argued that "whatever pleases us most, or excites the most agreeable sensation, is that which 'operates to induce a volition'; and to say otherwise is to assert that that which pleases us most does not." Bledsoe replied, first, that the experience of feeling emotion, desire, or affection was clearly unlike the experience of willing. To desire rain was not to put forth a volition; to be moved by a pleasant sensation was not to will; to be pleased was not to choose. Edwards's neglect of the difference had produced the absurd result that a volition in his philosophy was simultaneously active and passive. Bledsoe believed that consciousness could distinguish mental acts that were "self-active," original, producing causes from other mental experiences that were "necessitated," and that Edwards could not, with his approach, explain the differences in the subjective experiences. Bledsoe also accused Edwards of a number of logical errors, but the distinction between volition and sensibility formed the keystone of his argument.[50]

The critique of Edwards formed the starting point for Bledsoe's further reflections on theodicy, which continued after he moved South and associated himself with the Methodists, who eventually accepted him into their ministerial ranks. He was teaching at the University of Mississippi when he published his *Theodicy*, which traced the history of the problem of evil from Lucretius and the early Greeks to nineteenth-century Calvinists. The book was a polemic against determinism and a speculative explanation of metaphysical evil. Bledsoe repeated many of his earlier arguments against Edwards, but he expanded his criticisms to encompass such diverse figures as Calvin and Kant, Spinoza and Thomas Chalmers, Locke and the New Divinity theologians. He believed that Leibniz's *Essais de Theodicée* was the model of philosophical speculation on the issue, but he charged that even Leibniz had failed. The true solution, he thought, was a doctrine of human freedom, combined with a concept of divine moral government. The existence of sin and evil could be reconciled with the power and goodness of God only if the grand aim and design of God's moral government was the production of the greatest possible amount of moral good. Such a design presupposed the existence of temptation, the freedom to sin, and the possibility of misery, all being necessary to the attainment of virtue. Moral character, not happiness, was the goal of human existence, and sin and evil were necessary for the production of moral character.[51]

The publication of Bledsoe's *Theodicy* was a major event in Southern theology. One can still find marginal notes in nineteenth-century Methodist and Presbyterian periodicals that mention "Bledsoism" along with "Calvinism" and "Arminianism."[52] The reviewer in the Methodist *Quarterly Review* announced that Bledsoe had vindicated the divine government from impeachment.[53] *The Southern Presbyterian Review* accused him of deifying human reason and charged that his attack on the Edwardean doctrine of "motives" undermined confidence in the rationality of the world.[54] Even the Methodists were divided. The minister in Leesburg, Virginia, J. S. R. Clarke, wrote a lengthy rebuttal in the *Quarterly Review*. Clarke preferred Leibniz to Bledsoe because he believed that Bledsoe's *Theodicy* had denigrated God's power. A theodicy, he said, must vindicate not only divine goodness and holiness but also divine power and wisdom. Bledsoe had suggested that God did not prevent all moral evil because he could not, but Clarke disagreed:

> Might not the universe of God be free of all moral evil, and so kept by proper light and moral influence being brought suasively to bear upon all its moral agents, without at all fettering their wills? Who will dare to say that it might not?[55]

Why could not an infinitely powerful God create men and women with free wills who nevertheless could never sin? Bledsoe assumed that God could not work a contradiction. Clarke again disagreed: "Does it make any sense to say that infinite power can be confined by anything?" Clarke would say only that God, for reasons known only to himself, did not choose to perform a contradiction. Evil was a mystery. Clarke's review produced an immediate defense by one of Bledsoe's admirers.[56] But the debate continued even after the Civil war, as the refutation of Bledsoe became a standing challenge to Calvinist theologians.

The Calvinists, though, had their own intramural differences. In 1858 Robert J. Breckinridge (1800–1871) completed the first volume of a planned three-volume systematic theology, *The Knowledge of God Objectively Considered*, and his attempts at theodicy became, largely by accident, the subject of bitter contention. The son of Thomas Jefferson's attorney-general and a member of the Southern aristocracy, Breckinridge was a celebrity even before he published his theology. He had been a noted lawyer, a college president, the superintendent of public education in Kentucky, the pastor of a large church in Lexington, and an orator of national reputation. His diatribes against Roman Catholicism made him a hero among nativists. A contentious personality, a commanding presence, bedecked with an enormous beard and subject to angry outbursts, Breckinridge intimidated some of his admirers. One Southern minister who met him at a convention wrote his wife that

Breckinridge was "decidedly the most brilliant man in this country
... the most interesting man I have ever met in my life."[57]

To less admiring colleagues Breckinridge seemed disconcertingly conscious of his own originality as a theologian. No previous
theologian, he wrote in the preface of his 1858 text, had grasped
"the conception I have of this immense subject, or the method I
adopt in developing it, or the order I pursue in treating it."[58] The
boastfulness may have been misleading, for Breckinridge was in
fact beset by "many worldly cares" when he wrote his systematic
theology, among which was a nagging fear that his work would
fare poorly in "the judgment which God's people" would make.[59]
But he did believe that theology was a positive science that could
be stated as "uncontrovertibly as I would write Geometry."[60] Persuaded of the utter rationality of theology, he believed that he
could fit everything into his system—even evil.

Breckinridge's solution consisted largely of timeworn assertions about the fall of Adam, but almost as an afterthought to his
discussion of the divine attributes he also offered a metaphysical
explanation of evil that was indebted to Leibniz and his theological
successors, especially the German rationalists Christian Wolff and
Johann Friedrich Stapfer. "The reason why anything is possible,"
he said, "must be sought in the understanding of God." The divine
intelligence was the fountain of all potentialities, which Breckinridge, following Stapfer, defined as "essences" or divine intellections of possibility. God's intellections encompassed all possibilities, including evil and imperfection as well as goodness and
perfection. In calling the essences into existence, moreover, God's
will changed nothing in them, so that imperfection—metaphysical,
moral, or physical—was not due to his will but to the ideas in his
intellect, which were necessary and eternal. Since praise and blame
could be attached only to the will, God was not responsible for imperfections, which were themselves eternal essences.[61] Breckinridge did not fully amplify the implications of his scheme, and he
did not intend his remarks on essences and existences to occupy an
unusually prominent place in either his theological system or his
solution to the problem of evil. But his choice of words—or, to be
more accurate, his failure to use his own words—made his theodicy
especially vulnerable to criticism.

His seeming pretensions infuriated Robert L. Dabney, who claimed never to have encountered such "cool arrogance" in such a young professor (Breckinridge was fifty-eight). Dabney compared him to Falstaff bearing the dead body of Hotspur from the battlefield with the expectation that the spectators would credit him with great deeds.[62] Dabney's fulminations were in part a signal of damaged pride and institutional insecurities. After joining the faculty of the new theological school at Danville, Breckinridge had criticized the pedagogical methods used at Union Seminary, where Dabney taught. The creation of Danville was a threat to the other Presbyterian schools. Thornwell feared that cheaper living conditions in Kentucky would help draw students away from struggling Columbia Seminary. Dabney viewed Breckinridge as the symbol of Danville's potential prominence: "Breckinridge's undeserved glitter and prestige among our young men, has been a great injury to us."[63]

Dabney was therefore not inclined to find unusual merit in the new theological system. He told his friend Moses Hoge that it was a "preposterous book." "If you have gone entirely through it, you have more industry than I give you credit for, and more than me." And Dabney leaped at the book's remarks on theodicy, because he had found that Breckinridge copied them almost verbatim from Stapfer's *Institutiones theologiae polemicae universae Ordine Scientifico dispositae* (1743–1747). He saw an opportunity to expose his rival, to "stick a pin in, and letting out a part of the 'gas,' make him collapse to his fair dimensions." Consequently the friends of Union Seminary, led by Dabney and Moses Drury Hoge, decided to "take in hand a thorough and temperate exposure of this whole thing." They determined that Dabney should write a critical rebuttal, which they wanted to publish in the *Princeton Review*. They anticipated no difficulty, for as Dabney told Hoge, "Princeton hates Breckinridge fully as much as he hates them."[64] But Charles Hodge at Princeton was reluctant to intervene in an open quarrel between Union and Danville. His response was tart. He refused, as Dabney told Hoge, to permit Princeton "to be used as a cats paw to pull *our* chestnuts out of the fire."[65] So Dabney's evaluation appeared in the *Southern Presbyterian Review*, and his verdict was unequivocal: "Dr. Breckinridge's friends have committed a grave error in persuading him that he is a dialectician."[66]

Dabney accused Breckinridge of being an unwitting disciple of Wolff and the purveyor of a "wretched, antiquated piece of scholasticism." He had three explicit objections. No educated person, he said, believed that an "essence" could exist apart from concrete things; no Christian theologian could accept a theory that made God subject to a metaphysical necessity that determined the kind of universe he could create; and no reasonable philosopher could have overlooked the point that in the Wolffian system God's intellect contained an infinite number of possible universes, any one of which his will could have chosen. Therefore Breckinridge had not solved the problem of evil. Equally important, he stood exposed as a plagiarist.[67]

Breckinridge's book received some admiring reviews. Thornwell, by giving it his warm commendation without mentioning plagiarism or theodicy, provoked from Dabney the charge of "flunkeyism."[68] A reviewer in the *Southern Presbyterian Review* claimed that the book would take its place "by the side of the works of the great masters" and even asserted that Breckinridge had "borrowed nothing."[69] Another admirer acknowledged that Breckinridge had copied from Stapfer but insisted that he was merely repeating ideas that were the common property of Christendom.[70] Breckinridge himself denied that he was guilty of plagiarism and claimed that his original contribution was his systematic distinction between an objective and subjective knowledge of divine things. But Dabney would not accept even that claim.

Thoroughly imbued with Scottish philosophy, Breckinridge had begun his first volume, supposedly devoted to the "objective," not the subjective, knowledge of God, by appealing to the human consciousness of existence and of an external world. Dabney's criticism was inevitable: "throughout the 'objective' volume we find nearly as much of the subjective as of the objective."[71] But Dabney's own commitments to Scottish thought prevented him from seeing that Breckinridge's philosophy and his theology were both expressions of the drive toward rationality that Dabney himself fully shared. Breckinridge assumed from the start that the theologian should combine "a thorough Evangelism and a true Philosophy." He believed that theology was a rational endeavor because the world was a rational place. In fact, he thought that in solving the mystery of evil the theologian could demonstrate both the truth of religion and "its claims to a superhuman intelligence."[72] Theodicy was simply another of the evidences of Christianity. Dabney and Breckinridge argued with one another so vehemently because they had so much in common.

Underlying the denominational differences among the Southern theologians was a common outlook on God and the world, and the writings on theodicy were the natural expressions of a world-view that seemed unquestionable to most of the educated clergy and to many others as well. Indeed, the issue of theodicy was close to the heart of rational orthodoxy, a theology that proposed to justify faith and to explain the world. The elite Southern town clergy believed in the reasonableness of faith and the rationality of the world. But to say that theodicy was the quintessential theological task because it reflected a common world-view is not to say that the doctrines of divine benevolence and rationality simply held together a system of interrelated ideas. Rational orthodoxy was not a self-contained intellectual system; it was, rather, a complex of inherited religious ideas, more or less coherent, that were subject to subtle modification in changing social settings. In the Old South, the wording of the town ministers' sermons, the gentility of their manners, and the message of their theology reflected the aspirations of an urban constituency who, in seeking respectability, tended to distance themselves from the religious antics and social ineptitude of the unwashed and untutored. The theology was used, among other purposes, to attract and reassure men and women whose sense of personal identity was inseparable from their conviction that "reasonable" behavior—restraint, order, refinement, self-control, self-improvement, and similar virtues that sometimes seemed alien in Southern culture—was congruent with the deepest nature of things.

A pattern of thought that commands widespread allegiance must somehow reflect both an historic tradition and a concrete social setting. In the antebellum South, tradition and social demand coincided in the towns and cities. As a consequence a certain way of thinking about theology became deeply engrained among an influential company of clerical leaders. Their location in towns and cities did not produce the contents of their thought, but the peculiar demands of a town pastorate encouraged some of them to recover a particular mode of religious discourse.

The town pastors were not the sole adherents of rational orthodoxy, but they wrote the books, founded the journals, and established the institutions that nurtured it. They also were not inatten-
tive to other impulses in Southern and American religious culture,
specifically the growing appeal of "sentimentality" in popular religion.[73] The same minister who instructed his congregation about
evidential logic on one Sunday was likely to indulge the following
week in maudlin descriptions of domestic felicity and sorrow. Yet
for all its failings, rational orthodoxy did serve as a check on the
cult of sentiment. The logic may not have been very tight and hard,
in fact it was often noticeably circular and question-begging, but
it was at least a logic, an assertion that religion ought to make
sense.

The Civil War destroyed many of the institutions, the schools
and colleges, that had promoted the theology, and the economic
and social dislocation probably did more to undermine rational
orthodoxy in the South than any single intellectual event. The
devastation severely affected the fortunes of the professional and
commercial classes who had built a town milieu in which the orthodox clerical rationalists could thrive. Yet it would be wrong to
conclude that the theology melted away. Rational orthodoxy maintained its hegemony in many churches until late in the nineteenth
century. Some of the older theologians remained in positions of influence during and after Reconstruction, including John Adger and
John L. Giradeau at Columbia, Robert L. Dabney at Union, Basil
Manly, Jr., at Southern Baptist Theological Seminary, and Thomas O. Summers at Vanderbilt.

Indeed, rational orthodox theology stood in the background of
both religious liberalism and fundamentalism in the South. The
later fundamentalists viewed the Bible itself as a rationalistic system of divinely inspired propositions, while the liberals still sought
to prove the reasonableness of faith. Both represented the revision
of an older system, not its abandonment. Hence an understanding
of that pattern of ideas is not only essential for a comprehensive
grasp of Southern religion during the period when it was beginning
to reshape the consciousness of the Southern people but also indispensable for understanding the religion of the modern South.
The 1976 presidential election only serves to underline the significance of that task.[74]

NOTES

MANUSCRIPT COLLECTIONS CITED

Bernard Diary   Overton Bernard Diary, University of North Carolina, Chapel Hill

Breckinridge Letters   Robert J. Breckinridge Letters, Yale University, New Haven

Buck Letters   William C. Buck Family Letters, Louisiana State University, Baton Rouge

Cottrell Diary   Joseph B. Cottrell Diary, University of North Carolina, Chapel Hill

Dabney Papers   Robert Lewis Dabney Papers, Historical Foundation of the Presbyterian and Reformed Churches in the United States, Montreat, North Carolina

Dana Papers   Charles B. Dana and Family Papers, Louisiana State University, Baton Rouge

Garland Collection   Landon Garland Collection, Vanderbilt University, Nashville

Gildersleeve–Cooper Letters   Benjamin Gildersleeve–Thomas Cooper Correspondence, University of North Carolina, Chapel Hill

Gilman Collection   Samuel Gilman Collection, Harvard University, Cambridge

Green Classbook   William Mercer Green Papers, University of North Carolina, Chapel Hill

Hendrix Papers   Eugene Russell Hendrix Papers, Duke University, Durham

Henkel Papers   David Henkel Papers, University of North Carolina, Chapel Hill

Houston Papers   Samuel R. Houston Papers, Historical Foundation of the Presbyterian and Reformed Churches in the United States, Montreat, North Carolina

King Diary   Mitchell King Diary, University of North Carolina, Chapel Hill

Lacy Papers   Drury Lacy Papers, University of North Carolina, Chapel Hill

McKendree Collection   William McKendree Collection, Vanderbilt University, Nashville

McTyeire Collection   W. H. McTyeire Collection, Vanderbilt University, Nashville

Manly Collection   Basil Manly Collection, University of Alabama, Tuscaloosa

Manly Papers   Basil Manly, Sr., Papers, University of North Carolina, Chapel Hill

Manly, Jr., Papers   Basil Manly, Jr., Papers, University of North Carolina, Chapel Hill

Miles Papers   James Warley Miles Papers, Duke University, Durham

Miller Collection   Samuel Miller Collection, Princeton University, Princeton

Montgomery Papers   Joseph A. Montgomery Papers, Louisiana State University, Baton Rouge

Otey Papers   James Hervey Otey Papers, University of North Carolina, Chapel Hill

Palmer Papers   Benjamin M. Palmer Papers, Duke University, Durham

Paris Papers   John Paris Papers, University of North Carolina, Chapel Hill

Penick Papers   Daniel A. Penick Papers, University of North Carolina, Chapel Hill

Pierce Collection   George F. Pierce Collection, Georgia State Archives, Atlanta

Ravenscroft Papers   John Stark Ravenscroft Papers, University of North Carolina, Chapel Hill

Robertson Papers   Mary Jane Robertson Papers, Louisiana State University, Baton Rouge

Smith Diary   The Autobiographical Diary of George Gilman Smith, University of North Carolina, Chapel Hill

Smith Papers   Whitefoord Smith Papers, Duke University, Durham

Smyth Papers   Thomas Smyth Papers, Historical Foundation of the Presbyterian and Reformed Churches in the United States, Montreat, North Carolina

Stratton Papers   Joseph B. Stratton Papers, Louisiana State University, Baton Rouge

Taylor Papers   Sereno Taylor Diaries, Louisiana State University, Baton Rouge

Thornwell Collection   James Henley Thornwell Collection, Historical Foundation of the Presbyterian and Reformed Churches in the United States, Montreat, North Carolina

Thornwell Papers   James Henley Thornwell Papers, University of North Carolina, Chapel Hill

Waddel Papers   Moses Waddel Papers, University of North Carolina, Chapel Hill

Willie Notes   L. R. Willie Notes from Union Theological Seminary, 1838–1839, Duke University, Durham

Wilmer Papers   Richard Hooker Wilmer Papers, University of North
    Carolina, Chapel Hill
Winans Collection   William Winans Collection, University of Missis-
    sippi, Oxford
Young Papers   John Freeman Young Papers, University of North Caro-
    lina, Chapel Hill

ABBREVIATIONS FOR FREQUENTLY
CITED JOURNALS

JSH   *Journal of Southern History*
MQR   *Quarterly Review of the Methodist Episcopal Church, South*
SPR   *The Southern Presbyterian Review*

INTRODUCTION

1. Clement Eaton, *The Freedom of Thought Struggle in the Old South*
(New York, 1964; 1st ed., Durham, N. C., 1940), p. 233.

2. R. M. Weaver, "The Older Religiousness in the South," *Sewanee Review* 51 (1943):248–49.

3. John B. Boles, *The Great Revival 1787–1805* (Lexington, Kentucky,
1972), p. 195.

4. Henry Adams, *The Education of Henry Adams* (New York, 1931),
p. 57.

5. W. J. Cash, *The Mind of the South* (New York, 1941), p. 99.

6. Thomas Ralston, *Elements of Divinity* (Nashville, 1871; 1st ed.,
1847), p. 361.

CHAPTER ONE

1. Jeremiah Jeter to James Taylor, 30 March 1827, in George Taylor,
Life and Times of James B. Taylor (Philadelphia, 1872), p. 60.

2. Taylor, *Life of Taylor*, pp. 50, 100, 130–33.

3. Frank L. Owsley, *Plain Folk of the Old South* (Baton Rouge, 1950),
pp. 24–62.

4. Donald B. Dodd and Wyndle S. Dodd (eds.), *Historical Statistics of
the South, 1790–1970* (Tuscaloosa, 1973); *The Seventh Census of the
United States: 1850* (Washington, 1853).

5. J. D. B. DeBow, *Commercial Review of the South and West* 29
(1860):613–14.

6. James B. Taylor, *Virginia Baptist Ministers* (Philadelphia, 1859),

p. 280; Philip Lindsley, *The Works of Philip Lindsley*, ed. L. J. Halsey, 3 vols. (Philadelphia, 1866), 1:431, 258.

7. DeBow, *Review* 29 (1860):613–14.

8. Anon. to C. B. Dana, 1 March 1858, Dana Papers, L.S.U., Baton Rouge.

9. Amelia Montgomery to Joseph Montgomery, 27 February 1860, Montgomery Papers, L.S.U., Baton Rouge.

10. Mary Jane Robertson to anon., 28 June 1861, Robertson Papers, L.S.U., Baton Rouge.

11. "New Orleans and Charleston," *Review* 1 (1844):45–51; "Cities of the Valley of the Mississippi and Ohio," *Review* 1 (1844):145–53; "The City of Nashville," *Review* 1 (1844):503–8; "Commerce of American Cities," *Review* 4 (1847):391–404; "Public Improvements in Charleston," *Review* 7 (1849):398–402; L. W. Dorsett and A. H. Shaffer, "Was the Antebellum South Antiurban? A Suggestion," *JSH* 38 (February, 1972): 93–101; Hinton R. Helper, *The Impending Crisis of the South: How to Meet It* (New York, 1857), pp. 331–34.

12. Sallie Watson to Gideon Buck, 2 January 1860, Buck Letters, L.S.U., Baton Rouge.

13. *Lynchburg Daily Virginian*, 30 August 1858; *United States Catholic Miscellany*, 5 June 1822.

14. *The Albany Patriot*, 16 April 1845; *The Columbus* [Georgia] *Inquirer*, 26 May and 28 July 1832; *The* [Richmond] *Inquirer*, 4 July 1804; *The LaGrange Herald*, 7 and 28 September 1843.

15. Marvin Meyers, *The Jacksonian Persuasion: Politics and Belief* (New York, 1960), pp. 76–77.

16. Richard M. Bernard, "A Portrait of Baltimore in 1800: Economic and Occupational Patterns in an Early American City," *Maryland Historical Society Magazine* 69 (Winter, 1974):346–60. By 1850 Baltimore's population was 169,054.

17. Arthur Mazyck, *Guide to Charleston Illustrated* (Charleston, n.d.), pp. 28, 47–49; Fredrika Bremer, *The Homes of the New World; Impressions of America*, trans. Mary Howitt, 2 vols. (New York, 1854), 1:271.

18. John P. Little, *History of Richmond, Reprinted from the Southern Literary Messenger* (1851) (Richmond, 1933), p. 184; *Seventh Census of the United States: 1850.*

19. Landon Garland to Caroline Garland, 22 January 1848, Garland Collection, Vanderbilt.

20. Shadrach Nye to William McMahon, 1 November 1824, McKendree Collection, Vanderbilt.

21. J. O. Andrew, *Miscellanies: Comprising Letters, Essays, and Addresses* (Louisville, 1854), p. 17.

22. *The Life and Letters of Stephen Olin, D.D., LL.D* (New York, 1854), p. 141. My first two chapters, taken as a whole, contain the evidence for my assertions about the clerical perception of town life.

23. D. R. Hundley, *Social Relations in Our Southern States* (New York,

1860), pp. 30, 91–96, 170–366. See also M. R. Babcock to John F. Young, 24 May 1855, Young Papers, U.N.C., Chapel Hill; D. Clayton James, *Antebellum Natchez* (Baton Rouge, 1968), pp. 165–79; Richard Wade, *The Urban Frontier* (Boston, 1959); Link and Patrick (eds.), *Writing Southern History*, pp. 158–74.

24. T. O. Summers (ed.), *Biographical Sketches of Eminent Itinerant Ministers* (Nashville, 1858), p. 57; Tiberius G. Jones, *Duties of a Pastor to His Church* (Charleston, 1853), pp. 52–54; "Mercantile Morals," *SPR* 7 (1853):533; "Dr. Smith's Philosophy and Practice of Slavery," *MQR* 11 (1857):249; J. L. Dagg, *The Elements of Moral Science* (Macon, 1870; 1st ed., 1859), p. 203; "Spencer's Social Statics," *MQR* 10 (1856):200; James H. Thornwell, *Discourses on Truth* (1851), *The Collected Writings of James Henley Thornwell*, ed. John Adger, 3 vols. (Richmond, 1871), 2:466.

25. John England, *The Works of the Right Rev. John England, First Bishop of Charleston*, ed. I. A. Reynolds, 5 vols. (Baltimore, 1849), 5:33–34.

26. William Meade, *Old Churches, Ministers, and Families of Virginia*, 2 vols. (Philadelphia, 1900; 1st ed., 1857), 1:390; A. B. Van Zandt, "The Necessity of a Revelation," *Lectures on the Evidences of Christianity Delivered at the University of Virginia During the Sessions of 1850–51* (New York, 1852), p. 41; Basil Manly to Sarah Manly, 28 November 1835, Manly Collection, University of Alabama, Tuscaloosa; T. V. Moore, "Inspiration of the Scriptures," *MQR* 5 (1851):52; Charles F. Deems (ed.), *The Southern Methodist Pulpit* 3 (1848):52; Clement Eaton, "Class Differences in the Old South," *Virginia Quarterly Review* 33 (Summer, 1957):357–70; Robert E. Shalhope, "Race, Class, Slavery and the Antebellum Southern Mind," *JSH* 37 (1971):557–74.

27. Meade, *Old Churches*, 2:391.

28. Thomas Smyth, *The Complete Works of Rev. Thomas Smyth, D.D.*, ed. J. W. Flynn, 10 vols. (Columbia, S. C., 1909–12), 10:501, 493; 7:546.

29. Ibid., 5:543; 7:724; 10:457, 474, 479; 5:453, 460; Smyth, "An Appeal to the Conscience of the Christian, Conservative Bible-Loving Men and Women of the North," *New York Journal of Commerce*, 1 March 1861.

30. Frances M. Trollope, *Domestic Manners of the Americans* (New York, 1901; 1st ed., 1832), p. 102.

31. C. S. Deems (ed.), *Annals of Southern Methodism for 1857* (Nashville, 1858), pp. 104–24; DeBow (ed.), *Review* 7 (1849):398–402; George G. Smith, Jr., *History of Methodism in Georgia and Florida from 1785 to 1865* (Macon, 1877), p. 438; Andrew, *Miscellanies*, p. 17; John G. Jones, *A Complete History of Methodism as Connected with the Mississippi Conference of the Methodist Episcopal Church, South*, 2 vols. (Nashville, 1908), 2:321, 348.

32. M. J. Spalding, *Miscellanea: Comprising Reviews, Lectures, and Essays on Historical, Theological, and Miscellaneous Subjects* (Louisville, 1855), p. 394.

33. William H. Brisbane (ed.), *The Southern Baptist and General Intelligencer* 1 (Charleston, 3 January 1835):20.

34. Shadrach Nye to William McMahon, 1 November 1824, McKendree Collection, Vanderbilt; William Winans to W. H. Watkins, 26 October 1842, Letterbooks, Winans Collection, University of Mississippi, Oxford; J. P. K. Henshaw, *Memoir of the Life of the Rt. Rev. Richard Channing Moore* (Philadelphia, 1842), p. 72; William E. Hatcher, *Life of J. B. Jeter, D.D.* (Baltimore, 1877), p. 178; John Breckinridge (ed.), *The Annual of the Board of Education of the General Assembly of the Presbyterian Church in the United States* (Philadelphia, 1833), p. 11.

35. W. H. Wilmer to R. C. Moore, 27 January 1813, Henshaw, *Memoir*, p. 121.

36. William Meade to R. C. Moore, 4 March 1813, Henshaw, *Memoir*, p. 124.

37. William Meade, *Lectures on the Pastoral Office, Delivered to the Students of the Theological Seminary at Alexandria, Virginia* (New York, 1849), pp. 192, 198; "Bishop Elliott's Address," *The Southern Episcopalian* 2 (Charleston, 1855):176; "The Episcopal Church in the Up Country," *Southern Episcopalian* 2 (Charleston, 1855):370–72; Meade, *Old Churches*, 2:391; Henshaw, *Memoir*, p. 72; George G. Smith, *The Life and Times of George Foster Pierce, D.D., LL.D.* (Sparta, Georgia, 1888), p. 561.

38. Meade, *Old Churches*, 2:389.

39. M. R. Babcock to John Young, 24 May 1855, Young Papers, U.N.C., Chapel Hill.

40. Samuel Montgomery to Joseph Montgomery, 4 December 1840, Montgomery Papers, L.S.U., Baton Rouge.

41. Taylor, *Life of Taylor*, p. 50. See also William Winans to Kate Adams, 24 December 1853, Winans Collection, University of Mississippi, Oxford; W. H. McTyeire, "Sermons and Comments," McTyeire Collection, Vanderbilt.

42. R. J. Breckinridge, *The Christian Pastor* (n. p., 1845), p. 16; J. H. Thornwell, "Review of the Christian Pastor," *SPR* 1 (1847):141; R. J. Breckinridge, "Theological Seminaries," *Baltimore Religious and Literary Magazine* 6 (1840):399, 402; Thomas E. Peck, *Miscellanies of the Rev. Thomas E. Peck*, 2 vols. (Richmond, 1895), 1:297; E. C. Mayse, "Robert Jefferson Breckinridge: American Presbyterian Controversialist" (Th.D. diss., Union Theological Seminary in Virginia, 1974), p. 498.

43. J. H. Spencer, *A History of Kentucky Baptists from 1769 to 1885*, 2 vols. (Cincinnati, 1885), 1:557.

44. Basil Manly to Sarah Manly, 28 November 1835, Manly Collection. See also Walter B. Posey, *The Development of Methodism in the Old Southwest, 1783–1824* (Tuscaloosa, 1933); *The Presbyterian Church in the Old Southwest, 1778–1838* (Richmond, 1952); and *The Baptist Church in the Lower Mississippi Valley, 1776–1845* (Lexington, 1957); John D. Boles,

The Great Revival, 1787–1805 (Lexington, 1972); Dickson D. Bruce, Jr., *And They All Sang Hallelujah: Plain-Folk Camp-Meeting Religion, 1800–1845* (Knoxville, 1973).

45. Whitefoord Smith, "Address Delivered Before the Historical Society of the South Carolina Conference, November, 1857," Smith Papers, Duke.

46. Lovick Pierce, "A Semi-Centennial Discourse," p. 28, *Sermons and Essays by Ministers of the Methodist Episcopal Church, South*, ed. T. O. Summers (Nashville, 1857); Smith, *Life of Pierce*, p. 119; C. F. Deems, *Annals of Southern Methodism for 1855* (New York, 1856), pp. 259–71.

47. William McKendree, Papers; Eli Truitt to William McKendree, 27 August 1822, McKendree Collection, Vanderbilt.

48. William Winans to F. A. W. Davis, 8 November 1841; Winans to James Sewall, 18 October 1842, Winans Collection, University of Mississippi, Oxford.

49. Winans to Maria Huston, 16 December 1842, Winans Collection, University of Mississippi, Oxford.

50. Winans to Henry Slicer, 17 December 1842; Winans to James Sewall, 18 October 1842, Winans Collection, University of Mississippi, Oxford.

51. *The Southern Baptist and General Intelligencer*, 3 January 1835, p. 250.

52. R. B. C. Howell, *The Monthly Miscellany: A Religious and Literary Review* (Atlanta and Richmond, 1849), pp. 81–82.

53. Basil Manly, Jr., to Charles Manly, 21 August 1838, Manly, Jr., Papers; Basil Manly to anon., 14 February 1850, Manly Papers, U.N.C., Chapel Hill.

54. *Proceedings of the First Triennial Meeting of the Southern Baptist Convention, Held in Richmond, Virginia* (Richmond, 1846), p. 35; *Proceedings of the Second Triennial Meeting* (Savannah, 1847), p. 26.

55. *Proceedings of the Southern Baptist Convention, Convened in the City of Baltimore, 1853* (Richmond, 1853), pp. 18–19.

56. *Proceedings of the Second Triennial Meeting*, p. 26; *Proceedings 1853*, p. 57; *Proceedings of the Sixth Biennial Session of the Southern Baptist Convention, Held in Louisville, Kentucky, May, 1857* (Richmond, 1857), p. 25.

57. Landon Garland to Caroline Garland, 17 July 1857, Garland Collection, Vanderbilt.

58. James B. Finley, *Sketches of Western Methodism* (Cincinnati, 1855), p. 250; Peter Guilday, *The Life and Times of John England, First Bishop of Charleston*, 2 vols. (New York, 1927), 2:8; Summers (ed.), *Biographical Sketches*, p. 135; Spencer, *Kentucky Baptists*, 1:557; *Life of Olin*, 1:182; Albea Godbold, *The Church College of the Old South* (Durham, N. C., 1944), p. 56; Smith, *Life of Pierce*, p. 24.

59. Ernest A. Smith, *Martin Ruter* (New York, 1915), p. 37; William Winans to anon., 22 September 1841, Winans Collection, University of

Mississippi, Oxford; H. B. Bascom to William Wightman, 9 August 1844, Hendrix Papers, Duke.

60 James A. Davis, *The History of the City of Memphis* (Memphis, 1873), p. 242.

61. William Winans to B. M. Drake, 24 May 1849, Winans Collection, University of Mississippi, Oxford.

62. Smith, *Life of Pierce*, p. 24; Landon Garland to Caroline Garland, 17 July 1857, Garland Collection, Vanderbilt; "The Use of Tobacco," p. 7, *Sermons and Essays*, ed. Summers; *Southern Baptist and General Intelligencer*, 10 January 1835; Smith, *Methodism in Georgia and Florida*, p. 448; John B. McFerrin, *History of Methodism in Tennessee*, 3 vols. (Nashville, 1895), 3:76; *Life of Olin*, 1:41, 112.

63. John Melish, *Travels Through the United States of America* (Philadelphia, 1812), in Mills Lane (ed.), *The Rambler in Georgia* (Savannah, 1973), p. 25; Charles C. Jones, Jr., *Memorial History of Augusta, Georgia* (Syracuse, 1890), pp. 148, 297.

64. Smith, *Life of Pierce*, pp. 24–33, 117–21; Smith, *Methodism in Georgia and Florida*, pp. 423–36.

65. J. G. Jones, *Complete History of Methodism*, 2:142; Deems, *Annals 1855*, n.p.; George G. Smith, Smith Diary, 1:111, U.N.C., Chapel Hill.

66. Joseph Parks, *General Leonidas Polk C.S.A.: The Fighting Bishop* (Baton Rouge, 1962), p. 55.

67. F. A. Mood, *Methodism in Charleston* (Nashville, 1856), pp. 48–52.

68. Shadrach Nye to William McMahon, 1 November 1824; Eli Truitt to William McKendree, 27 August 1822, McKendree Collection, Vanderbilt; William Winans to Rev. Curtis, 20 September 1841, Winans Papers, University of Mississippi, Oxford.

69. Guilday, *Life of England*, 1:380–402; Alfonso Comeau, "A Study of the Trustee Problem in the St. Louis Cathedral in New Orleans, Louisiana, 1842–44," *The Louisiana Historical Quarterly* 31 (1948):897–972.

70. G. F. Taylor, "The Early History of the Episcopal Church in New Orleans, 1805–40," *The Louisiana Historical Quarterly* 22 (1939):428–78; N. H. Cobbs to J. H. Otey, 17 December 1852, Otey Papers, U.N.C., Chapel Hill.

71. Mitchell King, Diary, 1 February 1852–27 June 1853, King Diary, U.N.C., Chapel Hill; Louis F. Tasistro, *Random Shots and Southern Breezes*, 2 vols. (New York, 1842), 2:183.

72. O. P. Fitzgerald, *Dr. Summers: A Life Study* (Nashville, 1885), p. 55.

73. Basil Manly to J. L. Reynolds, 12 September 1841; Manly to Reynolds, 21 August 1849; Manly to T. P. Smith, 21 February 1855; Manly to Smith, 15 June 1855, Manly Collection, University of Alabama, Tuscaloosa.

74. Basil Manly to John Broadus, 14 May 1858, in A. T. Robertson, *Life and Letters of John Albert Broadus* (Philadelphia, 1901), p. 148.

CHAPTER TWO

1. Hundley, *Social Relations*, pp. 91–96, 170–366.
2. Margaret DesChamps Moore (ed.), "Letters of John Holt Rice to Thomas Chalmers, 1817–1819," *Virginia Magazine of History and Biography* 67 (1959):310.
3. Frederick A. Norwood, *The Story of American Methodism: A History of the United Methodists and Their Relations* (Nashville, 1974), p. 189.
4. *The Seventh Census of the United States: 1850* (Washington, 1853), p. lxvii. I included figures from thirteen states: Maryland, Virginia, North Carolina, South Carolina, Georgia, Florida, Alabama, Mississippi, Louisiana, Texas, Arkansas, Tennessee, and Kentucky. The report from the Aid Society was cited in Frederick Olmsted, *A Journey in the Seaboard Slave States in the Years 1853–1854*, 2 vols. (New York, 1904; 1st ed., 1856), 2:82.
5. The sample includes the following clergy, listed alphabetically according to denomination with birth and death dates, and with an indication of at least one of the towns, institutions, or offices with which they were prominently associated.

Presbyterians: John Adger (1810–1899, Charleston and Columbia, S. C.), George D. Armstrong (1813–1899, Norfolk, Va.), William M. Atkinson (1796–1849, Winchester, Va.), Samuel J. Baird (1817–1893, Baltimore), George A. Baxter (1771–1841, Lexington, Va., and Union Theological Seminary), Gideon Blackburn (1772–1838, Louisville and Danville, Ky.), John Breckinridge (1796–1846, Baltimore), Robert J. Breckinridge (1800–1871, Baltimore and Lexington, Ky.), Joseph Caldwell (1773–1835, Chapel Hill, N. C.), Alonzo Church (1793–1862, Athens, Ga.), R. M. Cunningham (1760–1839, Lexington, Ky.), R. L. Dabney (1820–1898, Union Theological Seminary), Benjamin Gildersleeve (b. 1791, Charleston), Thomas Goulding (1786–1848, Columbia, S. C.), Samuel Lyle Graham (1794–1851, Union Theological Seminary), Robert Henry (1792–1856, Charleston), Thomas C. Henry (1790–1827, Columbia and Charleston, S. C.), Moses Hoge (1752–1820, Shepherdstown, Va.), Moses Drury Hoge (1819–1899, Richmond), George Howe (1802–1883, Columbia, S. C.), Aaron W. Leland (1787–1871, Charleston and Columbia, S. C.), Philip Lindsley (1785–1855, Nashville), James Lyon (1814–1882, Columbus, Miss.), John Matthews (1772–1848, Shepherdstown, Va.), William McPheeters (1778–1842, Raleigh, N. C.), Benjamin Palmer (1819–1902, New Orleans), Benjamin Morgan Palmer (1781–1847, Charleston), William Swan Plumer (1802–1880, Richmond), John Holt Rice (1777–1831, Richmond), Nathan L. Rice (1807–1877, Bardstown and Paris, Ky.), Francis Sampson (1814–1854, Union Theological Seminary), Benjamin M. Smith (1811–1893, Danville, Va.), Thomas Smyth (1808–1873, Charleston), Conrad Speece (1776–1836, Augusta, Va.), James H. Thornwell (1812–1862, Columbia, S. C.), Moses Waddel

(1770–1840, Athens, Ga.), John Clarke Young (1803–1857, Danville, Ky.).

Baptists: John Armstrong (1798–1844, New Bern, N. C., and Columbus, Miss.), James P. Boyce (1827–1888, Columbia and Greenville, S. C.), W. T. Brantly, Jr. (1816–1882, Augusta and Atlanta, Ga.), W. T. Brantly, Sr. (1787–1845, Beaufort and Charleston, S. C., and Augusta, Ga.), John A. Broadus (1827–1895, Charlottesville, Va.), A. W. Clopton (1784–1833, Chapel Hill, N. C.), John L. Dagg (1794–1884, Penfield, Ga.), Richard Furman (1755–1825, Charleston), Henry Holcombe (1762–1824, Savannah), R. B. C. Howell (1801–1868, Nashville), J. B. Jeter (1802–1880, Richmond), John Kerr (1782–1842, Richmond), Basil Manly, Jr. (1825–1892, Richmond), Basil Manly, Sr. (1798–1868, Tuscaloosa, Ala., and Charleston, S. C.), Jonathan Maxcy (1768–1820, Columbia, S. C.), Jesse Mercer (1769–1841, Washington, Ga.), Silas Mercer Noel (1783–1839, Frankfort, Ky.), Billington Sanders (1789–1854, Penfield, Ga.), R. B. Semple (1769–1831, Fredericksburg and Bruington, Va.), Adiel Sherwood (1791–1879, Penfield and Griffin, Ga.), James Taylor (1804–1871, Richmond), John L. Waller (1809–1854, Shelbyville and Louisville, Ky.), and Alva Woods (1794–1887, Lexington, Ky., and Tuscaloosa, Ala.).

Methodists: Henry B. Bascom (1796–1850, Danville and Louisville, Ky.), A. T. Bledsoe (1809–1877, Oxford, Miss., and Charlottesville, Va.), William Capers (1790–1855, Charleston and Columbia, S. C., and Savannah, Ga.), B. M. Drake (1800–1860, New Orleans), Ignatius Few (1789–1845, Savannah, Columbus, Macon, Ga.), H. H. Kavanaugh (b. 1802, Frankfort, Ky.), Robert L. Kennon (b. 1789, Louisville), George Lane (1815–1848, Oxford, Ga.), John Lane (1787–1855, Vicksburg, Miss.), Hezekiah G. Leigh (1795–1853, Raleigh, N. C., Norfolk and Petersburg, Va.), A. B. Longstreet (1790–1870, Oxford, Ga., Oxford, Miss., and Columbia, S. C.), William McKendree (1757–1835, Bishop of the Western District of Southern Methodism), Robert Paine (1799–1882, Aberdeen, Miss.), George F. Pierce (1811–1884, Macon and Oxford, Ga.), Thomas Ralston (1806–1885?, Louisville), Edward Drumgoole Sims (1805–1845, Ashland, Va., and Tuscaloosa, Ala.), William A. Smith (1802–1870, Richmond, Norfolk, Va.), Thomas O. Summers (1812–1882, Nashville).

Episcopalians: Jasper Adams (1793–1841, Charleston), Thomas Atkinson (1807–1881, Baltimore, and Norfolk, Va.), Frederick Dalcho (1770–1836, Charleston), L. S. Ives (1797–1867, Bishop of North Carolina), Reuel Keith (1792–1842, Alexandria and Williamsburg, Va.), James Madison (1749–1812, Williamsburg, Va.), William Meade (1789–1862, Richmond), Richard Channing Moore (1762–1841, Richmond), James Hervey Otey (1800–1863, Franklin and Memphis, Tenn.), Leonidas Polk (1806–1864, New Orleans), John S. Ravenscroft (1772–1830, Richmond and Bishop of North Carolina), Daniel Stephens (1778–1850, Staunton, Va., and Columbia, Tenn.), R. H. Wilmer (1816–1900, Bishop of Alabama), W. H. Wilmer (1782–1827, Alexandria, Va.).

Lutherans: John Bachman (1790–1874, Charleston), Paul Henkel (1754–1825, New Market, Va.).

Roman Catholics: J. B. M. David (1761–1841, Bardstown, Ky.), John England (1786–1842, Charleston), Benedict Flaget (1763–1850, Bardstown and Louisville), Francis P. Kenrick (1796–1863, Bardstown), John McGill (1809–1872, Richmond), M. J. Spalding (1810–1872, Louisville).

My biographical information came from the articles in Allen Johnson and Dumas Malone (eds.), *Dictionary of American Biography* (New York, 1928–1937), William B. Sprague, *Annals of the American Pulpit* (New York, 1860), and the individual biographical studies listed in the footnotes to this chapter, especially n. 66.

The attempt to break the analysis into discrete time periods did not change the character of the group profile, though, as one might expect, ministers whose careers were at their peak during the forties and fifties tended to have a bit more exposure than their predecessors to college and seminary education.

My list is by no means exhaustive. It might have included, for instance, Charles Colcock Jones (1804–1863), the central figure of Robert Manson Myers's epic *The Children of Pride* (New Haven, 1972), who was minister for a time in Savannah; or Patrick Neison Lynch (1817–1882), the third Roman Catholic Bishop of Charleston; or Augustin Verot (1805–1876), a professor at St. Mary's College in Baltimore, who later became Bishop of Florida. See Michael V. Gannon, *Rebel Bishop: The Life and Era of Augustin Verot* (Milwaukee, 1964).

6. B. F. Riley, *History of the Baptists of Alabama* (Birmingham, 1895), p. 64; Howell, *Monthly Miscellany*, p. 81; Smith, *Life of Pierce*, p. 561.

7. M. J. Spalding, *Sketches of the Life, Times, and Character of the Right Reverend Benedict Joseph Flaget, First Bishop of Louisville* (Louisville, 1852), p. 236; Tasistro, *Random Shots*, 2:187.

8. Lovick Pierce, "Semi-Centennial Discourse," *Sermons and Essays by Ministers of the Methodist Episcopal Church, South*, p. 28; Smith, *Life of Pierce*, p. 119; Whitefoord Smith, "Address," Smith Papers, Duke; Deems (ed.), *Annals* (1855), pp. 259–71; Clement Eaton, *A History of the Old South* (3rd ed., New York, 1975), p. 458.

9. These statistics are based on a sample of 253 clergy in 24 towns within 7 states in 1860: Jackson, Vicksburg, and Natchez, Miss.; Frankfort, Louisville, and Lexington, Ky.; Tuscaloosa, Montgomery, and Mobile, Ala.; Athens, Augusta, Macon, Albany, and Savannah, Ga.; Beaufort, Spartanburg, Columbia, and Charleston, S. C.; Charlottesville, Alexandria, and Richmond, Va.; Nashville, Jackson, and Memphis, Tenn. The figures are taken from the manuscript Population Schedules of the Eighth Census, 1860, available on microfilm from the National Archives.

10. In discussing family background I was imprecise—using such qualified terms as "slightly more," "slightly less," and "almost"—because I could find firm information about the family backgrounds of only 80 men out of

the 100: 35 were the sons of farmers and planters, 14 of merchants and businessmen, 14 of ministers, 13 of other professionals and civil servants, and 4 of artisans. Probably more than half spent a portion of their childhood in towns and cities: 49 were apparently born in cities or towns while 45 were listed only as being born in counties (though some of them may have lived in towns later). I could not obtain sufficient information about the remaining six. I would not, moreover, wish to overstate the difference between small towns and the countryside in considering childhood experience.

11. M. M. Henkle, *The Life of Henry Bidleman Bascom, D.D., LL.D.* (Louisville, 1854), p. 329.

12. In addition to the Princeton graduates the sampling includes alumni of Andover (5), Union in Virginia (4), The Episcopal Theological Seminary of Virginia (2), Indiana Theological Seminary (1), Newton Theological Seminary (1), Columbia (1), St. Mary's Baltimore (1), Nantes (1), Clermont (1), Bardstown (1), and one student—Thornwell—who attended Andover and studied informally at Harvard for a year but found neither institution to his liking.

13. Fourteen attended Southern state colleges: South Carolina College (4), The University of Virginia (2), The University of North Carolina (4), and the University of Georgia (4). Nineteen attended private and church-affiliated colleges in the South.

14. H. C. Owsley (ed.), *The South: Old and New Frontiers: Selected Essays of Frank Lawrence Owsley* (Athens, Ga., 1969), pp. 45–46.

15. For the national averages see Leo Soltow, *Men and Wealth in the United States, 1850–1870* (New Haven, 1975). I calculated the clerical average from a sample of 254 Protestant and 3 Jewish clergy in 24 towns within 7 states (see n. 9). I drew all of my data on wealth from the manuscript population schedules of the eighth census, 1860.

16. Not every minister listed his denominational affiliation in the census. I drew my figures from lists of those who did; they included 41 Baptists, 88 Methodists, 42 Episcopalians, and 31 Presbyterians. I could not calculate the average wealth of Roman Catholics, for they often had no personal holdings, and church officials often listed the value of church property under their own names.

17. William Winans to P. H. Diffenwirth, 18 March 1842, and Winans to R. H. Rivers, October 1848, Winans Papers, University of Mississippi, Oxford.

18. John Lambert, *Travels Through Lower Canada and the United States of America* (London, 1810), in Lane (ed.), *Rambler in Georgia*, p. 46; *Minutes of the Synod of Georgia* (Milledgeville, 1848), p. 33; Clifford M. Drury, *William Anderson Scott: "No Ordinary Man"* (Glendale, Calif., 1967), pp. 72, 82; Olmsted, *Journey*, 2:83; Taylor, "History of the Episcopal Church," *Louisiana Historical Quarterly* 22 (1939):428–78; G. W. Williams, *The Rev. Frederick Dalcho, M.D.* (Charleston, 1960), p. 9.

19. Basil Manly to J. L. Reynolds, 18 September 1839; Manly to Reyn-

olds, 12 September 1841, Manly Collection, University of Alabama, Tuscaloosa.

20. *Minutes of the Synod of Georgia* (Macon, 1845), p. 28; Jones, *Duties of a Pastor*, p. 90; Ernest L. Hazelius, *History of the American Lutheran Church* (Zanesville, Ohio, 1846), p. 249; R. B. C. Howell, *The Early Baptists of Virginia* (Philadelphia, 1857), p. 127; Harriet Martineau, *Society in America*, 2 vols. (New York, 1837), 2:351; *Southern Christian Advocate*, 7 October 1842.

21. "Clarke County, State of Georgia, Court of Ordinary, Tax Digest, 1856–66"; "Chatham County, State of Georgia, Superior Court, Tax Digests, 1835"; "Tax Digest, Newton County, Georgia, 1851," Georgia State Archives; but see especially the manuscript slave schedules of the 1860 census, available on microfilm from the National Archives. I suspect that the percentages of ministerial slaveholders in the towns were even higher than I indicate, for I included only ministers whom I could clearly identify. Eugene Genovese says that in South Carolina between 1780 and 1800 about 40% of the clergy owned slaves; see his *Roll, Jordan, Roll* (New York, 1974), p. 202. The Reverend James Smylie, who wrote one of the first Biblical defenses of slavery, owned fifty-three persons in 1830; he was the third largest slaveholder in Amite County, Mississippi, according to information in the Montgomery Papers.

22. Based on a sample of 257 clergy in 24 towns within 7 states, as given in the manuscript population schedules of the 1860 census (see n. 9).

23. Martineau, *Society in America*, 2:351.

24. Stow Persons, *The Decline of American Gentility* (New York, 1973).

25. Anthony Upton, "The Road to Power in the Early Nineteenth Century," *The Virginia Magazine of History and Biography* 62 (July, 1954): 259–80; *Life of Olin*, p. 60; *The Seventh Census of the United States: 1850*, p. lxvii; Anson West, *History of Methodism in Alabama* (Nashville, 1893), p. 80; Persons, *American Gentility*, pp. 4–31; Daniel H. Calhoun, *Professional Lives in America: Structure and Aspiration, 1750–1850* (Cambridge, Mass., 1965), pp. 65–82.

26. *Life of Olin*, p. 50; *Seventh Census*, pp. lxvii, lxiv.

27. Eaton, *History of the Old South*, pp. 278–79.

28. C. H. Williams, "Early Ante-Bellum Montgomery: A Black-Belt Constituency," *JSH* 7 (November, 1941):495–525.

29. "The City of Nashville," *Review* 1 (1848):503–8; *Seventh Census, 1850*, p. lxvii.

30. Manuscript population schedules of the eighth census, 1860, provided data on the number of professionals in the smaller towns and cities, though my figures are low, because some Southerners who listed themselves as merchants and practitioners of other occupations were also attorneys or doctors. Seven of the clergy in my sampling of one hundred had attended medical school; sixteen had studied law.

31. My conclusions about professional wealth are based on a sample of

424 lawyers in 22 towns within 7 states and 515 doctors in 23 towns within 7 states, according to the population schedules of the eighth census, 1860. See n. 9. For figures on laborers' wages, see Eaton, *History of the Old South*, p. 279.

32. Martha C. Mitchell, "Health and the Medical Profession in the Lower South, 1845–1860," *JSH* 10 (November, 1944):424–46; Upton, "Road to Power," *Virginia Magazine of History and Biography* 62:259–80.

33. John Holt Rice, *Virginia Evangelical and Literary Magazine* 6 (1823):424.

34. Frances Trollope, *Domestic Manners of the Americans*, 2 vols. (New York, 1901; 1st ed., 1832), 1:103; Bremer, *Homes of the New World*, 2: 647.

35. George Howe, *A Discourse on Theological Education* (New York, 1844), p. 118.

36. R. H. Rivers, *The Life of Robert Paine, D.D.* (Nashville, 1916), p. 179.

37. Joseph H. Baker (ed.), *The Baptist Chronicle and Monthly Monitor* 1 (November, 1840):80–82. See also Lindsley, *Works*, 1:443.

38. Howe, *Discourse*, p. 118; C. D. Mallary, *Memoirs of Elder Jesse Mercer* (New York, 1844), p. 407; Rice, *Magazine* 6 (1823):424; Lindsley, *Works*, 1:438, 443.

39. Mitchell, "Medical Profession," *JSH* 10:440–45. Perry Miller, *The Life of the Mind in America from the Revolution to the Civil War* (New York, 1965); Calhoun, *Professional Lives*, pp. 65–82; William J. Sassnett, *Progress: Considered with Particular Reference to the Methodist Episcopal Church, South* (Nashville, 1855), p. 262; Jones, *Duties of a Pastor*, p. 43; Alva Woods, *President Woods' Addresses* (Tuscaloosa, 1838), n.p.; Richard Channing Moore, *The Doctrines of the Church* (Philadelphia, 1820), p. 6; Howe, *Discourse*, p. 118; James Hervey Otey, "Plans for a Theological and Literary Institution," 16 February 1835, Otey Papers, U.N.C., Chapel Hill.

40. John H. Moore (ed.), "The Abiel Abbot Journals: A Yankee Preacher in Charleston Society, 1818–1827," *South Carolina Historical Magazine* 68 (1967):51–73, 115–39, 232–54; William Winans to Kate Adams, 24 December 1853, Winans Papers, University of Mississippi, Oxford; Tasistro, *Random Shots*, 2:187; Taylor, *Life of Taylor*, p. 35; Fitzgerald, *Dr. Summers*, pp. 153–54; Smith, *Life of Pierce*, p. 41; Basil Manly, Diary, 1830–34, and Basil Manly to Sarah Manly, 6 November 1835, Manly Collection, University of Alabama, Tuscaloosa; James H. Thornwell to his wife, 29 May 1851, Thornwell Papers, U.N.C., Chapel Hill; L. C. Garland to his mother, 23 February 1848, Garland Papers, Vanderbilt.

41. William B. Hamilton, "The Southwestern Frontier, 1795–1817," *JSH* 10 (November, 1944):389–403; Carl Bode, *The American Lyceum: Town Meeting of the Mind* (New York, 1956), pp. 31–32, 79–82, 155–56; James Silk Buckingham, *The Slave States of the South* (London, 1842), in Lane (ed.), *Rambler in Georgia*, p. 168.

42. W. M. Waeky to William Winans, 18 September 1842, Winans Papers, University of Mississippi, Oxford; Thomas Cary Johnson, *The Life and Letters of Benjamin Morgan Palmer* (Richmond, 1906), p. 146; Isaac Otey to James H. Otey, 6 May 1833, Otey Papers, U.N.C., Chapel Hill; Sereno Taylor Diaries, 6 January 1849, Taylor Papers, L.S.U., Baton Rouge; *United States Catholic Miscellany* 10, 25 December 1830. John Bachman, *The Unity of the Human Race Examined on the Principles of Science* (Charleston, 1850) and Thomas Smyth, *The Unity of the Human Races Proved to be the Doctrine of Scripture, Reason, and Science, Works* 7, were two examples of theological treatises that originated as presentations of local philosophical societies.

43. Smith, *Life of Pierce*, p. 41.

44. William M. Wightman, *Life of William Capers, D.D., Including an Autobiography* (Nashville, 1902), p. 190.

45. "Use of Tobacco," pp. 7, 13, and Lovick Pierce, "Devotedness to Christ," p. 18, in Summers (ed.), *Sermons and Essays*; Moore, *Doctrines of the Church*, p. 6.

46. Moore, *Doctrines of the Church*, p. 6; Jones, *Duties of a Pastor*, p. 41; Robert Fleming (ed.), *The Georgia Pulpit: or Minister's Yearly Offering, Containing Sermons and Essays from Georgia Baptist Ministers* (Richmond, 1847), p. 67; Jesse Mercer, *Christian Index* (1834), in Mallary, *Memoirs*, p. 185; Lindsley, *Works*, 1:443.

47. Summers (ed.), *Biographical Sketches*, p. 56.

48. J. H. Thornwell, Journal, 14 June 1836, Thornwell Collection, Montreat; Hatcher, *Life of Jeter*, p. 523; Summers (ed.), *Biographical Sketches*, p. 56; Meade, *Lectures on the Pastoral Office*, p. 192; William Winans to Richard Abbey, 25 October 1842, Winans Papers, University of Mississippi, Oxford.

49. Tasistro, *Random Shots*, 2:183–84. He was not speaking simply of the Southern clergy, however.

50. J. H. Thornwell, *Review of Paley's Moral Philosophy*, p. 25, in Miscellaneous Papers, Smyth Library, Columbia Theological Seminary.

51. Shaftesbury, *An Inquiry Concerning Virtue* (1699), *British Moralists: Being Selections From Writers Principally of the Eighteenth Century*, ed. L. A. Selby-Bigge, 2 vols. (New York, 1964), 1:39; Francis Hutcheson, *An Inquiry Concerning Moral Good and Evil* (1725), *British Moralists*, 1:130–31; Adam Smith, *The Theory of Moral Sentiments* (1759), *British Moralists*, 1:229.

52. Joseph Butler, *Sermons* (1726), *British Moralists*, 1:200–203.

53. Dagg, *Moral Science*, pp. 194–95, which was an adaptation of Francis Wayland, *The Elements of Moral Science* (1835). All the textbooks in moral philosophy carried the same message; see below, chap. 6.

54. Thornwell, *Discourses on Truth*, p. 534; Wightman, *Life of Capers*, p. 190.

55. Joseph B. Cottrell, Diary, 1854–92, U.N.C., Chapel Hill. See also

the manuscript population schedules of the eighth census in Alabama, 1860, and the manuscript slave schedules of the eighth census, Alabama, 1860.

56. Howell, *Monthly Miscellany*, pp. 81–82.

57. Jack Lumpkin, "Ministerial Education" (1832), *Georgia Pulpit*, p. 112. See also Riley, *Baptists of Alabama*, p. 87; Alva Woods, *Intellectual and Moral Culture* (Lexington, 1828), p. 9.

58. J. W. M. Williams to Basil Manly, Jr., 10 April 1846, Manly, Jr., Papers, U.N.C., Chapel Hill.

59. Jones, *Duties of a Pastor*, p. 103.

60. C. F. Deems (ed.), *The Southern Methodist Pulpit* 4 (1851):52. See also Francis Flournoy, *Benjamin Mosby Smith, 1811–1893* (Richmond, 1947), p. 62; William M. Green, *Life and Papers of A. L. P. Green, D.D.* (Nashville, 1877), p. 96; William Wightman, *Ministerial Ability* (Nashville, 1856), p. 15.

61. Wightman, *Ministerial Ability*, p. 13.

62. Summers (ed.), *Sermons and Essays*, pp. 4–5.

63. E. Merton Coulter, "What the South Has Done about Its History," *JSH* 2 (February, 1936):3–28.

64. John Ellis Edwards, *Life of the Rev. John Wesley Childs* (Richmond, 1852), p. 15.

65. Theodore P. Green, *America's Heroes: The Changing Models of Success in American Magazines* (New York, 1970), p. 40; *The Evangelical Museum* 1 (Fayetteville, N. C., January, 1828):30; Adam Clarke, *The Preacher's Manual* (New York, 1820), pp. 108–9. See also Thomas Coke, *Four Discourses on the Duties of a Minister of the Gospel*, in Clarke, *Preacher's Manual*, p. 222. Such works complemented the secular literature: Persons, *American Gentility*, pp. 43–50, discusses Charles Butler, *The American Gentleman* (Philadelphia, 1836) and other instances of the genre.

66. Among the biographical and autobiographical statements written by clergy active during the antebellum period were John Adger, *My Life and Times* (Richmond, 1899); John A. Broadus, *Memoir of James Petigru Boyce, D.D., LL.D.* (Nashville, 1927; 1st ed., 1893); Joseph Caldwell, *Autobiography of the Rev. Joseph Caldwell, D.D.* (n.d.); Jesse Campbell, *Georgia Baptists: Historical and Biographical* (Richmond, 1847); Theodore Clapp, *Autobiographical Sketches and Recollections During a Thirty-five Years' Residence in New Orleans* (Boston, 1857); John Ellis Edwards, *Life of the Rev. John Wesley Childs* (Richmond, 1852); Robert Emory, *The Life of the Rev. John Emory* (New York, 1841); James B. Finley, *Sketches of Western Methodism: Biographical, Historical, and Miscellaneous* (Cincinnati, 1855); William Henry Foote, *Sketches of North Carolina: Historical and Biographical* (New York, 1846); M. M. Henkle, *The Life of Henry Bidleman Bascom* (Louisville, 1854); J. P. K. Henshaw, *Memoir of the Life of the Rt. Rev. Richard Channing Moore, D.D.* (Philadelphia, 1842); R. B. C. Howell, *The Early Baptists of Virginia* (1857); Leroy M. Lee, *The Life and Times of the Rev. Jesse Lee* (1848); Charles

D. Mallary, *Memoirs of Elder Edmund Botsford* (Charleston, 1832); Charles D. Mallary, *Memoirs of Elder Jesse Mercer* (New York, 1844); William Maxwell, *A Memoir of the Rev. John H. Rice, D.D.* (Philadelphia, 1835); William Meade, *Old Churches, Ministers, and Families of Virginia* (Philadelphia, 1872); William H. Milburn, *Ten Years of Preacher-Life: Chapters from an Autobiography* (New York, 1859); Robert Paine, *Life and Times of William McKendree* (1857); B. M. Palmer, *The Life and Letters of James Henley Thornwell, D.D., LL.D.* (Richmond, 1875); Levi Purviance, *The Biography of Elder David Purviance* (Dayton, 1848); R. H. Rivers, *The Life of Robert Paine, D.D.* (Nashville, 1916; 1st ed., 1884); M. J. Spalding, *Sketches of the Life, Times, and Character of the Right Reverend Benedict Joseph Flaget, First Bishop of Louisville* (Louisville, 1852); A. Steele, *Christianity in Earnest, As Exemplified in the Life and Labors of the Rev. Hodgson Casson* (Nashville, 1855); Edward Stevenson, *Biographical Sketch of the Rev. Valentine Cook, A.M.* (Nashville, 1858); Thomas O. Summers (ed.), *Biographical Sketches of Eminent Itinerant Ministers* (Nashville, 1858); James Taylor, *Biography of Elder Lott Carey* (1837); James Taylor, *Memoir of Luther Rice* (1840); James Taylor, *Lives of Virginia Baptist Ministers* (Philadelphia, 1859); W. H. Watkins, "Character and Life of the Rev. B. M. Drake, D.D." (1860), in T. L. Mellen (ed.), *Life and Labors of the Rev. William Hamilton Watkins* (Nashville, 1886); William Wightman, *Life of William Capers, D.D., Including an Autobiography* (Nashville, 1902). One should also consult the many biographical sketches in such papers as Henry Holcombe's *Georgia Analytical Repository* (Savannah, Georgia) or *The Monthly Miscellany: A Religious and Literary Review* (Atlanta and Richmond).

67. Taylor, *Lives*, pp. 49, 61, 66, 74, 97–98, 131–33, 143–44, 160–61, 171, 383.

68. Jeter, "Introduction," *Lives*, Taylor, p. ix.

69. Fitzgerald, *Dr. Summers*, pp. 152, 25–231; Thomas Summers, Introductory Essay, A. Vinet, *Pastoral Theology: The Theory of a Gospel Ministry* (Nashville, 1861), p. xx.

70. Summers (ed.), *Sketches*, pp. 57, 76, 114, 141, 312.

71. J. E. Edwards, "Biographical Sketch of Bishop Doggett," in *Sermons by the late Rev. David Seth Doggett*, ed. T. O. Summers, 2 vols. (Nashville, 1882), 1:xviii.

72. William Winans to W. B. Hines, 20 March 1852, Winans Collection, University of Mississippi, Oxford.

73. J. B. Jeter (ed.), *The Sermons and Other Writings of the Rev. Andrew Broaddus* (New York, 1855), p. 35. See the criticisms in Adam Clarke, *Preacher's Manual*, p. 122, an English work popular among American Methodists, which argued that "Allegorical preaching debases the taste, and fetters the Understanding."

74. T. O. Summers (ed.), *MQR* 13 (1859):282.

75. Edwards, "Biographical Sketch," p. xvii. See also Summers (ed.), *Sketches*, pp. 58, 100, 314; William H. Foote, *Sketches of Virginia, His-*

torical and Biographical (Philadelphia, 1855), p. 199; Jones, *Duties of a Pastor*, p. 29; Campbell, *Georgia Baptists*, p. 37.

76. Lionel Trilling, *Sincerity and Authenticity* (Cambridge, Mass., 1971), p. 112; Alexis de Tocqueville, *Democracy in America*, 2 vols. (New York, 1961; 1st ed., 1835), 2:76–85.

77. Quoted in Martin Marty, *Righteous Empire* (New York, 1970), p. 74.

78. Basil Manly to Basil Manly, Jr., 28 September 1847, Manly Collection, University of Alabama, Tuscaloosa.

79. William Smithson (ed.), *The Methodist Pulpit South* (Washington, 1858), n.p.; Henkle, *Life of Bascom*, p. 334.

80. See Henry Smith Stroupe, *The Religious Press in the South Atlantic States, 1802–1865* (Durham, N. C., 1956).

81. William Winans to D.V. (?), 31 May 1852, Winans Collection, University of Mississippi, Oxford; William Stokes (ed.), *The Southern Baptist Preacher, or Sermons by Living Baptist Ministers in the South* (Washington, Georgia, 1839), n.p.; Foote, *Sketches of Virginia*, p. 258; Clarke, *The Preacher's Manual*, p. 163; Wilbur Fisk to John Keener, 15 May 1834, Hendrix Papers, Duke.

82. Greene, *America's Heroes*, pp. 26, 40; John Holt Rice to Thomas Chalmers, 25 July 1817, in Moore (ed.), "Letters of Rice," *Virginia Magazine of History and Biography* 67:312.

83. Ibid.; Foote, *Sketches of Virginia*, p. 304.

84. Johnson, *Life of Palmer*, p. 126; Henkle, *Life of Bascom*, p. 303.

85. Charles Sydnor, *The Development of Southern Sectionalism, 1819–1848* (Baton Rouge, 1948), p. 64; *Seventh Census, 1850*, p. lx; Owsley (ed.), *South*, pp. 45–46; David B. Potts, "American Colleges in the Nineteenth Century: From Localism to Denominationalism," *History of Education Quarterly* 11 (Winter, 1971):363–70; Natalie A. Taylor, "The Ante-Bellum College Movement: A Reappraisal of Tewksbury's Founding of American Colleges and Universities," *History of Education Quarterly* 13 (Fall, 1973):261–71.

86. Godbold, *Church College*, pp. 56–58, 146; Rivers, *Life of Paine*, p. 179; Daniel Penick to Drury Lacy, 27 November 1854, Penick Papers, U.N.C., Chapel Hill; B. A. Houghton to William Winans, 16 January 1836, Winans Papers, University of Mississippi, Oxford.

87. Mallary, *Memoirs of Mercer*, pp. 178–83; see also T. O. Summers, *Holiness: A Treatise on Sanctification* (Richmond, 1851), p. 19; Howe, *Discourse*, p. 196; Samuel Gilman, *Contributions to Religion* (Charleston, 1860), p. 65.

88. Mallary, *Memoirs of Mercer*, p. 185.

89. *Life of Olin*, p. 182; William Winans, "The Gospel Ministry," in Summers (ed.), *Sermons and Essays*, p. 12.

90. Bertram Wyatt-Brown, "The Antimission Movement in the Jacksonian South: A Study in Regional Folk Culture," *JSH* 36 (November, 1970):501–29.

91. Robert Davidson, *History of the Presbyterian Church in the State of Kentucky* (New York, 1847), p. 230; John Holt Rice to Archibald Alexander, 5 March 1823, in Moore (ed.), "Letters of Rice," *Virginia Magazine of History and Biography* 67:57.

92. Wightman, *Life of Capers*, p. 202; Smith, *Life of Pierce*, p. 58; Fitzgerald, *Dr. Summers*, p. 59; Henkle, *Life of Bascom*, p. 98; McFerrin, *Methodism in Tennessee*, p. 424.

93. Nicholas Snethen, *Essays on Lay Representation and Church Government, Collected from the Wesleyan Repository, The Mutual Rights, and The Mutual Rights and Christian Intelligencer, from 1820 to 1829* (Baltimore, 1835), p. xxv.

94. Sassnett, *Progress*, pp. 306, 262. Winans thought that even Sassnett had granted too much to the progressives; see Winans to Sassnett, June 1856, Winans Collection, University of Mississippi, Oxford. Winans regretted the introduction of "a learned ministry, exquisite music, splendid churches, and imposing ceremonies." See Winans to D. D. Venne, 15 March 1848, Winans Collection.

95. *The Southern Baptist Messenger, Devoted to the Service of the Old School Baptists* (Covington, Georgia, July 15, 1857), p. 99.

96. *The LaGrange Herald*, 28 September 1843.

97. *Southern Baptist Messenger*, 15 February 1853, p. 31; Riley, *Baptists of Alabama*, p. 122.

98. William Winans to C. K. Marshall, 18 October 1852; Winans to C. K. Marshall, 11 July 1856, Winans Collection, University of Mississippi, Oxford.

99. Jeremiah Jeter, *Campbellism Examined* (New York, 1855), pp. 82, 343; Alexander Campbell, *The Millennial Harbinger* 2 (Bethany, Virginia, n.d.):15, 27, 312.

CHAPTER THREE

1. Niels Henry Sonne, *Liberal Kentucky, 1780–1828* (New York, 1939), p. 79; James Gallaher, *The Western Sketch-Book* (Boston, 1850), pp. 32–33; Sister Mary Ramona Mattingly, *The Catholic Church on the Kentucky Frontier* (Washington, D.C., 1936), p. 195; Martin J. Spalding, *Sketches of the Early Catholic Missions of Kentucky* (Louisville, 1844), p. 83; Robert Davidson, *History of the Presbyterian Church in the State of Kentucky* (New York, 1847), p. 102. The continuities between liberalism and orthodoxy have received attention from Sidney Mead, *The Lively Experiment* (New York, 1963), pp. 38–54 and Conrad Wright, *The Liberal Christians* (Boston, 1970), chap. 1.

2. Eaton, *Freedom of Thought*, p. 12; Robert C. McLean, "A Yankee Tutor in the Old South," *North Carolina Historical Review* 47 (Winter, 1970):79; Moore, *Doctrines of the Church*, p. 24; Henshaw, *Memoir*, p. 121.

3. Herbert Morais, *Deism in Eighteenth Century America* (New York, 1934), pp. 154–55.

4. Jones, *Duties of a Pastor*, p. 23; Leonidas Rosser, *Reply to the Evils of Infant Baptism* (Richmond, 1855), p. 98.

5. Fletcher Green, *The Role of the Yankee in the Old South* (Athens, Ga., 1972), p. 93; Sprague (ed.), *Annals of the American Pulpit*, 4:177; Davidson, *History of the Presbyterian Church*, p. 283; Mattingly, *Catholic Church*, p. 183; William Hooper, *Fifty Years Since: An Address Before the University of North Carolina Alumni* (Raleigh, 1859), p. 39.

6. Meade, *Old Churches*, 1:29.

7. Gallaher, *Western Sketch-Book*, p. 68.

8. Spencer, *Kentucky Baptists*, 1:501.

9. Jasper Adams, *Elements of Moral Philosophy* (Cambridge, 1837), p. 323.

10. Greenough White, *A Saint of the Southern Church: Memoir of the Right Reverend Nicholas Hamner Cobbs, Doctor of Divinity, First Bishop of the Diocese of Alabama* (New York, 1897), p. 15.

11. Thomas Paine, *The Age of Reason, Being an Investigation of True and Fabulous Theology, The Writings of Thomas Paine*, ed. Moncure Daniel Conway, 4 vols. (New York, 1896), 4:27, 30, 38, 52, 57–60, 65, 76, 90, 95–96.

12. James H. Smylie, "Clerical Perspectives on Deism: Paine's *Age of Reason* in Virginia," *Eighteenth Century Studies* 6 (Winter, 1972–73): 209.

13. Paine, *Writings*, 4:184, 191.

14. Ibid., p. 88. See Sidney Mead, *The Nation with the Soul of a Church* (New York, 1975), pp. 48–77, and Mead, *Lively Experiment*, pp. 38–54.

15. Philip Freneau, *Letters on Various Interesting and Important Subjects* (Philadelphia, 1799), pp. 37–38, cited in Martin Marty, *The Infidel: Freethought and American Religion* (Cleveland, 1961), p. 25. See also James Gallaher (ed.), *Calvinistic Magazine* 1 (1827):63; Foote, *Sketches of Virginia*, p. 233; Sarah Lemmon, "Nathaniel Blount: Last Clergyman of the Old Church," *North Carolina Historical Review* 50 (October, 1973): 362; T. O. Summers, "The Theological Works of Thomas Paine," *MQR* 7 (1854):486.

16. Charles S. Sydnor, "The Beginning of Printing in Mississippi," *JHS* 1 (February, 1935):49; Richard Watson, *An Apology for the Bible. In a Series of Lectures Addressed to Thomas Paine*, ed. T. O. Summers (Nashville, 1856).

17. Olmsted, *Journey in the Seaboard Slave States*, 2:592.

18. Andrew Broaddus, *The Age of Reason and Revelation: or Animadversions on Mr. Thomas Paine's Late Piece, Intitled The Age of Reason* (Richmond, 1795), pp. 13, 22–23.

19. Ibid., p. 24.

20. Ibid., pp. 25–32, 43.

21. Moses Hoge, *The Sophist Unmasked; In a Series of Letters Addressed to Thomas Paine* (Shepherdstown, 1797), pp. 257–62.

22. Gallaher (ed.), *Calvinistic Magazine* 1 (1827):95.

23. Thomas R. Dew, *Southern Literary Messenger* 2 (November, 1836):768.

24. Clarence Gohdes, "Some Notes on the Unitarian Church in the Ante-Bellum South: A Contribution to the History of Southern Liberalism," *American Studies in Honor of William Kenneth Boyd*, ed. David K. Jackson (Durham, N. C., 1940), pp. 327–66; Eaton, *Freedom of Thought*, pp. 314–20; Arthur A. Brooks, *The History of Unitarianism in the Southern Churches* (Boston, n.d.), pp. 1–25; George H. Gibson, "Unitarian Congregations in Ante-Bellum Georgia," *Georgia Historical Quarterly* 54 (Summer, 1970):148–57; Clement Eaton, "Winifred and Joseph Gales, Liberals in the Old South," *JSH* 10 (November, 1944):461–74.

25. "On the Unitarian Controversy," *Virginia Evangelical and Literary Magazine* 5 (Richmond, 1822):31.

26. Brooks, *History of Unitarianism*, pp. 3–25.

27. Thomas Jefferson, *The Writings of Thomas Jefferson*, ed. A. A. Lipscomb and A. E. Bergh, 20 vols. (Washington, 1904), 15:392.

28. Ibid., 15:272–76.

29. Adrienne Koch, *The Philosophy of Thomas Jefferson* (Chicago, 1964; 1st ed., 1943), pp. 44–45. See also Lula Jane Gilmer, "Some Aspects of the Ethical and Religious Thought of Thomas Jefferson" (M.A. thesis, Duke University, 1937); Daniel J. Boorstin, *The Lost World of Thomas Jefferson* (New York, 1960; 1st ed., 1948); W. D. Gould, "The Religious Opinions of Thomas Jefferson," *Mississippi Valley Historical Review* 20 (September, 1933):191–209; and George H. Knole, "The Religious Ideas of Thomas Jefferson," *Mississippi Valley Historical Review* 30 (September, 1943):187–204.

30. Jefferson, *Writings*, 15:75.

31. Koch, *Thomas Jefferson*, pp. 65–75.

32. Jefferson, *Writings*, 15:240.

33. Ibid., 15:426.

34. Gilbert Chinard, *Jefferson et les Ideologues d'apres sa Correspondance Inedite avec Destutt de Tracy, Cabanis, J.-B. Say, et Auguste Comte* (Baltimore and Paris, 1925), pp. 25, 231.

35. Jefferson, *Writings*, 16:91.

36. Jefferson to Clark Sheldon, 5 December 1825, cited in Chinard, *Jefferson*, p. 282.

37. Jefferson, *Writings*, 15:75.

38. Ibid., 14:149. Jefferson also spoke highly of Dugald Stewart, but the Scottish philosophy was in conflict at several points with Ideology. In fact, Stewart ridiculed Tracy and his followers. I think that Jefferson liked Stewart for two reasons: (1) Stewart's *Elements of the Philosophy of the Human Mind*, which Jefferson read, emphasized the immediate, practi-

cal relevance of philosophy, and (2) Jefferson liked the Scottish notion of a moral sense. I find no evidence, however, that the Scottish criticism of sensationalist epistemology had the slightest effect on Jefferson's docrine of knowledge.

39. Chinard, *Jefferson*, p. 175.

40. Jefferson, *Writings*, 14:149; 15:323.

41. Ibid., 15:425–30; 14:72.

42. Ibid., 15:1–3, 323, 383–85; 14:144–51; 10:379–85.

43. Boorstin, *Thomas Jefferson*, pp. 27–56.

44. Jefferson, *Writings*, 10:379–85; 15:219–24.

45. Ibid., 13:350; 12:236; 14:233.

46. Ibid., 10:374–78, 379–85; 6:256–61; 12:314–16.

47. Ibid., 10:380.

48. Ibid., 6:261.

49. Ibid., 10:174; 15:240, 269–76.

50. G. W. Burnap, "Unitarian Christianity Expounded and Defended," in Samuel Gilman, et al., *The Old and the New* (Charleston, 1854), pp. 126–28.

51. See my analysis of Scottish philosophy and Southern theology in chap. 5.

52. Gilman, *Contributions to Religion: Consisting of Sermons, Practical and Doctrinal* (Charleston, 1860), pp. 24–25; Gilman to John G. Palfrey, 26 May 1828; Gilman to Dorothea Dix, 1851; Gilman to R. W. Emerson, 10 April, 14 April, 21 December 1827, Gilman Collection, Harvard; Gilman, "Brown's Philosophy of the Human Mind," *Southern Review* 3 (1829): 153–55.

53. Gilman, *Revealed Religion: A Dudleian Lecture Delivered in the Chapel of the University at Cambridge* (Boston, 1848), p. 24; Gilman, *Old and New*, pp. 53–54.

54. Gilman, *Revealed Religion*, pp. 3–24.

55. Gilman, *Unitarian Christianity Free from Objectionable Extremes: A Sermon Preached at the Dedication of the Unitarian Church in Augusta, Georgia* (Charleston, 1828), pp. 19, 28.

56. Gilman, *Revealed Religion*, pp. 3–24.

57. Gilman, *Old and New*, pp. 62–68.

58. Ibid., pp. 29, 62–68, 52, 96.

59. Daniel Walker Howe, "A Massachusetts Yankee in Senator Calhoun's Court: Samuel Gilman in South Carolina," *New England Quarterly* 44 (June, 1971):197–220; Gohdes, "Notes on the Unitarian Church," *American Studies in Honor of William Kenneth Boyd*, pp. 327–66; Brooks, *History of Unitarianism*, pp. 3–25.

60. Ralph Luker, "God, Man, and the World of James Warley Miles, Charleston's Transcendentalist," *Historical Magazine of the Protestant Episcopal Church* 39 (June, 1970):101–36. On romanticism see Sydney Ahlstrom, "The Romantic Religious Revolution and the Dilemmas of Religious History," *Church History* 46 (June, 1977):149–70.

61. James W. Miles, *Philosophic Theology; or, Ultimate Grounds of All Religious Belief Based in Reason* (Charleston, 1849), pp. 12, 86, 180, 188.

62. Ibid., pp. 15–17, 86–87, 93–107, 110–12, 155–57. I am grateful to Prof. William Longton for permitting me to read his unpublished essay, "The Thought of James Warley Miles."

63. Ibid., pp. 17, 27, 52, 70; James Warley Miles to anon., 1857, Miles Papers, Duke.

64. Miles to Mrs. Thomas John Young, 28 July 1864, Miles Papers, Duke.

65. Miles, *Philosophic Theology*, pp. 17–31, 68–71, 58–59, 199–203.

66. Ibid., p. 115.

67. Miles to Mrs. Thomas John Young, 12 April 1854, October 1858, Miles Papers, Duke; Miles to David McCord, 24 April 1851, in "Letters of James Warley Miles to David James McCord," ed. James Easterby, *The South Carolina Historical and Genealogical Magazine* 44 (April, 1942): 188.

68. William Henry Milburn, *Ten Years of Preacher-Life: Chapters from an Autobiography* (New York, 1859); William Henry Milburn, *The Pioneer Preacher* (New York, 1857).

69. Ralston, *Elements*, p. 744. The quotation comes from the second edition of 1871, but it summarizes an antebellum consensus.

CHAPTER FOUR

1. See, e.g., the sermons in John Stark Ravenscroft, *The Works of the Right Reverend John Stark Ravenscroft, D.D.*, 2 vols. (New York, 1830); Fleming (ed.), *Georgia Pulpit*; S. C. Jennings (ed.), *The Presbyterian Preacher* (Pittsburgh, 1823–1837); or the other collected sermons noted in chap. 2.

2. Giovanni Perrone, *Kompendium der katholischen Dogmatik* (Landeshutt, 1852), p. 342. See also Avery Dulles, *A History of Apologetics* (London, 1971), pp. 150–97.

3. Raymond M. Bost, "The Reverend John Bachman and the Development of Southern Lutheranism" (Ph.D. diss., Yale University, 1963), p. 194.

4. Mayse, "Robert Jefferson Breckinridge" (Th.D. diss., Union Seminary, Richmond, 1974), p. 503; Howe, *Discourse*, p. 229; Thornwell, *Works*, 1:32; Broadus, *Memoir of Boyce*, p. 268; *History of the Establishment and Organization of the Southern Baptist Theological Seminary, Greenville, South Carolina, to which is appended the first annual Catalogue 1859–60* (Greenville, S. C., 1860), p. 46.

5. "Francisci Turretini Opera," *SPR* 2 (1848):136–37. See also Frank Bell Lewis, "Robert Lewis Dabney: Southern Presbyterian Apologist" (Ph.D. diss., Duke University, 1946), p. 162.

6. Franciscus Turretinus, *Institutio Theologiae Elencticae* (Amsterdam, 1701), pp. 32, 49–53, 185–208.

7. John Hunt, *Religious Thought in England*, 3 vols. (London, 1870), 1:271.

8. Baden Powell, "On the Study of the Evidences of Christianity," *Essays and Reviews* (London, 1861; 1st ed., London, 1860), p. 94.

9. Mark Pattison, "Tendencies of Religious Thought in England, 1688–1750," *Essays and Reviews*, p. 258.

10. Albert Outler (ed.), *John Wesley* (New York, 1964), pp. 393–96.

11. John Wesley, *The Works of the Rev. John Wesley, A.M.*, 14 vols. (London, 1842), 14:285–88.

12. The description of Watson comes from J. R. Graves, *Notes of Application and Illustration* (Nashville, 1856), p. 226.

13. Pattison, "Tendencies of Religious Thought," *Essays and Reviews*, p. 259.

14. Ralston, *Elements*, p. 4; "Review of Elements of Divinity," *MQR* 1 (1847):422–51. Ralston listed the differences between the editions of 1847 and 1871.

15. A. H. Redford, *Life and Times of H. H. Kavanaugh, D.D.* (Nashville, 1884), p. 326.

16. Ralston, *Elements*, p. 12.

17. Thornwell, *Works*, 1:31; "Essays on Divinity," *Virginia Evangelical and Literary Magazine* 1 (1819):9; Samuel Cassells, "The Origin of our Ideas Concerning a God," *SPR* 2 (1848):203–15.

18. Ralston, *Elements*, pp. 14–15.

19. Henkle, *Life of Bascom*, pp. 137–39, 230, 254, 270, 326.

20. William Winans to Maria Huston, 5 December 1850, Winans Collection, University of Mississippi, Oxford; Henkle, *Life of Bascom*, p. 269.

21. Henry Caswell, *America and the American Church* (London, 1839), pp. 219–22.

22. Samuel Baker to William McKendree, 17 August 1824, McKendree Collection, Vanderbilt.

23. Thomas Ralston, Introduction, *Posthumous Works of the Rev. Henry B. Bascom*, 3 vols. (Nashville, 1917), 2:ix, xi.

24. "The Posthumous Works of the Reverend Henry B. Bascom," *MQR* 9 (1855):614.

25. Bascom did not use the word "correlation," and I am aware of the danger of making him sound "modern" by using a term associated with the theology of Paul Tillich. But the word perfectly expresses what he was trying to do.

26. H. B. Bascom, "Lectures on the Relative Claims of Christianity and Infidelity," *Works*, 2:64.

27. Ibid., p. 62.

28. A. B. Van Zandt, "The Necessity of a Revelation: and the Condition of Man Without It," *Lectures on the Evidences*, p. 55; see also *SPR* 2 (1848): 213.

29. Ralston, *Elements*, p. 367; Van Zandt, "Necessity of a Revelation," *Lectures on the Evidences*, p. 43; Thornwell, *Works*, 1:57, 76; Aaron Leland, "On the Proper Agency of Reason, in Matters of Religion," *The Southern Preacher* (Philadelphia, 1824), pp. 281–99; "The Christian Religion Vindicated from the Charge of Being Hostile to Knowledge," *Virginia Evangelical and Literary Magazine* 1 (1818):226; George Armstrong, *The Theology of Christian Experience* (New York, 1858), p. 35; James A. Lyon, "The New Theological Professorship—Natural Science in Connection with Revealed Religion," *SPR* 12 (1859):188.

30. Van Zandt, "Necessity of a Revelation," *Lectures on the Evidences*, p. 52; *MQR* 11 (1857):49.

31. *MQR* 11 (1857):49.

32. Clement Read, "Charge Delivered to John Rice," p. 33, in John H. Rice, *An Inaugural Discourse, Delivered on the First of January 1824* (Richmond, 1824).

33. T. C. Johnson, *Scientific Interests in the Old South* (New York, 1936), pp. 39–43; Godbold, *Church College*, pp. 144–45.

34. "Review of Thomas Dick, *The Christian Philosopher*," *MQR* 11 (1857):461; Johnson, *Scientific Interests*, pp. 35–36.

35. Bachman, *Unity of the Human Race*, Preface, n.p.; Green, *Role of the Yankee*, p. 102.

36. Green, *Role of the Yankee*, p. 102.

37. Bachman, *Unity of the Human Race*, pp. 9, 292.

38. L. W. Green, "The Harmony of Revelation and Natural Science; With Especial Reference to Geology," *Lectures on the Evidences*, p. 463.

39. Green, "Harmony of Revelation and Natural Science," *Lectures on the Evidences*, pp. 463–76; T. V. Moore, "God's Method of Saving the World," *MQR* 11 (1855):76; C. C. Pinckney, *The Testimony of Science to the Truth of Revelation* (Charleston, 1854), pp. 3–4; Ralston, *Elements*, p. 171; T. V. Moore, "English Infidelity," *MQR* 6 (1852):9; Richard Gladney, "Natural Science and Revealed Religion," *SPR* 12 (1860):445–78; "An Address on the Sphere, Interest, and Importance of Geology," *SPR* 3 (1849–50):662; B. M. Smith, *The Testimony of Science to the Truth of the Bible* (Charlottesville, 1850).

40. *MQR* 11 (1857):46–48; see also D. Martindale, "Footprints of the Creator," *MQR* 5 (1851):508; W. N. Pendleton, "The Chronology of Creation," *MQR* 10 (1856):162, 178.

41. Karl Barth, *Die protestantische Theologie im 19. Jahrhundert*, 2 vols. (Hamburg, 1960; 1st ed., 1946), 1:133.

42. William Paley, *Natural Theology, The Works of William Paley, D.D.*, 7 vols. (London, 1825), 5:129–206. See also D. L. LeMahieu, *The Mind of William Paley: A Philosopher and His Age* (Lincoln, Neb., 1976), pp. 55–90.

43. E. F. Rockwell, "The Alphabet of Natural Theology," *SPR* 10 (1857–58):411–36.

44. See the reviews in *SPR* 2 (1848–49):164–65; *MQR* 8 (1854):611, 11 (1857):285, 5 (1851):34–35, and 13 (1859):271.

45. Howard Mumford Jones, "The Influence of European Ideas in Nineteenth Century America," *American Literature* 7 (1935):241–73; *The Columbian Star*, 22 February 1822.

46. Johnson (ed.), *Miscellanies of Thomas E. Peck*, 2:293, 295.

47. *SPR* 12 (1859):188–89.

48. Adger, *Life and Times*, p. 424.

49. William Childs Robinson, *Columbia Theological Seminary and the Southern Presbyterian Church* (n.p., 1931), pp. 168–77; Adger, *Life and Times*, pp. 423–25; Tankersley, *College Life*, p. 81.

50. The articles appeared from 1854 to 1859.

51. Smyth, *Works*, 9:25–26, 92–93, 299–302.

52. Ibid., pp. 30–46.

53. "Scripturalism and Rationalism," *SPR* 5 (1851):275.

54. "On the Submission of the Understanding Required in Scripture," *Virginia Evangelical and Literary Magazine* 2 (1819):52.

55. Ralston, *Elements*, pp. 546, 549, 550.

56. R. L. Dabney, *Syllabus and Notes of the Course of Systematic and Polemic Theology Taught in Union Theological Seminary, Virginia* (Richmond, 1871), pp. 15–54, 83.

57. Ibid., pp. 81, 85.

58. Ralston, *Elements*, p. 605; Smyth, *Works*, 9:92–93.

59. *MQR* 11 (1857):283.

60. Richard Watson, *Theological Institutes: Or, A View of the Evidences, Doctrines, Morals, and Institutions of Christianity* (30th ed., New York, 1850), pp. 71, 95.

61. R. J. Breckinridge, "The General Internal Evidence of Christianity," *Lectures on the Evidences*, p. 330.

62. Van Zandt, "Necessity of a Revelation," *Lectures on the Evidences*, pp. 31–33.

63. Joseph Butler, *Analogy of Religion, Natural and Revealed, to the Constitution and Course of Nature* (New York, 1872; 1st ed., 1736), pp. 272–319.

64. Ralston, *Elements*, p. 701.

65. Breckinridge, "General Internal Evidence," *Lectures on the Evidences*, pp. 336–39; Van Zandt, "Necessity of a Revelation," p. 26; Ralston, *Elements*, p. 691; H. B. Bascom, *Sermons from the Pulpit* (Louisville, 1850), p. 34.

66. Ralston, *Elements*, p. 701; "The Analogy of Religion," *MQR* 8 (1854):215; Robertson, *Life of Broadus*, p. 76; William S. Plumer, "Man Responsible for His Belief," *Lectures on the Evidences*, p. 4; James H. Thornwell, "Miscellaneous Manuscripts," Thornwell Collection, Montreat; B. M. Smith, "Popular Objections to Christianity," *Lectures on the Evidences*, p. 369.

67. Leslie Stephen, *History of English Thought in the Eighteenth Century*, 2 vols. (New York, 1881), 1:254–73.

68. Ralston, *Elements*, p. 611.

69. LeMahieu, *Mind of William Paley*, pp. 1–28, 91–114.

70. Henry Ruffner, "Miracles, Considered as an Evidence of Christianity," *Lectures on the Evidences*, pp. 61–62.

71. David Hume, "Of Miracles," *Hume on Religion*, ed. Richard Wollheim (London, 1963), pp. 211–12.

72. Ralston, *Elements*, p. 611.

73. Bascom, *Sermons*, p. 208; Ruffner, "Miracles," *Lectures on the Evidences*, pp. 70–75; Green, "Harmony of Revelation and Natural Science," ibid., pp. 478–81; G. F. Holmes to J. H. Thornwell, 16 September 1856, Thornwell Collection, Montreat; Ralston, *Elements*, pp. 612–16; Josiah P. Tustin, *The Evidences of Christianity* (Charleston, 1854), p. 115.

74. Hans Frei, *The Eclipse of Biblical Narrative* (New Haven, 1974), pp. 66–85.

75. Ibid. See also Watson, *Theological Institutes*, pp. 194–204; Tustin, *Evidences*, p. 120; "Evidences of Christianity," *The Virginia Evangelical and Literary Magazine* 2 (1819):303–8; William T. Brantley, *Sermons* (n.d.), pp. 13–34; L. R. Willie, "Lecture Notes," Willie Notes, Duke; J. M. Pendleton, *Short Sermons on Important Subjects* (Nashville, 1860), pp. 20–27; Charles Dana, "Do Men Need a Revelation from God?" 16 November 1849, Dana Papers; T. A. Anderson, "A Brief Sketch of the Evidences of Christianity," *Calvinistic Magazine* 1 (1827):108.

76. Dulles, *History of Apologetics*, pp. 150, 196.

77. E. W. Hengstenberg, *Christologie des Alten Testaments und Commentar über die messianischen Weissagungen der Propheten*, 2 vols. (Berlin, 1829–35), 1:22, 333–34, 352–62.

78. E. W. Hengstenberg, *Christology of the Old Testament*, trans. Reuel Keith, 3 vols. (Alexandria, 1836); see the citations in *MQR* 10 (1856): 609; 9 (1855):610; for seminary reading lists, see "Diocesan Seminary," *The Southern Episcopalian* 5 (July, 1858):183; Howe, *Discourse*, pp. 215, 233.

79. Charles D. Dorough, "Religion in the Old South: A Pattern of Behavior and Thought" (Ph.D. diss., University of Texas, 1944), p. 318, citing the unpublished research of Orval Filbeck. See also Godbold, *Church College*, p. 126; G. W. Paschal, *History of Wake Forest College 1834–1865* (Wake Forest, 1935), p. 361; James B. Sellers, *History of the University of Alabama, 1818–1902*, 2 vols. (University, Alabama, 1953), 1:55; Henry M. Bullock, *A History of Emory University* (Nashville, 1936), p. 37; Robert N. Daniel, *Furman University* (Greenville, S. C., 1951), p. 20; Daniel W. Hollis, *University of South Carolina: South Carolina College*, 2 vols. (Columbia, 1951), 1:123–25; Spright Dowell, *A History of Mercer University 1833–1953* (Macon, 1958), p. 89; E. Merton Coulter, *College Life in the Old South* (Athens, Ga., 1928), p. 39; James Allen Cabaniss,

A History of the University of Mississippi (Oxford, 1949), pp. 9, 24, 196.
I also had access to numerous college and seminary catalogues in the Smyth
Collection, Columbia Theological Seminary, Decatur, Ga.

80. *MQR* 8 (1854):228. Thornwell was also uneasy: see Palmer, *Life
of Thornwell*, p. 224. For additional references to the evidential tradition,
see Frederick Dalcho, *The Evidence from Prophecy for the Truth of Christianity, and the Divinity of Christ* (Charleston, 1820); Pendleton, *Sermons*,
pp. 20–27; Samuel Montgomery to Joseph Montgomery, 4 December 1840,
Montgomery Papers, L.S.U., Baton Rouge; W. J. Scott, *Biographic Etch-
ings of Ministers and Laymen of the Georgia Conference* (Atlanta, 1895),
p. 77; Brantley, *Sermons*, pp. 13–163; Adam Empie, *Remarks on the Distinguishing Doctrine of Modern Universalism* (New York, 1825), p. 59;
James Hervey Otey, Journal, 2:21, Otey Papers, U.N.C., Chapel Hill; *The
Monthly Miscellany: A Religious and Literary Review* (1849):78; "Essays
on Divinity," *Virginia Evangelical and Literary Magazine* 2 (1819):15–
19; William H. Wilmer, *The Episcopal Manual: A Summary Explanation
of the Doctrine, Discipline, and Worship of the Protestant Episcopal Church
of the United States of America* (Philadelphia, 1841; 1st ed., 1815), pp.
102–3.

81. W. C. Dana, "A Reasonable Answer to the Skeptic," *SPR* 11 (1857–
58):394.

82. Thornwell, "Canon" and "Inspiration," Thornwell Collection, Mon-
treat; "The Inspiration of the Holy Scripture," *MQR* 11 (1857):280; F. S.
Sampson, "The Authority of the Sacred Canon and the Integrity of the
Sacred Text," *Lectures on the Evidences*, pp. 143–50.

83. Frei, *Eclipse of Biblical Narrative*, p. 91.

84. Leroy M. Lee, "Pulpit Hermeneutics," *MQR* 7 (1852):118, 128,
405–9.

85. Frei, *Eclipse of Biblical Narrative*, pp. 256–66.

86. Ibid., pp. 247–49.

87. T. V. Moore, "Inspiration of the Scriptures," *MQR* 5 (1851):23;
T. O. Summers, "The Philosophy of Infidelity," *MQR* 5 (1851):363; "Au-
gustus Neander's Life of Jesus Christ," *SPR* 2 (1848):147; R. L. Dabney,
"Breckinridge's Theology," *Discussions Evangelical and Theological* (Lon-
don, 1967; 1st ed., 1890), p. 49; "Two Different Modes of Interpreting
Scripture," *Virginia Evangelical and Literary Magazine* 7 (1824):192;
"Review of Stuart's Letters to the Rev. Wm. E. Channing," ibid., 2 (1819):
558.

88. Dabney, *Discussions Evangelical and Theological*, p. 49; *MQR* 5
(1851):363.

89. William A. Mueller, *A History of Southern Baptist Theological
Seminary* (Nashville, 1959), p. 85; *MQR* 7 (1852):117; Robinson, *Columbia Theological Seminary*, pp. 16, 159; *SPR* 5 (1851):275; George
Howe, "Review of Bunsen's Bibelwerk," *SPR* 14 (1861):107; Joseph Baker
(ed.), *The Baptist Chronicle and Monthly Monitor* 1 (1840–1841):107.

90. Jerry Wayne Brown, *The Rise of Biblical Criticism in America, 1800–1870* (Middletown, Ct., 1969), p. 52.

91. "Hugh Miller on the Testimony of the Rocks," *MQR* 11 (1857): 626; see also *MQR* 5 (1851):502; 10 (1856):162, 178; 11 (1857):46; "The Testimony of Geology and Astronomy to the Truth of the Hebrew Records," *Southern Baptist Review and Eclectic* 1 (1855):723.

92. Ralston, *Elements*, p. 73; *MQR* 5 (1851):34–45, 164–65; 8 (1854): 611.

93. *MQR* 5 (1851):33.

94. Alexander Campbell, *The Christian System, in reference to the Union of Christians and a Restoration of Primitive Christianity* (Cincinnati, 1839; 1st ed., 1835), pp. 126–27, 12, 15, 20; Robert Richardson (ed.), *Memoirs of Alexander Campbell* (Nashville, 1956; 1st ed., 1897), pp. 267–73; Alexander Campbell, *Debate on the Evidences of Christianity*, 2 vols. (Cincinnati, 1829), 1:33.

95. L. Sullivan Ives, *The Trials of a Mind in its Progress to Catholicism* (Boston, 1854), pp. 29, 41.

96. England, *Works*, 1:87–88; 2:67.

97. Guilday, *Life of England*, 1:76, 95, 121; 2:434.

98. England, *Works*, 1:17, 89.

99. Ibid., 1:88.

100. J. Adam Moehler, "Sendschreiben an Herrn Bautain," *Gesammelte Schriften und Aufsätze*, 2 vols. (Regensburg, 1840), 2:142–64. For a summary of European Catholic theological positions, see Dulles, *History of Apologetics*.

101. Ludivico Abelly, *Medulla Theologica; Ex Sacris Scripturis, Conciliorum, Pontificumque Decretis* (Munich, 1650), p. 129; Louis Bailly, *Theologica Dogmatica et Moralis Ad Usum Seminariorum* (Lugduni, 1846), 1:12.

102. Perrone, *Kompendium der katholischen Dogmatik*, pp. 3–15, 17–53, 316–21, 326, 333, 340, 342; Abelly, *Medulla*, pp. 40–58, 129; Bailly, *Theologica*, 1:12–32, 46–123, 250–304.

103. Guilday, *Life of England*, 1:69.

104. England, *Works*, 1:141.

105. Ibid., 1:57–58, 77.

106. E. Levesque, "Saint Sulpice," *Dictionnaire de Theologie Catholique* 14/1 (Paris, 1939):802–31.

107. Thomas W. Spalding, *Martin John Spalding: American Churchman* (Washington, 1973), p. 16; Spalding, *Life of Flaget*.

108. The work was entitled *Our Faith, the Victory: Or a Comprehensive View of the Principal Doctrines of the Christian Religion* (1865).

109. Spalding, *Martin John Spalding*, pp. 26, 99.

110. Martin J. Spalding, *Lectures on the Evidences of Catholicity, Delivered in the Cathedral of Louisville* (Louisville, 1857), pp. 131–52, 220–66.

111. Spalding, *Martin John Spalding*, p. 91; M. J. Spalding, *Miscellanea*, pp. 387–90.

112. Spalding, *Martin John Spalding*, p. 59; M. J. Spalding, *Life of Flaget*, p. 17.

113. Guilday, *Life of England*, 1:367; Donna Merwick, *Boston Priests, 1848–1910: A Study of Social and Intellectual Change* (Cambridge, Mass., 1973), pp. 12–40; England, *Works*, 2:73, 251.

114. Cited in J. H. Thornwell, *The Arguments of Romanists from the Infallibility of the Church and the Testimony of the Fathers in Behalf of the Apocrypha Discussed and Refuted* (New York, 1845), p. 358.

CHAPTER FIVE

1. Cited in Johnson, *Life of Palmer*, p. 150.

2. Cited in Theodore Dwight Bozeman, "Science, Nature, and Society: A New Approach to James Henley Thornwell," *The Journal of Presbyterian History* 50 (1972):307.

3. Thornwell, Journal, 14 June 1836, Thornwell Collection, Montreat.

4. Thornwell, "An Address Delivered Before the Literary Societies of Davidson College, N.C. on the First Day of August, 1837," Thornwell Collection, Montreat. For biographical information, see Palmer, *Life of Thornwell*; Thomas Law, "Dr. Thornwell as a Preacher and a Teacher," *Centennial Addresses Delivered Before the Synod of South Carolina* (Spartanburg, 1913), pp. 6–12; John M. Wells, *Southern Presbyterian Worthies* (Richmond, 1936), p. 34; Paul Leslie Garber, "A Centennial Appraisal of James Henley Thornwell," *A Miscellany of American Christianity: Essays in Honor of H. Shelton Smith*, ed. Stuart Henry (Durham, 1963).

5. "Thornwell's Inaugural Address," *The Southern Presbyterian* (1857): n.p.

6. T. L. McBryde and Committee to Thornwell, 14 October 1857, Thornwell Collection, Montreat.

7. Sydney Ahlstrom, "The Scottish Philosophy and American Theology," *Church History* 2 (September, 1955):257–72.

8. Ralston, *Elements*, p. 611.

9. Thomas Reid, *The Works of Thomas Reid*, 3 vols. (New York, 1822), 1:131.

10. Ibid., 2:25.

11. Ibid., 1:132.

12. Ibid., 2:52, 74.

13. Ibid., 2:74, 90.

14. Ibid., 2:44, 83.

15. Ibid., 1:152; 2:260.

16. Ibid., 1:362–63; 2:311–71. See Andrew-Seth Pringle-Pattison, *Scottish Philosophy* (Edinburgh, 1885), pp. 73–141, and Selwyn A. Grave, *The Scottish Philosophy of Common Sense* (Oxford, 1960).

17. Reid, *Works*, 1:131, 191, 362–63; 2:311.

18. William Winans to W. B. Hines, 20 March 1852, Winans Collection, University of Mississippi, Oxford.

19. Dugald Stewart, *Elements of the Philosophy of the Human Mind* (Brattleborough, Vt., 1813), pp. 12–15, 16, 23–54, 86, 376.

20. Ibid., p. 86.

21. William Hamilton, *Lectures on Metaphysics*, 2 vols. (Boston, 1859): 1:34; 2:530.

22. Robert B. Come, "The Influence of Princeton on Higher Education in the South before 1825," *William and Mary Quarterly*, 2nd ser. 2 (October, 1945):362–94.

23. Nathan Bangs, "Introduction," Reid, *Works*, 1:iii; William Winans to Nathan Bangs and Thomas Mason, 10 March 1823, Winans Collection, University of Mississippi, Oxford.

24. For additional examples of Scottish philosophy in Southern theological works, see Ralston, *Elements*, pp. 166–69, 187; Bascom, *Posthumous Works*, 3:20–23; Henkle, *Life of Bascom*, p. 57; Watson, *Theological Institutes*, p. 277; Rivers, *Life of Paine*, p. 48; R. H. Rivers, *Elements of Moral Philosophy* (Nashville, 1859), p. 27; Albert T. Bledsoe, *A Theodicy; or Vindication of the Divine Glory, as Manifested in the Constitution and Government of the Moral World* (New York, 1856; 1st ed., 1854), p. 96; James H. Otey, Journals, 1, 10 June 1840, Otey Papers, U.N.C., Chapel Hill; Adam Empie, *Remarks on the Distinguishing Doctrine*, pp. 7, 37; "Letters from William and Mary, 1798–1801," *The Virginia Magazine of History and Biography* 29 (April, 1921):146; Adams, *Moral Philosophy*, p. 18; B. M. Palmer, *An Address Delivered Before the Philomathean and Euphemian Literary Societies of Erskine College* (Due West, S. C., 1854), pp. 7–29; Enoch Pond, "Philosophy in the Church," *SPR* 4 (1850–51):157; Dabney, *Lectures*, p. 65; Robert J. Breckinridge, *The Knowledge of God Objectively Considered* (New York, 1858), p. 324; Paschal, *Wake-Forest College*, p. 361; Jonathan Maxcy, "An Anniversary Sermon," *American Eloquence; Consisting of Orations, Addresses, and Sermons; Being the Literary Remains of the Rev. Jonathan Maxcy, D.D.* (New York, 1845), p. 271; Dagg, *Moral Science*, p. iii.

25. Thomas Cooper to Benjamin Gildersleeve, 2 July 1831, Gildersleeve-Cooper Letters, U.N.C., Chapel Hill.

26. "The Collected Works of Dugald Stewart," *MQR* 11 (1857):619.

27. Thornwell to M. J. Williams, 26 August 1850, in Palmer, *Life of Thornwell*, p. 344.

28. Thornwell, "The Philosophy of Religion," *SPR* 3 (1849–50):493, 496, 531; Thornwell, "The Office of Reason in Regard to Revelation," *SPR* 1 (1847):33.

29. Thornwell Collection, Montreat; *SPR* 3 (1849–50):496, 503, 529, 557, 593. Through Hamilton's influence some clergy associated Scottish philosophy with Kantianism. J. D. Morrell's well-known *Historical and Critical View of the Speculative Philosophy of Europe in the Nineteenth*

Century also interpreted the Scottish philosophy as a proto-Kantian movement.

30. *SPR* 3 (1849–50):519.

31. Thornwell, *Works*, 2:609; *SPR* 3 (1849–50):509.

32. Thornwell, "Inaugural Address," *Southern Presbyterian* (1857): n.p.

33. John L. Dagg, *Manual of Theology* (Charleston, 1857), pp. 28–63, 133.

34. R. D. Ragsdale, *The Story of Georgia Baptists* (Atlanta, 1932), p. 109; *Annual Catalogue, Southern Baptist Theological Seminary* (Greenville, S. C., 1860), p. 46.

35. Dagg, *Manual of Theology*, pp. iv, 14.

36. Ibid., p. iv.

37. Ibid., pp. 112, 116, 61, 68.

38. Ibid., pp. 20–21.

39. Ibid., pp. 123–25.

40. Ibid., pp. 125, 139. On Dagg, see Robert G. Gardner, "John Leadley Dagg: Pioneer American Baptist Theologian" (Ph.D. diss., Duke University, 1957).

41. John Bocock, "Modern Theology—Taylor and Bledsoe," *SPR* 9 (1856):503.

CHAPTER SIX

1. Thornwell, *Discourses on Truth*, pp. 456–527.

2. "Review of *Discourses on Truth*," *MQR* 9 (1855):134.

3. Thornwell, *Discourses on Truth*, pp. 456–59, 467, 502, 527; Thornwell, *Review of Paley's Moral Philosophy*, p. 23.

4. The ministers were Lindsley, Longstreet, McGuffey, Manly, Olin, Smith, Dagg, Bascom, Rivers, Thornwell, Young, Ruffner, Church, Adams, Ralston, and Dabney. Others were Thomas R. Dew, George Tucker, David Swain, and Francis Lieber.

5. England, *Works* 3:119; Antony Koch and Arthur Preuss, *A Handbook of Moral Theology*, 5 vols. (St. Louis, 1925), 1:71; Francis Kenrick, *Theologia Moralis* (2nd ed., Malines, 1860–61), 1:xiv. On the slavery issue, see H. Shelton Smith, *In His Image, But . . .: Racism in Southern Religion, 1780–1910* (Durham, N. C. 1972), pp. 129–65.

6. Ralph Cudworth, *Treatise Concerning Eternal and Immutable Morality, British Moralists*, 1:258.

7. Samuel Clarke, *On Natural Religion, British Moralists*, 2:11.

8. Shaftesbury, *Inquiry Concerning Virtue, British Moralists*, 1:6–63.

9. Francis Hutcheson, *An Inquiry into the Original of our Ideas of Beauty and Virtue, British Moralists*, 1:83, 115, 153.

10. Joseph Butler, *Sermons* and *Dissertations upon Virtue, British Moralists*, 1:181.

11. R. H. Rivers, *Elements of Moral Philosophy* (Nashville, 1859), pp. 63–64.

12. Butler, *Sermons* and *Dissertation*, 2:201, 209–10, 246.

13. Richard Price, *A Review of the Chief Questions and Difficulties of Morals*, *British Moralists*, 2:106, 114, 124, 142–43, 144–49.

14. Reid, *Works*, 3:264, 304–5, 307, 309.

15. Ibid., pp. 172, 268–77, 273.

16. John Witherspoon, *The Works of the Rev. John Witherspoon*, 4 vols. (Philadelphia, 1802), 3:374, 379.

17. Basil Manly to Sarah Manly, 30 September 1837, Manly Papers, U.N.C., Chapel Hill.

18. Francis Wayland, *The Elements of Moral Science*, ed. Joseph L. Blau (Cambridge, 1963; 1st ed., 1835), pp. 62–82.

19. Deems (ed.), *Southern Methodist Pulpit*, p. 67; "Conscience—Its Nature, Office, and Authority," *SPR* 7 (1852–53):461; Dabney, *Lectures*, p. 60; Thornwell, *Review of Paley's Moral Philosophy*, p. 24.

20. Thornwell, *Discourses on Truth*, p. 466; Rivers, *Moral Philosophy*, pp. 49–57, 127–31. See also Thornwell, *Review of Paley's Moral Philosophy*, pp. 24–25; Dabney, *Lectures*, p. 61; Adams, *Moral Philosophy*, p. 14; H. B. Bascom, *Works*, 3:185.

21. Thornwell, *Review of Paley's Moral Philosophy*, p. 24; Bascom, *Mental and Moral Philosophy*, p. 16; see also Dagg, *Moral Science*, p. 15; Thornwell, *Discourses on Truth*, pp. 467, 496.

22. Rivers, *Life of Paine*, pp. 44, 49.

23. William Winans to R. H. Rivers, October 1848, and Winans to Rivers, 7 November 1853, Winans Collection, University of Mississippi, Oxford; "Rivers's Elements of Moral Philosophy," *MQR* 14 (1860):182–88; "Rivers's Moral Philosophy," *MQR* 13 (1859):625–26.

24. Rivers, *Moral Philosophy*, p. 143.

25. Dagg, *Moral Science*, p. 49; Rivers, *Moral Philosophy*, pp. 49, 63, 125, 143; Thornwell, *Discourses on Truth*, pp. 514–22; Dabney, *Lectures*, pp. 58, 64; *SPR* 6 (1853):456.

26. Thornwell, *Review of Paley's Moral Philosophy*, p. 27; Adams, *Moral Philosophy*, p. 18; Van Zandt, "Necessity of a Revelation," *Lectures on the Evidences*, p. 47; Dagg, *Moral Science*, p. 72.

27. Rivers, *Moral Philosophy*, p. 26.

28. Dagg, *Moral Science*, p. 66; see also Rivers, *Moral Philosophy*, pp. 58–59; Thornwell, *Review of Paley's Moral Philosophy*, p. 29; Adams, *Moral Philosophy*, pp. 12–28; Dabney, Lectures, pp. 65–68; R. S. Gladney, "Moral Philosophy," *SPR* 9 (1855–56):118.

29. Dagg, *Moral Science*, p. 37.

30. D. H. Meyer, *The Instructed Conscience: The Shaping of the American National Ethic* (Philadelphia, 1972).

31. Dagg, *Moral Science*, p. 93.

32. Thornwell, *Review of Paley's Moral Philosophy*, p. 29; Adams, *Moral Philosophy*, p. 2.

33. *SPR* 9 (1855–1856):118.

34. Dabney, *Lectures*, p. 68.

35. Ibid., p. 65.

36. This was the heading to *A Parte of a Register*, a manuscript collection described in Albert Peel (ed.), *The Second Parte of a Register: Being a Calendar of Manuscripts Under that title intended for Publication by the Puritans about 1593* (Cambridge, 1915), 1:12, 30–33.

37. E. Brooks Holifield, *The Covenant Sealed: The Development of Puritan Sacramental Theology in Old and New England, 1570–1720* (New Haven, 1974), p. 40.

38. Baird Tipson, "How Can the Religious Experiences of the Past Be Recovered? The Examples of Puritanism and Pietism," *Journal of the American Academy of Religion* 43 (December, 1975):695–707. See also Edmund Morgan, *Visible Saints: The History of a Puritan Idea* (Ithaca, 1963).

39. *MQR* 9 (1855):456; Robert Emory, *The Life of the Rev. John Emory, D.D.* (New York, 1841), p. 235.

40. Richard Sibbes, *The Soules Conflict with it selfe, and Victory over itself by Faith* (London, 1635), "intro.," n.p.

41. Holifield, *Covenant Sealed*, p. 41.

42. Ralston, *Elements*, p. 438; George F. Pierce, "The Distinctive Doctrines of Methodism," Pierce Collection, Georgia State Archives.

43. Outler (ed.), *John Wesley*, p. 392; Tipson, "Religious Experiences," *Journal of the American Academy of Religion* 43:695–707.

44. John Wesley, *Sermons on Several Occasions* (New York, 1847), 2:236; Outler (ed.), *John Wesley*, pp. 227–28, 285–86.

45. Timothy Smith, *Revivalism and Social Reform* (2nd ed., New York, 1965), pp. 116–34; Smith, *Life of Pierce*, p. 189.

46. Ralston, *Elements*, pp. 458–59.

47. Pierce, "Distinctive Doctrines," Pierce Collection, Georgia State Archives; Ralston, *Elements*, pp. 345–50.

48. Moses Hoge, *Strictures Upon a Pamphlet Lately Published by Jeremiah Walker* (Philadelphia, 1793), pp. 29–37, 54–62; L. R. Willie, "Notes, Union Theological Seminary, 1838–39," Duke.

49. Ralston, *Elements*, p. 351.

50. "Diary of the Rev. Joseph B. Stratton, D.D.," 24 December 1850, Stratton Papers, L.S.U., Baton Rouge; Thornwell, Journal, 19 July 1836, Thornwell Collection, Montreat; Otey, Journals, vol. 8, 27 January 1852, Otey Papers, U.N.C., Chapel Hill; Thornwell Jacobs (ed.), *Diary of William Plumer Jacobs* (Atlanta, 1937), pp. 48–49; Winans to Elijah Steele, 24 August 1842, Winans Collection, University of Mississippi, Oxford; William Burleigh to Thomas Smyth, 3 January 1860, Smyth Papers, Montreat; Robertson, *Life of Broadus*, p. 103.

51. Ralston, *Elements*, p. 136; Thomas Smyth, "The Province of Reason, Especially in Matters of Religion," *SPR* 7 (1853–54):279; Thornwell, *Discourses on Truth*, p. 602. Anne Firor Scott found the same pattern in

the diaries of Southern women in her *The Southern Lady: From Pedestal to Politics 1830–1930* (Chicago, 1970), pp. 1–21.

52. Rivers, *Moral Philosophy*, p. 144. See also Thornwell, *Review of Paley's Moral Philosophy*, pp. 5–6; Dagg, *Moral Science*, pp. 46–47; James Henley Thornwell, "The Principles of Moral and Political Economy," *SPR* 7 (1853–54):9; "The Agathon of Scripture; Or, the Rule, Basis, and Effects of Spiritual Virtue," *SPR* 6 (1852–53):287.

53. Rivers, *Moral Philosophy*, p. 145.

54. Ibid., p. 204.

55. Ibid., pp. 81, 83, 137.

56. Bascom, *Works*, 3:10; Dagg, *Moral Science*, p. 15.

57. Rivers, *Moral Philosophy*, pp. 37–48, 187.

58. Dagg, *Moral Science*, pp. 89, 92.

59. Thornwell, *Discourses on Truth*, pp. 454, 601; Dabney, *Lectures*, p. 290; *SPR* 7 (1853–54):279; Bascom, *Works*, 3:183; Dagg, *Moral Science*, p. 92; Adams, *Moral Philosophy*, p. 279.

60. Reid, *Works*, 3:139; Stewart, *Elements of the Philosophy of Mind*, passim.

61. Stratton, Diary, 15 July 1849, Stratton Papers, L.S.U., Baton Rouge.

62. Adams, *Moral Philosophy*, p. 150.

63. Dagg, *Moral Science*, p. 243; Rivers, *Life of Paine*, pp. 197–98.

64. Cited in James, *Antebellum Natchez*, p. 250.

65. Rivers, *Moral Philosophy*, p. 27.

66. Adams, *Moral Philosophy*, p. 11.

67. Gilman to J. G. Palfrey, 26 May 1828, and Gilman to R. W. Emerson, 10 April, 14 April, and 21 December 1827, Gilman Collection, Harvard.

68. Adams, *Moral Philosophy*, p. 84.

69. See Eugene Genovese, *The Political Economy of Slavery: Studies in the Economy and Society of the Slave South* (New York, 1967); *The World the Slaveholders Made* (New York, 1971); and *Roll, Jordan, Roll: The World the Slaves Made* (New York, 1974).

70. See R. W. Fogel and S. L. Engerman, *Time on the Cross: The Economics of American Negro Slavery* (Boston, 1974); Paul David and Peter Temin, "Slavery: the Progressive Institution," *Journal of Economic History* 34 (1974):739–83; Paul A. David and Peter Temin, "*Time on the Cross*: Two Views—Capitalist Masters and Bourgeois Slaves," *Journal of Interdisciplinary History* 5 (Winter, 1975):445–58; and especially Herbert Gutman, *Slavery and the Numbers Game: A Critique of Time on the Cross* (Urbana, Illinois, 1975).

71. Thornwell, *Discourses on Truth*, p. 466; Thornwell, *Report on the Subject of Slavery, Presented to the Synod of South Carolina* (Columbia, South Carolina, 1852), p. 4; Adams, *Moral Philosophy*, p. 84; Rivers, *Moral Philosophy*, p. 294.

72. Rivers, *Moral Philosophy*, p. 294.

73. Richard D. Brown, "Modernization: A Victorian Climax," *American Quarterly* 27 (December, 1975):533–48.

74. Rivers, *Moral Philosophy*, p. 201. See Daniel Walker Howe, "American Victorianism as a Culture," *American Quarterly* 27 (December, 1975): 507–32.

75. Adams, *Moral Philosophy*, pp. 84–85.

76. Rivers, *Moral Philosophy*, pp. 221, 228; Adams, *Moral Philosophy*, p. 84.

77. Dagg, *Moral Science*, pp. 268–77; Adams, *Moral Philosophy*, pp. 335–51.

78. Adams, *Moral Philosophy*, p. 230.

79. Smyth, *Works*, 8:678.

80. Ibid., 5:59.

81. Ibid., 8:719–20.

82. Ibid., 10:492; 8:696–700, 716, 720, 744, 754.

83. Ibid., 6:97; 5:30; 6:97.

84. Ibid., 6:97; 8:718.

85. Ibid., 8:743.

86. Ibid., 5:441; 8:719.

87. Smyth, "An Appeal," *New York Journal of Commerce*, 1 March 1861, New York Public Library.

88. Thomas E. Clarke, "Thomas Smyth: Moderate of the Old South" (Ph.D. diss., Union Theological Seminary in Virginia, 1970), p. 119.

89. Smyth, *Works*, 8:26, 75, 136, 338. Reviews are cited from the Edinburgh *Witness*, the *Scottish Guardian*, and *Harper's New Monthly Magazine*.

90. James Robinson to Thomas Smyth, 6 July 1846, in Smyth, *Autobiographical Notes*, p. 391.

91. Smyth, *Works*, 5:668. See *Autobiographical Notes*, p. 391.

92. Smyth, "An Appeal," *New York Journal of Commerce*, 9 March 1861.

93. Ibid., 1 March, 9 March, and 26 March 1861.

94. Smyth, *Works*, 5:449, 457; 10:454.

95. Ibid., 10:457, 479; 5:453, 460.

96. Ibid., 5:447; 10:466. For conflicting interpretations of the Protestant Ethic in the South, see C. Vann Woodward, "The Southern Ethic in a Puritan World," *William and Mary Quarterly* 25 (July, 1968):343–70, and Edmund S. Morgan, "The Puritan Ethic and the American Revolution," *William and Mary Quarterly* 24 (January, 1967):3–43. See also David Bertelson, *The Lazy South* (New York, 1967).

97. Smyth, *Works*, 3:2, 10:490, 495; Ernest Trice Thompson, *The Spirituality of the Church* (Richmond, 1961).

CHAPTER SEVEN

1. *MQR* 8 (1854):133.

2. A. C. Dayton, *Theodosia Ernest, the Heroine of Faith* (Nashville,

1856); Dayton, *Theodosia Ernest* (Nashville, 1858).

3. Leonidas Rosser, *Baptism: Its Nature, Obligation, Mode, Subjects, and Benefits* (Richmond, 1854), p. 14.

4. Holifield, *Covenant Sealed*, pp. 2, 41.

5. Ibid., pp. 12, 49–50.

6. G. W. H. Lampe, *The Seal of the Spirit* (London, 1951), pp. 59–60, 169, 245.

7. Ulrich Zwingli, *Huldreich Zwinglis Sämtliche Werke* IV, ed. Emil Egli et al., vol. 91, *Corpus Reformatorum* (Lepizig, 1927), pp. 292–95. See Holifield, *Covenant Sealed*, p. 6.

8. Holifield, *Covenant Sealed*, pp. 27–108; Owen Chadwick, *The Victorian Church*, 2 vols. (London, 1966), 1:250–70.

9. Sprague (ed.), *Annals*, 5:617–25.

10. Ravenscroft, *Works*, 1:247.

11. Ravenscroft to anon., 16 July 1821, Ravenscroft Papers, U.N.C., Chapel Hill; E. C. Chorley, *Men and Movements in the American Episcopal Church* (New York, 1950), p. 164.

12. Ravenscroft to "Dear Madam," 11 July 1820, Ravenscroft Papers, U.N.C., Chapel Hill.

13. Ravenscroft to anon., 16 July 1821, Ravenscroft Papers, U.N.C., Chapel Hill.

14. Ravenscroft to "Dear Madam," 11 July 1820, Ravenscroft Papers, U.N.C., Chapel Hill.

15. Ravenscroft, *Works*, 1:253.

16. Ibid., pp. 243–44.

17. Ravenscroft to "Dear Madam," 11 July 1820, Ravenscroft Papers, U.N.C., Chapel Hill.

18. Ravenscroft, *Works*, 1:30.

19. Ibid., 1:177.

20. Ravenscroft to "Dear Madam," 11 July 1820, Ravenscroft Papers, U.N.C., Chapel Hill; Ravenscroft, *Works*, 1:284–85; Ravenscroft to W. H. Wilmer, 22 January 1821, Ravenscroft Papers, U.N.C., Chapel Hill.

21. Chorley, *Men and Movements*, p. 246; White, *Saint of the Southern Church*, pp. 76–77; Moore, *Doctrines of the Church*, p. 13.

22. Ravenscroft, Journal, 30 June 1823, Ravenscroft Papers, U.N.C., Chapel Hill.

23. Chorley, *Men and Movements*, p. 78.

24. Wilmer, *Episcopal Manual*, pp. 142–45.

25. Ravenscroft to Wilmer, 22 January 1821, and Wilmer to Ravenscroft, 7 February 1821, Ravenscroft Papers, U.N.C., Chapel Hill. See George Bull, *Opera Omnia* (London, 1703).

26. William Meade, *Companion to the Font and Pulpit* (Washington, 1846), pp. 13, 29, 45, 52–55, 78; Meade, *Lectures on the Pastoral Office*, p. 171. See also William Hodges, *Baptism Tested by Scripture and History* (Philadelphia, 1858), pp. 134–59; Alexander Hay, *A Treatise on Baptism* (New York, 1842), pp. 60–83.

27. George E. DeMille, *The Catholic Movement in the American Episcopal Church* (Philadelphia, 1950), p. 41.

28. White, *Saint of the Southern Church*, p. 74.

29. Ibid., p. 78; William Winans to Charles Marshall, 5 June 1843, Winans Collection, University of Mississippi, Oxford; Chorley, *Men and Movements*, p. 202. Otey preached the sermons in 1843; they were published in 1852 as *Doctrine, Discipline, and Worship of the American Branch of the Catholic Church, Explained and Unfolded in Three Sermons.*

30. Bost, "John Bachman" (Ph.D. diss., Yale, 1963), p. 318.

31. Holifield, *Covenant Sealed*, p. 5.

32. Alton Koenning, "Henkel Press: A Force for Conservative Lutheran Theology in Pre-Civil War Southeastern America" (Ph.D. diss., Duke University, 1972), p. 96.

33. *Minutes, South Carolina Synod*, 1829, p. 15, cited in Bost, "John Bachman" (Ph.D. diss., Yale, 1963), p. 316.

34. Bost, "John Bachman" (Ph.D. diss., Yale, 1963), pp. 264, 287, 339. See John Bachman, "A Sermon on the Doctrines and Disciplines of the Evangelical Lutheran Church," reprinted in vol. 1 of *The Works of John England*, ed. Reynolds.

35. Koenning, "Henkel Press" (Ph.D. diss., Duke, 1972), p. 42.

36. "Copy of a Brief Extract from the Minutes of the Lutheran Synod of North Carolina" and "Documents Gathered by Andrew Hoyle in Connection with Charges Against David Henkel," Henkel Papers, U.N.C., Chapel Hill.

37. David Henkel, *Answer to Mr. Joseph Moore, the Methodist; With a Few Fragments on the Doctrine of Justification* (New Market, Virginia, 1825), pp. 14–16, 76, 82.

38. Raymond Bost, W. R. Fritz, et al., *A History of the Lutheran Church in South Carolina* (Columbia, 1971), pp. 201–2; Hugh George Anderson, *Lutheranism in the Southeastern States 1860–1886: A Social History* (The Hague, 1969), pp. 23, 37, 75.

39. Alexander Campbell, *Christian Baptism: With Its Antecedents and Consequences* (Bethany, Virginia, 1853), pp. 249–76.

40. Outler (ed.), *John Wesley*, pp. 321–22; see Ole E. Borgen, *John Wesley on the Sacraments* (Zurich, 1972); John W. Parris, *John Wesley's Doctrine of the Sacraments* (London, 1963); and Paul S. Sanders, "An Appraisal of John Wesley's Sacramentalism in the Evolution of Early American Methodism" (Th.D. diss., Union Theological Seminary, New York, 1954).

41. Richard Watson, "The Nature, Subjects, and Mode of Christian Baptism," *Pamphlets for the People* 4 (Nashville, n.d.), pp. 1–60.

42. Sanders, "John Wesley's Sacramentalism" (Th.D. diss., Union Theological Seminary, New York, 1954), pp. 415–21.

43. James Chapman, *Baptism, With Reference to its Import, Modes, History, and Present Use* (Nashville, 1856), p. 322.

44. Rosser, *Reply*, pp. 17, 19; Summers, *Baptism: A Treatise on the*

Nature, Perpetuity, Subjects, Administrator, Mode, and Use of the Initiating Ordinance of the Christian Church (Richmond, 1853), p. 141.

45. Summers, *Baptism*, p. 148.

46. Rosser, *Baptism*, p. 215.

47. Ibid., p. 221.

48. P. H. Mell, *Baptism in its Mode and Subjects* (Charleston, 1853), p. 224.

49. Rosser, *Baptism*, p. 246; Summers, *Baptism*, p. 22; George Langhorne, "Rosser on Baptism," *MQR* 9 (1855):120.

50. Rosser, *Reply*, p. 122; S. S. Bryant, *A Sermon on the Nature and Mode of Baptism* (Greensborough, N. C., 1843), p. 7; Rosser, *Baptism*, p. 246; "The Divine Covenants," *MQR* 13 (1859):528–42.

51. Summers, *Baptism*, p. 157.

52. Ibid., pp. 21, 158; Chapman, *Baptism*, p. 327; Bryant *Baptism*, p. 7; Rosser, *Baptism*, pp. 15–16; William Winans to N. B. Raiford, 29 June 1852, Winans Collection; S. S. Bryant, *A Sermon on the Obligation and Benefits of Infant Baptism* (Greensborough, N. C., 1843), p. 11; Henry Slicer, *An Appeal to the Candid of All Denominations, in Which the Obligation, Subjects, and Mode of Baptism are Discussed* (New York, 1841), pp. 23–24.

53. Rosser, *Baptism*, p. 12.

54. Summers, *Baptism*, p. 158; see also Rosser, *Baptism*, pp. 12, 19, 21; *MQR* 9 (1855):120; "Regeneration More Than Baptism," *Methodist Pamphlets for the People*, ed. T. O. Summers, 2 (Nashville, 1857):10.

55. Summers, *Baptism*, p. 14; Chapman, *Baptism*, pp. 319, 322.

56. *MQR* 9 (1855):122; Richard Tydings, *A Refutation of the Doctrine of Uninterrupted Apostolic Succession* (Louisville, 1844), p. 14.

57. "Advertisement," in Leroy Lee, *The Great Supper Not Calvinistic* (Nashville, 1856), n.p.

58. Leonard Woods, *Lectures on Infant Baptism* (Andover, 1828); Samuel Miller, *Infant Baptism Scriptural and Reasonable* (Philadelphia, 1835).

59. S. J. Cassels, *Lectures on Paedobaptism* (New York, 1834), p. 19.

60. "The Influence of Presbyterianism on the Intellect and Piety," *SPR* 9 (1855–56):166.

61. Holifield, *Covenant Sealed*, pp. 16, 17.

62. "The Abrahamic Covenant," *SPR* 1 (1848):86; Cassels, *Lectures*, p. 99; John M'Farland, *Series of Letters on the Relation, Duties, Rights, Privileges, and Duties of Baptized Children* (Lexington, Ky., 1828), p. 33. See also Daniel Baker, *A Plain and Scriptural View of Baptism* (Philadelphia, 1853); J. T. Hendrick, *Letters on the Subjects and Mode of Baptism* (Maysville, Ky., 1843); and *A Debate Between Rev. A. Campbell and Rev. N. L. Rice on the Action, Subject, Design, and Administration of Christian Baptism* (Lexington, Ky., 1844). This was the position of most 17th century English Puritans: see Holifield, *Covenant Sealed*, p. 98.

63. Holifield, *Covenant Sealed*, p. 98.

64. F. J. Powicke, "Some Unpublished Correspondence of the Rev. Richard Baxter and the Rev. John Eliot, 'Apostle to the American Indians,' 1656–1682," *Bulletin of the John Rylands Library* 20 (1931):138–76, 422–66.

65. Cassels, *Lectures*, p. 103.

66. M'Farland, *Letters*, p. 32; George D. Armstrong, *The Doctrine of Baptism* (New York, 1857), pp. 244–45.

67. The image comes from the New England Puritan Increase Mather. See Edmund Morgan, *The Puritan Family* (New York, 1966), pp. 161–65, and Holifield, *Covenant Sealed*, p. 189.

68. Mell, *Baptism*, pp. 219, 224, 263.

69. Joseph Brown to Samuel Miller, 27 January 1842, Miller Collection, Princeton.

70. *Minutes of the Synod of Georgia, 1845* (Augusta, 1846), p. 23.

71. M'Farland, *Letters*, p. 35; "The Abrahamic Covenant," p. 86; Cassels, *Lectures*, p. 99.

72. Armstrong, *Doctrine of Baptism*, pp. 245, 247.

73. M'Farland, *Letters*, p. 33.

74. R. B. C. Howell, *The Evils of Infant Baptism* (Charleston, 1852), pp. 279–80.

75. Rufus B. Spain, "R. B. C. Howell, Tennessee Baptist, 1801–1868 (M.A. Thesis, Vanderbilt, 1948).

76. Howell, *Evils of Infant Baptism*, pp. 44, 51, 63.

77. Fleming (ed.), *Georgia Pulpit*, p. 139.

78. John L. Dagg, *Manual of Theology: A Treatise on Church Order* (Charleston, 1858), p. 194; Howell, *Evils of Infant Baptism*, p. 85.

79. Mell, *Baptism*, p. 290; Howell, *Evils of Infant Baptism*, pp. 75–78.

80. Holifield, *Covenant Sealed*, p. 137.

81. Howell, *Evils of Infant Baptism*, pp. 81, 88.

82. Rosser, *Reply*, p. 46.

83. Dagg, *Church Order*, p. 176; Howell, *Evils of Infant Baptism*, p. 81.

84. Dagg, *Church Order*, pp. 73, 195.

85. Ibid., p. 136; Mell, *Baptism*, p. 290; Howell, *Evils of Infant Baptism*, p. 130.

86. Dagg, *Church Order*, p. 79.

87. Philip Schaff, *What is Church History?* (Philadelphia, 1846), p. 9.

88. On the Church issue in the South, see Thornwell, *Works*, 1:43, 2:44; Bascom, *Little Iron Wheel*, pp. 21, 233; J. R. Graves, *The Great Iron Wheel* (Nashville, 1856), p. vii; R. L. Stanton, *Brief Notice of a Series of Letters Entitled Episcopacy Maintained* (New Orleans, 1845); Thomas Smyth, Diary, Smyth Papers; *SPR* 2 (1848):1–67; 12 (1860):476–90; *MQR* 6 (1852):534–51.

89. John W. Nevin, "Thoughts on the Church," *The Mercersburg Review* 10 (1858):181; Nevin, "Introduction," *The Principle of Protestantism*, Philip Schaff (Philadelphia, 1964; 1st ed. Chambersburg, Pa., 1845), p. 51.

90. R. B. C. Howell, *Terms of Sacramental Communion* (Philadelphia, 1841), p. 32; Orseneth Fisher, *The Christian Sacraments* (New Orleans, 1854); Leonidas Rosser, *Open Communion* (Richmond, 1858), p. 180; Ralston, *Elements*, p. 999; Meade, *Lectures on the Pastoral Office*, p. 177; Henshaw, *Memoir*, p. 458; Dabney, *Lectures*, pp. 246, 257; Adger, *Life and Times*, p. 211; Armstrong, *Doctrine of Baptism*, p. 249; "Thoughts on Sacramental Occasions," *SPR* 3 (1850):677–79; Moses Hoge, *Sermons Selected from the Manuscripts of the Late Moses Hoge, D.D.* (Richmond, 1821), p. 340; M'Farland, *Letters*, p. 40; Dagg, *Church Order*, p. 214; Mallary, *Memoirs of Mercer*, p. 303; Richard Fuller, *Baptism and the Terms of Communion* (Charleston, 1852), pp. 215–46; Fleming (ed.), *Georgia Pulpit*, p. 149; J. C. M. Breaker, *Terms of Communion* (Nashville, 1859), pp. 12–39; James B. Taylor, *Restricted Communion: Or, Baptism an Essential Prerequisite to the Lord's Supper* (Charleston, 1856), p. 85.

91. Dagg, *Church Order*, p. 203; Howell, *Sacramental Communion*, p. 58; Fleming (ed.), *Georgia Pulpit*, p. 50; Hoge, *Sermons*, p. 338; *Unitarian Miscellany and Christian Monitor* 5 (1821):1–4; Summers, *Baptism*, p. 154; Summers, *Holiness*, p. 38.

92. Chorley, *Men and Movements*, pp. 70, 175; Bachman, "Sermon on the Doctrines," in *Works of John England*, 1:351; Moore, *Doctrines of the Church*, p. 316; Thornwell, Papers, Thornwell Collection, Montreat; Fuller, *Baptism and the Terms of Communion*, p. 225; Ralston, *Elements*, p. 997.

93. E. Brooks Holifield, "Mercersburg, Princeton, and the South: The Sacramental Controversy in the Nineteenth Century," *Journal of Presbyterian History* 54 (Summer, 1976):238–57.

94. W. M. Smythe, "The Lord's Supper," *SPR* 3 (1850):412.

95. "The General Assembly and the German Reformed Church," *The Presbyterian Critic and Monthly Review* 1 (1855):132.

96. Adger, *Life and Times*, pp. 77, 318, 322–25.

97. Thomas C. Johnson, *The Life and Letters of Robert Lewis Dabney* (Richmond, 1903), pp. 138, 159.

98. Dabney, *Lectures*, pp. 617, 809–11. Dabney's students published his lectures in 1871.

99. Adger, *Life and Times*, pp. 313–25.

100. Dabney, *Discussions Evangelical and Theological*, pp. 47–48; Dabney, *Lectures*, p. 811.

101. Holifield, *Covenant Sealed*, pp. 2–3, 221, 227; E. David Willis, *Calvin's Catholic Christology* (Leiden, 1966), pp. 3–7.

102. David Henkel, *Against the Unitarians: A Treatise on the Person and Incarnation of Jesus Christ* (New Market, Virginia, 1830), p. 111.

103. Adger, *Life and Times*, pp. 313–25.

104. Dabney, *Lectures*, pp. 75, 615–17; Dabney, *Discussions Evangelical and Theological*, p. 44.

105. Adger, *Life and Times*, pp. 311, 314, 326.

106. Ibid., pp. 311–13.

107. Dabney, *Lectures*, pp. 615–16, 810.

108. Ibid., pp. 803–12.

109. England, *Works*, 1:257, 416, 503; 2:64.

110. Ibid., 1:257, 504; 2:63–64, 67–69.

CHAPTER EIGHT

1. Asa Shinn, *On the Benevolence and Rectitude of the Supreme Being* (Baltimore, 1840), p. v.

2. Donald G. Mathews, "Religion in the Old South: Speculation on Methodology," *South Atlantic Quarterly* 73 (Winter, 1974):34–52.

3. Carl Bangs, *Arminius: A Study in the Dutch Reformation* (Nashville, 1971), pp. 196–202, 308–43.

4. Cited in Gerald Cragg, *From Puritanism to the Age of Reason* (Cambridge, 1950), p. 34. My interpretation of Restoration theology is indebted to Cragg.

5. See H. Shelton Smith, *Changing Conceptions of Original Sin: A Study in American Theology Since 1750* (New York, 1955), pp. 10–19.

6. Outler (ed.), *John Wesley*, pp. 427–72.

7. Lee, *Great Supper Not Calvinistic*, p. xx; "The Life and Writings of Arminius," *MQR* 8 (1854):540–65; Ralston, *Elements*, pp. 140, 263.

8. George G. Smith, Jr., *The History of Methodism in Georgia and Florida, from 1785 to 1865* (Macon, Ga., 1881), p. 109.

9. Ralston, *Elements*, p. 263; Lee, *Great Supper Not Calvinistic*, p. 48.

10. Hoge, *Strictures Upon a Pamphlet*, p. 39.

11. Ralston, *Elements*, p. 292.

12. Ibid., pp. 291–92.

13. Gallaher, *Calvinistic Magazine* 1 (1827):282.

14. Thornwell, *Works*, 2:105–201.

15. Ralston, *Elements*, p. 375; T. O. Summers, "The Calvinistic Doctrine of Imputed Righteousness Unscriptural and Absurd," *Pamphlets for the People*, 2:19.

16. Thornwell, *Works*, 2:377; Andrew Broaddus, *The Doctrine of Justification by the Imputed Righteousness of Jesus Christ Opened and Defended* (Fredericksburg, 1793), n.p.

17. Thornwell, *Works*, 2:378.

18. John Bocock, "Bledsoe's Theodicy," *SPR* 9 (1854):531.

19. Bledsoe, *Theodicy*, pp. 98, 119.

20. Jonathan Edwards, *Freedom of the Will*, ed. Paul Ramsey (New Haven, 1957), pp. 142, 156–59, 164, 181; Edwards, *On Original Sin*, *The Works of President Edwards in Ten Volumes* (New York, 1830), 2:343, 383.

21. Hoge, *Strictures Upon a Pamphlet*, p. 30; *SPR* 2 (1847):108; 9 (1856):506; 5 (1851–1852):535–51; Willie, "Notes from Union Theological Seminary," Willie Notes, Duke.

22. Ralston, *Elements*, pp. 161–89; A. T. Bledsoe, *An Examination of*

President Edwards' Inquiry into the Freedom of the Will (Philadelphia, 1845), p. 38; *MQR* 5 (1851):212–34; 8 (1854):563; 7 (1853):31–45; Lee, *Great Supper Not Calvinistic*, p. 143; Pierce, "Distinctive Doctrines," Pierce Collection, Georgia State Archives; E. H. Myers, "Reasons for Rejecting the Calvinistic Doctrine of Election," *Pamphlets for the People*, 2:13–68.

23. Ralston, *Elements*, p. 259.

24. *SPR* 2 (1847):106; 5 (1851–52):366–79.

25. Breckinridge, *Knowledge of God Objectively Considered*, p. xii.

26. Sidney Mead, *Nathaniel William Taylor 1786–1858* (Chicago, 1942), pp. 97–127.

27. Jonathan Edwards, Jr., "Three Sermons Delivered At New Haven on the Necessity of the Atonement," *The Atonement: Discourses and Treatises by Edwards and Others*, ed. and intro. by Edwards A. Park (Boston, 1859), p. 4.

28. Park, Introduction, *The Atonement*, pp. ix–lxxix; Edwards, "Three Sermons," pp. 4, 6, 20–21, and Jonathan Maxcy, "A Discourse Designed to Explain the Doctrine of the Atonement," *The Atonement*, ed. Park, pp. 87–110.

29. Maxcy, "Discourse," ibid., p. 90.

30. E. T. Thompson, *Presbyterians in the South: 1607–1861* (Richmond, 1963), 1:354–55.

31. A. W. Leland to Thomas Smyth, 12 August 1834, Smyth Papers, Montreat.

32. Robinson, *Columbia Theological Seminary*, pp. 11–32, 209–12.

33. Dagg, *Manual*, p. 219; Ralston, *Elements*, pp. 196–202; Thornwell, *Works*, 2:247, 256; Thornwell, *Discourses on Truth*, p. 461; Plumer, "Man Responsible for His Belief," *Lectures on the Evidences*, p. 19; Summers, *Pamphlets for the People*, 2:18. James E. Tull, *Shapers of Baptist Thought* (Valley Forge, Pa., 1972), p. 95, discusses the governmentalism of the English Baptist Andrew Fuller (1754–1815), who was highly influential among Southern Baptists.

34. Dabney, *Lectures*, p. 510; N. L. Rice, *The Old and New Schools* (n.p., n.d.), p. 74.

35. W. E. Channing, "Unitarian Christianity," *Three Prophets of Religious Liberalism*, ed. Conrad Wright (Boston, 1961), p. 74.

36. N. W. Taylor, *Concio ad Clerum: A Sermon Delivered in the Chapel of Yale College, September 10, 1828* (New Haven, 1828), in Sydney Ahlstrom (ed.), *Theology in America* (Indianapolis, 1967), pp. 242–49. See Smith, *Changing Conceptions of Original Sin*, pp. 86–136.

37. Earl A. Pope, "The Rise of the New Haven Theology," *Journal of Presbyterian History* 44 (March, 1966):24–44; Frank H. Foster, *A Genetic History of the New England Theology* (Chicago, 1907), pp. 369–97; George Marsden, *The Evangelical Mind and the New School Presbyterian Experience: A Case Study of Thought and Theology in Nineteenth Century America* (New Haven, 1970), pp. 47–54.

38. Maxwell, *Memoir of Rice*, pp. 369, 452.

39. *Inaugural Address of the Rev. G. A. Baxter on His Induction into the Professorship of Christian Theology in Union Theological Seminary, With the Charge to the Professor by the Rev. W. Hill, D.D.* (Richmond, 1832), p. 18.

40. Marsden, *Evangelical Mind*, pp. 89–96.

41. Thompson, *Presbyterians in the South*, 1:355–59; Gallaher (ed.), *Calvinistic Magazine* 1 (1827):35; W. L. Breckinridge, *Letters Addressed to the Members of the Presbyterian Churches, Under the Care of the Synod of Kentucky* (Danville, 1835), pp. 7, 13, 24.

42. Rice, *Old and New Schools*, n.p.

43. Thompson, *Presbyterians in the South*, 1:390–408; Robinson, *Columbia Theological Seminary*, p. 212; Samuel J. Baird, "Edwards and the Theology of New England," *SPR* 10 (1857–1858):574–92.

44. Staunton Field, "Reviewer Reviewed," *MQR* 9 (1855):390.

45. Wilmer, *Episcopal Manual*, pp. 74–75; Colin McIver (ed.), *The Southern Preacher* (Philadelphia, 1824), p. 305; Mat Bolls to James Smylie, 12 September 1831, Montgomery Papers, L.S.U., Baton Rouge; *SPR* 9 (1856):496.

46. *A Theological Discussion Held in Americus, Georgia, on the 14th, 15th, and 16th of March, 1850, Between the Rev. Lovick Pierce, D.D., Methodist, and the Rev. C. F. R. Shehane, Universalist* (Notasulga, Alabama, 1850), p. 8.

47. Eaton, *Freedom of Thought*, p. 316. See also C. F. R. Shehane, *A Key to Universalism* (Griffin, Georgia, 1854), pp. 105–53; *Discussion Between Rev. James L. Chapman, and Rev. C. F. R. Shehane, on the Important Query in relation to the Final Destiny of Man* (Notasulga, Alabama, 1850), pp. 15–27; John C. Burris, *Letters to Rev. Lovick Pierce, D.D.* (Notasulga, Alabama, 1853), pp. 25–87; "Universalism Disproved," *Calvinistic Magazine* 1 (1827):91; Empie, *Remarks on Modern Universalism*, pp. 13–64; George H. Williams, "American Universalism: A Bicentennial Historical Essay," *Journal of the Universalist Historical Society* 9 (1971): 1–46.

48. Pope, "Rise of the New Haven Theology," *Journal of Presbyterian History* 44 (1966):33; Foster, *Genetic History*, pp. 107–225; Mead, *Taylor*, pp. 97–129.

49. John B. Bennett, "Albert Taylor Bledsoe: Social and Religious Controversialist of the Old South" (Ph.D. diss., Duke University, 1942); J. W. Cooke, "Albert Taylor Bledsoe: An American Philosopher and Theologian of Liberty," *Southern Humanities Review* 8 (Spring, 1974):215–28.

50. Bledsoe, *Examination of Edwards*, pp. 8–77, 126.

51. Bledsoe, *Theodicy*, pp. 97, 150–75; Bledsoe, "The Divine Government," *MQR* 6 (1852):281–90.

52. Bennett, "Albert Taylor Bledsoe" (Ph.D. diss., Duke, 1942), p. xii.

53. "Bledsoe's Theodicy," *MQR* 8 (1854):132.

54. *SPR* 8 (1854–55):516–45; 9 (1856):492–512.

55. *MQR* 9 (1855):107.

56. Ibid., 8 (1854):282; 9 (1855):108, 384–402.

57. Drury Lacy to Willena Lacy, 16 May 1839 and 28 May 1842, Lacy Papers, U.N.C., Chapel Hill.

58. Breckinridge, *Knowledge of God Objectively Considered*, p. xii.

59. Breckinridge to Sprague, 9 October 1857, Breckinridge Letters, Yale.

60. Breckinridge to John Adger, 21 January 1857, cited in Mayse, "Breckinridge" (Th.D. diss., Union Theological Seminary, Richmond, 1974), p. 512.

61. Breckinridge, *Knowledge of God Objectively Considered*, pp. 275, 483, 502.

62. Dabney, *Discussions Evangelical and Theological*, p. 63.

63. Johnson, *Life of Palmer*, pp. 150–51; Dabney to Moses Hoge, 2 February 1858, Dabney Papers, Montreat.

64. Dabney to Hoge, 2 February 1858, Dabney Papers, Montreat.

65. Dabney to Hoge, 14 April 1858, Dabney Papers, Montreat.

66. Dabney, *Discussions Evangelical and Theological*, p. 71.

67. Ibid., p. 65.

68. Dabney to Hoge, 2 February 1858, Dabney Papers, Montreat.

69. *SPR* 10 (1857–1858):481–82.

70. *Andover and Danville* (n.p., n.d.), pp. 9–12.

71. Dabney, *Discussions Evangelical and Theological*, p. 34.

72. Breckinridge, *Knowledge of God Objectively Considered*, pp. 34, 330.

73. On the cult of sentimentality, see Ann Douglas, *The Feminization of American Culture* (New York, 1977), pp. 1–43, 80–117.

74. E. Brooks Holifield, "The Three Strands of Jimmy Carter's Religion," *The New Republic* 174 (June 5, 1976):15–17; William Lee Miller, "The Yankee From Georgia," *The New York Times Magazine* (July 3, 1977), pp. 16–20, 35.

INDEX OF PERSONS

Abelly, Louis, 104, 128
Adams, Jasper, 25, 64, 218n; on moral science, 51, 146
Adams, John, 58–59
Addison, Joseph, 45
Adger, John, 207, 217n; on sacraments, 177–83
Agassiz, J. L., 82
Alexander, Archibald, 95, 197
Alleine, Joseph, 140
Anderson, Isaac, 195
Andrew, James O., 19, 30
Anselm of Canterbury, 75
Aquinas, Thomas, 73, 75, 105
Arminius, Jacobus, 187
Armstrong, George, 171, 217n
Amstrong, John, 27, 218n
Arnold, Thomas 68
Asbury, Francis, 20
Atkinson, Thomas, 218n
Atkinson, William, 217n
Audubon, J. J., 82

Babcock, M. R., 14
Bachman, John, 81–82, 219n; on sacraments, 163, 165
Bailly, Louis, 104, 105, 128
Baird, Samuel, 217n
Balch, Hezekiah, 194
Bangs, Nathan, 119
Barnes, Albert, 178, 198
Bascom, Henry B., 27, 218n; natural theology, 78–80; moral science, 135
Bass, Henry, 19
Bauer, G. L., 98
Baumgarten, S. L., 99
Bautain, Louis-Eugene, 103
Baxter, George, 197, 217n
Baxter, Richard, 40, 75, 140
Beattie, James, 117
Bellamy, Joseph, 178, 193, 199

Bentham, Jeremy, 135
Berkeley, George, 113–15
Blackburn, Gideon, 217n
Bledsoe, A. T., 191, 199–202, 218n
Bocock, John, 125
Bonald, Louis de, 104
Boring, Isaac, 20
Bossuet, Jacques B., 108
Boyce, James, 218n
Brantly, W. T., Jr., 218n
Brantly, W. T., Sr., 218n
Breckinridge, John, 217n
Breckinridge, Robert J., 15, 119, 178, 179, 217n; on theodicy, 202–7
Breckinridge, W. L., 198
Bremer, Fredrika, 10, 33
Broaddus, Andrew, 53–55
Broadus, John, 218n
Brownson, Orestes, 109
Buckland, William, 99
Bull, George, 160, 161
Bullfinch, Stephen, 66
Burnap, G. W., 63
Bushnell, Horace, 71
Butler, Joseph, 37, 95, 96; on conscience, 131, 133, 134; on consistency, 89–90

Cabanis, P. J. G., 58
Caldwell, David, 119
Caldwell, Joseph, 50, 217n
Calvin, John, 74; on Christology, 180–81; on sacraments, 161, 168–69, 176
Campbell, Alexander, 49, 100
Campbell, George, 91
Capers, William, 19, 38, 42, 95, 218n
Carroll, John, 106
Cassels, S. J., 169
Cates, Edmund, 29

Chalmers, Thomas, 99
Channing, William E., 63, 65, 71;
    on theodicy, 196; on unitarianism,
    56–57
Chapman, James L., 168
Chapman, John, 90
Charles II, 187
Charnock, John, 75
Chase, Perry, 29
Chateaubriand, René François de,
    103
Chubb, Thomas, 53
Church, Alonzo, 28, 217n
Clapp, Thomas, 66
Clarke, Adam, 41, 42, 119
Clarke, James F., 66
Clarke, J. S. R., 202
Clarke, Samuel, 90, 129–30, 134,
    146
Clay, Henry, 78
Cleland, Thomas, 29
Clopton, A. W., 218n
Cobbs, H. H., 161
Coleridge, S. T., 67, 68, 94
Collins, Anthony, 93
Colwell, Stephen, 21
Converse, A. A., 198
Cooper, Anthony Ashley, 130–31
Cooper, James Fenimore, 9
Cooper, Thomas, 58, 95, 119
Cornette, Andrew, 81
Cottrell, Joseph, 38–39
Cousin, Victor, 67, 200
Craighead, Thomas, 198
Cranmer, Thomas, 157
Cudworth, Ralph, 129
Cunningham, R. M., 217n

Dabney, Robert L., 15, 98, 119, 207,
    217n; on atonement, 195; on moral
    science, 137; on reason, 84, 87–88;
    on sacraments, 178–83; on the-
    odicy, 204–5
Dagg, John L., 120, 122–25, 218n;
    on baptism, 174; on moral science,
    136–37, 145
Dalcho, Frederick, 218n
David, J. B. M., 219n
DeBow, J. D. B., 7–8, 9
Descartes, René, 129
Dew, Thomas R., 56

DeWette, Wilhelm, 98
Dix, Dorothea, 63
Dodwell, Henry, 76
Drake, B. M., 218n

Edwards, Jonathan, 178, 194, 200;
    on atonement, 193; on will, 191
Eichhorn, Albert, 64
Elliott, Stephen, 14, 95
Elliott, Stephen (of South Carolina),
    30
Emerson, Ralph Waldo, 66, 70, 71
Emery, Jacques André, 106
England, John, 11, 20, 109, 128,
    219n; on the Mass, 183–84; on
    reason, 102–3, 105; on slavery,
    128
Ernesti, Johann August, 98

Few, Ignatius, 43, 95, 218n
Flaget, Benedict J., 106, 108, 219n
Fletcher, John, 189
Flourens, Pierre, 59
Forrest, John, 21
Frei, Hans, 97
Freneau, Philip, 53
Furman, Richard, 218n

Garland, Landon, 10, 81
Gerhard, John, 74
Gildersleeve, Benjamin, 217n
Gilman, Caroline, 66
Gilman, Samuel, 63–66, 85, 146
Giradeau, John L., 126, 207
Goulding, Thomas, 195, 217n
Graham, S. L., 217n
Graham, William, 119
Gregory XVI, 20, 104
Griesbach, Johann, 64
Grotius, Hugo, 193

Hamilton, William, 118, 120–21
Hampden, R. H., 68
Harrison, Peyton, 15
Hay, John, 91
Hazelius, E. L., 163
Hedge, Levi, 111
Henderson, Matthew, 29
Hengstenberg, Ernst, 94
Henkel, David, 164
Henkel, Paul, 164, 219n

Henry, Robert, 120, 217n
Henry, T. C., 217n
Hermes, Georg, 103
Hill, William, 197
Hitchcock, Edward, 83, 99
Hobart, J. H., 159
Hobbes, Thomas, 129
Hodge, Charles, 111, 176–78, 204
Hoge, Moses, 55, 204, 217n
Holcombe, Henry, 218n
Holley, Horace, 66
Holmes, George F., 96
Hooker, Richard, 161
Hopkins, Samuel, 178, 193–94, 199
Howe, George, 34, 98, 195, 217n
Howell, R. B. C., 17, 39, 172–75, 218n
Hoyt, Nathan, 29
Hume, David: epistemology, 91–93, 112–114, 121; ethics, 131, 133, 135
Hundley, Daniel, 11, 24, 27
Hutcheson, Francis, 130–31, 134
Hutton, James, 83

Ives, L. Sullivan, 101, 162, 218n

Jefferson, Thomas, 57–62, 229n
Jennings, L. R. L., 29
Jenyns, Soame, 90
Jeter, Jeremiah, 41–42, 218n
Johnson, Richard, 96
Jones, Charles C., 219n
Justin, 73

Kant, Immanuel, 68, 103, 116, 118, 121, 239n; on ethics, 150
Kavanaugh, H. H., 218n
Keble, John, 162
Keith, Reuel, 94–95, 161, 218n
Kemp, James, 160
Kennedy, William, 43
Kennon, R. L., 42, 218n
Kenrick, Francis P., 106, 128, 219n
Kerr, W. C., 81, 218n
Kiel, K. A. G., 98
King, Mitchell, 21
Kirkland, John, 63
Knapp, Albert, 99

Lammenais, Felicité de, 104
Lane, George, 218n

Law, Edmund, 160
Law, William, 76
LeConte, Joseph, 83
Lee, Leroy, 97
Leland, Aaron, 195, 217n
Leibniz, Gottfried W., 191, 201
Leigh, Hezekiah, 218n
Leslie, Charles, 55
Lessing, Gottfried, 94
Lieber, Francis, 150
Ligouri, Alphonsus, 128
Lindsley, Philip, 8, 37, 217n
Locke, John, 64, 67, 71; epistemology, 112–17, 119–20, 130, 132; on reasonableness of Christianity, 76
Longstreet, A. B., 95–96, 218n
Luther, Martin, 74, 156, 163
Lynch, P. N., 109, 219n
Lyon, James, 84, 217n

McCorkle, Samuel, 55, 119
McCosh, James, 126
McGill, John, 107
McIlvaine, Charles, 200
McKendree, William, 16, 37, 43, 218n
McPheeters, William, 217n
Madison, James, 218n
Maistre, Joseph de, 104
Manly, Basil, Jr., 17, 98, 207, 218n
Manly, Basil, Sr., 22–23, 30, 44
Martenson, H. L., 69
Martineau, Harriet, 44
Matthews, John, 217n
Maury, Matthew, 83
Maxcy, Jonathan, 194, 218n
Meade, William, 11, 14, 51, 218n; on sacraments, 159, 161–62
Means, Alexander, 81
Melanchthon, Philip, 74, 78, 181
Mercer, Jesse, 36, 46–47, 218n
Middleton, Conyers, 52, 91
Miles, James Warley, 66–71
Mill, John Stuart, 125
Miller, Hugh, 82, 99
Miller, Samuel, 40
Milsaps, W. G., 29
Moehler, J. A., 104
Montgomery, Amelia, 8
Montgomery, Samuel, 15

Moore, Richard C., 13, 141, 158, 218n
Morgan, Thomas, 53
Morrell, John, 67
Muir, James, 55

Neander, Augustus, 21, 68
Nevin, John Williamson, 71, 175–78
Nitzsch, Carl, 68, 69
Noel, S. M., 218n
Norton, Andrews, 69

Olin, Stephen, 31, 47
Olmsted, F. L., 53
Origen, 73
Oswald, James, 117
Otey, J. H., 162, 218n
Owen, John, 75

Paine, Robert, 95, 136, 218n
Paine, Thomas, 52–56, 56
Paley, William: on evidences, 55, 83, 89, 91–93, 95–96, 105; on moral philosophy, 135
Palmer, Benjamin, 217n
Palmer, Benjamin Morgan, 217n
Parker, Theodore, 66
Pattison, Mark, 76, 77
Peck, Thomas, 84, 177
Perkins, John, 84
Perrone, Giovanni, 104, 107
Perry, G. B., 29
Pierce, George, 19, 140, 142, 218n
Pierce, Lovick, 19, 36, 141
Pierpont, John, Jr., 66
Pius IX, 109
Plumer, William, 198, 217n
Polk, Leonidas, 20, 218n
Price, Richard, 131–32, 134
Priestley, Joseph, 59, 61
Pusey, Edward B., 162

Ralston, Thomas, 92, 143, 218n; on atonement, 189–90; on reason, 77–78, 86–87, 90, 91, 99; on witness of the Spirit, 140
Ravenscroft, John, 158–63, 218n
Reid, Thomas, 63, 64, 145; epistemology, 112–18, 119, 122, 125; ethics, 132–33, 134

Reimarus, Hermann, 94
Rice, John Holt, 24, 33, 81, 119, 217n; editor, 45; on New Divinity, 197
Rice, Nathan L., 198, 217n
Rivers, R. H., 34, 135–36, 143–45
Robinson, Stuart, 177
Ross, Frederick, 198
Rosser, Leonidas, 167
Sampson, Francis, 217n
Sanders, Billington, 218n
Sassnett, William, 48
Schaff, Philip, 175
Schlegel, Frederick von, 108
Schleiermacher, F. D. E., 66, 67, 94
Schmucker, Samuel, 164
Scott, Archibald, 36
Sedgwick, Adam, 99
Semler, Johann, 98–99
Semple, R. B., 218n
Sherwood, Adiel, 218n
Silliman, Benjamin, 83, 99
Simmons, W. G., 81
Sims, E. D., 27, 218n
Sinclair, Elijah, 19–20
Smith, B. M., 27, 217n
Smith, William A., 218n
Smylie, James, 221n
Smyth, Thomas, 11, 143, 217n; on reason, 85–86; on slavery, 152–53; on theological ethics, 149–154
Spalding, Martin, 13, 107–8, 219n
Sparks, Jared, 56, 66
Speece, Conrad, 119, 217n
Stapfer, Johann Friedrich, 203, 204
Stephens, Daniel, 218n
Stewart, Dugald, 63, 64; epistemology, 117, 120, 122, 125; ethics, 134, 145
Strauss, David Friedrich, 69, 98
Stuart, Moses, 63, 98, 99, 100
Summers, Thomas O., 42, 207, 218n; on baptism, 167–68
Sweet, William W., 142

Taylor, George, 15
Taylor, James, 5–7, 41, 218n
Taylor, John, 188
Taylor, Nathaniel William, 111, 194–96, 199
Thornwell, James Henley, 15, 37,

95, 205, 217n; on atonement, 190; on epistemology, 110–12, 119, 120–22; on imputation, 190; on moral philosophy, 127, 135; on sacraments, 178
Ticknor, George, 66
Tillotson, John, 188
Tindal, Matthew, 52
Tocqueville, Alexis de, 12, 44
Tolet, Francis de, 106
Tracy, Destutt de, 58–59
Turretin, Francis, 74–75, 180
Tyler, Bennet, 196

Van Zandt, A. B., 80, 89
Verot, Augustin, 219n

Waddel, Moses, 119, 217n
Walker, A. N., 29
Walker, James, 111
Waller, John L., 218n
Ware, Henry, 63
Watkins, W. H., 29
Watson, Richard, 76–77, 88, 166
Watson, Richard (of Cambridge), 55, 90, 91
Watts, Isaac, 40

Wayland, Francis, 134, 150
Wesley, John, 41, 119, 200; on piety, 140–42; on reason, 76–77; on sacraments, 165–66, 176; on theodicy, 189
Whately, Richard, 68
White, Blanco, 105
Whitefield, George, 139
Wilmer, R. H., 218n
Wilmer, W. H., 13, 161, 218n
Winans, William, 16
Wirt, William, 31
Wiseman, Nicholas, 107
Witherspoon, John, 118, 119, 134
Wolff, Christian, 99, 203
Wollaston, William, 131
Woodrow, James, 83–85
Woods, Alva, 95, 218n
Woods, Leonard, 194, 195, 197
Woolston, Thomas, 53

Young, John C., 218n
Young, John F., 14

Zwingli, Ulrich, 75; on sacraments, 157, 169, 176

INDEX OF SUBJECTS

Age of Reason, 52–56
Alexandria, Va., 13, 55
American Journal of Science, 83
American Lutherans, 164
Amherst College, 83, 99
Andover Seminary, 34, 63, 110, 194, 220n
Arminianism, 187–93
Assurance of salvation, 140
Athens, Ga., 9, 28, 30, 32, 35
Atonement, 189–90, 193–96
Augsburg Confession, 163
Augusta Academy, 118
Augusta College, 78
Augusta, Ga., 19–20, 34, 56, 66, 102

Baltimore, Md., 56, 63, 66, 106, 128; description, 10; deism, 51
Baptism: as covenantal condition, 158–63; as seal, 165–71; as sign, 171–75
Baptist Chronicle and Monthly Monitor, 34
Baptist doctrines, 120, 122–25, 171–76, 183, 187–89 passim
Baptist Preacher, 44
Bardstown, Ky., 106
Beaufort, S. C., 30
Belfast College, 12
Belmont, Miss., 8
Biblical criticism, 21, 41; deist, 52–53; European, 96, 98; liberal, 64–65, 69–70; rational orthodox, 98–100, 103; typological, 174
Biographies, 40, 224n
Blount Academy, 119
Boosterism, 8

Cabalistic tradition, 21
Calvinism, 187–99
Calvinistic Magazine, 198
Cambridge Platonism, 129

Cambridge University, 91
Canton, Miss., 15
Centenary College, 34, 136
Centre College, 119
Chapel Hill, N. C., 50
Charleston College, 10, 64, 68, 95, 146
Charleston, S. C., 22, 34, 35, 81, 82, 149; Catholicism, 20, 26, 102, 109; clerical wealth, 29; description, 10–12; liberalism, 51, 56, 63, 65, 67, 85
Charleston schism, 20
Christian movement, 49, 100
Christology, 179–80
Church: doctrine of the, 66, 71, 157–86
The Citadel, 38
Class distinctions, 8–12, 48–49, 66, 149
Clermont, 106, 220n
Close communion, 176
Colleges: founding of, 45–47
Columbia Theological Seminary, 30, 83, 85, 220n; textbooks, 75, 98, 195; theology, 110–11, 119, 177, 198
Columbian College, 27
Columbian Star, 5, 83
Columbus, Miss., 84
Commercial Review of the South and West, 9
Connecticut Evangelical Magazine, 45
Conscience, 133, 135–38
Consciousness: in philosophy, 115–26, 134–37
Covenant theology, 155–56, 157–75
Cult of honor, 38
Cumberland Presbyterian schism, 48

Danville, Ky., 78
Danville Theological Seminary, 75, 178, 204
Danville, Va., 27
Davidson Academy, 119
Davidson College, 81
Deism, 50–51; arguments against, 51–56, 62, 65, 75–76, 85–96
Dort: Synod of, 187

Eberhard-Karls University, Tübingen, 69, 99, 104
Edinburgh University, 118
Education of clergy, 24–27, 45–47, 118–19
Elite clergy: defined, 25–28
Emory College, 48, 81, 95
Episcopal doctrines, 75–76, 157–65, 175
Episcopal Theological Seminary in Virginia, 95, 161, 200, 220n
Epistemology, 57–62, 63–70, 66–71, 86, 110–26
Erskine College, 95
Evidences: of Catholicity, 104–9; of Christianity, 85–96, 104–9

Finitum non capax infiniti, 86, 108
Florence, Ala., 10
Frankfort, Ky., 77
Fredericksburg, Va., 167
Freedom of the will, 191–92. *See also* Arminianism, theodicy
Furman College, 95

General Theological Seminary, 67, 159
Gentility: as ideal, 36–49
Geology: and religion, 83–85, 99
Great Awakening, 139–40
Greensboro, Ga., 36
Greenville College, 194

Hampden-Sidney College, 27, 33, 55, 81, 95, 119
Harvard College, 57, 63, 110, 111
Hermeneutics. *See* Biblical criticism

Ideology, 58
Imputation, 180–81, 190

Indiana Theological Seminary, 220n
Institutiones morales, 128
Introspection, 140–42
Issy, 101, 106

Jackson, Tenn., 32
Jeffersonian religion, 57–62
Journals: of sermons, 44; of theology, 45

King's College, Aberdeen, 112

LaGrange College, Alabama, 34, 95, 136
LaGrange College, Tennessee, 95
LaGrange, Ga., 49
Landmark Baptists, 175
Landowning: by clergy, 30–31
Lay authority, 20. *See also* trusteeism
Leesburg, Va., 202
Lexington, Ky., 34, 51, 66, 77–78, 107, 202
Liberalism, 50–71
Lord's Supper, 175–85
Louisiana State University, 96
Louisville, Ky., 10, 25, 56, 77–78, 107–8
Lutheran doctrines, 74, 156, 163–65
Lyceums, 35–36
Lynchburg, Va., 9

Macon, Ga., 30
Martin Academy, 119
Maryville College, 195
Materialism, 58–59
Maysville, Ky., 77
Memphis, Tenn., 18, 32
Mercersburg Review, 176
Mercersburg theology, 66, 176–77
Methodist doctrines, 76–77, 140–43, 165–69, 175, 186–202 passim
Methodist Pulpit South, 44
Methodist Quarterly Review. See Quarterly Review of the Methodist Episcopal Church, South
Methodist revival, 139–40
Miracles: debate over, 91–92
Mississippi College, 95
Mobile, Ala., 18, 32
Montgomery, Ala., 18, 32

Moral Philosophy, 37, 60–62, 127–54

Nantes, 220n
Nashville, Tenn., 8, 17, 39, 42, 172; clerical wealth, 29; description, 10; liberalism, 56; professionals, 32
Natchez, Miss., 14, 17, 29
Nativism, 26, 108, 202
Natural theology, 72–85, 121
Neologians, 97, 100
Neo-Thomism, 101–9
New Divinity, 193–94
New Haven theology, 196–98
New Market, Va., 164
New Orleans, La., 8, 9, 22, 34, 56, 66; Catholics, 20; Methodists, 16–17
New School Presbyterians, 178, 196–98
New Side Presbyterians, 139
Newton Theological Seminary, 220n
Nominalists, 74
Norfolk, Va., 20, 35

Oakland College, 95
Oglethorpe College, 83, 95
Old School Presbyterians, 196–98
Old Side Presbyterians, 139
Original Sin, 188–89
Orleans, 101
Oxford, Ga., 19
Oxford movement, 67, 162

Pensacola, Fla., 38
Perkins Professorship of Natural Science, 84
Petersburg, Va., 80
Physico-theology, 83
Piety: and moral philosophy, 138–45
Plains, Miss., 15
Platonism, 59–60, 129
Population: urban, 7, 10
Populists: clerical, 47–49
Presbyterial Critic, 84, 177
Presbyterian doctrines, 74–75, 169–71, 175–83, 186–93, 184–206 passim

Princeton Review, 45, 176, 204
Princeton Theological Seminary, 12, 41, 84, 111
Princeton University, 118–19
Professional: defined, 31–36
Prophecy: as proof, 93–95
Primitive Baptists, 47
Protestant Episcopal Pulpit, 44
Protestant Ethic, 154
Protestant Methodist Church, 48
Puritanism, 138–43, 156, 175, 187

Quarterly Review of the Methodist Episcopal Church, South, 45, 78; on philosophy, 119; on piety, 140; on theology, 43, 79, 90, 96, 155, 201–2

Racism, 52, 82, 145, 148, 152. See also slavery
Randolph-Macon College, 47, 81, 95
Rational orthodoxy: defined, ix, 3–4, 77–110, 186–99
Rebirth, 140
Revelation: arguments for, 85–96
Relation: as ethical category, 146–49
Revivals, 15, 56, 139–40
Richmond College, 6
Richmond, Va., 5–7, 12, 15, 22, 33, 41, 53, 97, 158; clerical wealth, 29–30; description, 10; liberalism, 51, 56
Roanoke College, 95
Roman Catholic doctrines, 73, 101–9, 128, 183–85
Romanticism, 66–71, 108

Sacraments, 155–85
St. Joseph's College, 106
St. Mary's, Baltimore, 106, 220n
St. Mary's, Ireland, 102
St. Patrick's, Carlow, 101, 105
St. Thomas Seminary, 106, 107, 220n
Salado, Tex., 9
Salaries: of clergy, 29–30
Sanctification, 141
Savannah, Ga., 19, 22, 29–30, 56, 66
Science: and religion, 80–85
Scottish Realist Philosophy, 63–64,

262   THE GENTLEMEN THEOLOGIANS

67, 87, 205, 239n; epistemology, 110–18; ethics, 127–54; relation to theology, 118–27
Seminary of St. John the Baptist, 109
Separate Baptists, 139
Sermons, 43–45, 72
Skepticism, 50–57
Slaveholding: by clergy, 30–31, 39, 66, 221n
Slavery, 11, 28, 56, 171, 177, 197; and moral philosophy, 145, 148, 152–53
South Carolina College, 22, 58, 95, 110, 120, 150, 194
Southern Baptist and General Intelligencer, 17
Southern Baptist Convention, 17
Southern Baptist Preacher, 44
Southern Baptist Pulpit, 44
Southern Baptist Review, 44
Southern Baptist Theological Seminary, 75, 98
Southern Literary Messenger, 56
Southern Methodist Pulpit, 39, 44
Southern Preacher, 44
Southern Presbyterian Pulpit, 44
Southern Presbyterian Review, 45; on piety, 169; on theology, 83, 85, 177, 204, 205
Southern Pulpit, 44
Southern Religious Telegraph, 198
Spartanburg, S. C., 29, 30
Spectator, 45
Spirituality of the Church, 154
Spring Hill College, 81
Staunton, Va., 27
Sulpicians, 106, 109

Theodicy, 186–207
Theological Institute of Connecticut, 196
Theological Repertory, 159
Theological Seminary of the Evangelical Lutheran Synod of South Carolina, 163
Thirty-Nine Articles, 158
Town life, 5–24
Transcendentalism, 66–71, 111
Transubstantiation, 183
Transylvania University, 78, 95, 119

Trusteeism, 20
Tuscaloosa, Ala., 10, 30, 122
Typology, 174
Tusculum Academy, 119

Union Theological Seminary in Virginia, 27; textbooks, 75; theology, 87, 119, 137, 178, 197, 198, 204, 220n
Unitarian doctrines, 21, 56–57, 62–66, 85–86, 110
United States Catholic Miscellany, 102, 128
Unity of the human race, 82
Universalists, 199
University of Alabama, 22, 95, 122
University of Glasgow, 112
University of Georgia, 19, 96, 119, 220n
University of Halle, 27, 99
University of Mississippi, 96, 201
University of Nashville, 172, 198
University of North Carolina, 27, 50, 55, 220n
University of Virginia, 6, 58, 220n
Urban College, Rome, 101, 106–7
Utilitarianism, 129, 134–35, 150

Versailles, Ky., 77
Vicksburg, Miss., 17, 18
Victorianism, 148–49
Virginia Baptist Seminary, 6
Virginia Evangelical and Literary Magazine, 33, 44, 45, 56

Wake Forest College, 81, 95
Washington, Ga., 169
Watchman of the South, 198
Wealth: doctrine of, 11–12, 153–54; of clergy, 15, 22, 28–32, 34, 219n; of lawyers and physicians, 32
Wesleyan piety, 140–43; and theology, 187–93
Wesleyan University, 136
Wheeling, Va., 56
William and Mary College, 51, 56, 158
Witness of the Spirit, 140

Yale Divinity School, 83, 99, 111, 194, 196